M.J. NEWBY

ON MATURITY:

Upbringing, Education and the Recovery of Adulthood

An Authors OnLine Book

Text Copyright © M. J. Newby 2014

Cover design by Terrence Compton ©
Cover: based on a photograph of an ancient
footpath near Symondsbury, Dorset

British Library Cataloguing Publication Data.
A catalogue record for this book is available from the British Library

ISBN 978-0-7552-0737-4

Authors OnLine Ltd
19 The Cinques
Gamlingay, Sandy
Bedfordshire SG19 3NU
England

This book is also available in e-book format, details of which are available at www.authorsonline.co.uk

For Anja, JJ, Issy, Jayden, Athan, Xanthe and Luca

CONTENTS

PREFACE

'Sit down to write what you have thought, and not to think what you shall write.' (Wm Cobbett Grammar of the English Language 1818)

My journey begins knowing that we can be physically mature yet behave like children. Conversely, we can be physically immature, very young or physically stunted, yet be mature in manner of life. What might this mean and how can upbringing and education enable us and our progeny to live more grown-up lives? What is maturity? Is it but rarely attained in the developed world? Is it specific to each cultural tradition, or are there shared features indicating its meaning for the global world of today and tomorrow? I would not profess to have all the answers. On the other hand, to have none, even to dismiss the question as itself immature, is no option. There seems little point in lamenting human immaturity if we don't see ways to transcend it, and to contrast maturity with popular cultures which, at least in the 'developed' world, so pervasively harm people's lives.

Ill-thought-out, popularly assumed ideas of mature living abound in the so-called 'developed' world. Indeed, in many ways the rich world has reversed its own growth through greed, self-adulation and complacency. We appear not prepared to moderate, let alone sacrifice, a lifestyle built upon possessions, rivalry, celebrity, and various means of instant gratification. Remove the presence of threat from our daily lives and we are tempted to cease contemplation altogether: so ubiquitous yet unperceived are the forces of mis-education that threaten our present and our children's future. Refusal to think critically and imaginatively lies at the heart of all this.

This work comes from a life of earnest inner journeying. Whether I like it or not, without facing certain questions and pursuing ways of answering them, I am hardly on the path to maturity. If I ask myself 'How am I doing?' the answer will often be found easily. I examine the task and

apply its criteria of success, thus arriving at a conclusion. This helps me know how to improve my performance. By contrast, there are questions about how I am doing as a human being in a most general sense. `What`, for example, `is my life doing for the world and its future?` `How shall I be remembered by my loved ones?` `What have I shown others by my life?` `What and who did I love?` `Did I know how to love at all?` `What were the qualities I possessed?` `Was I really a person who gave others joy?`

The other day I walked through the forest in Queensland with daughter and grandson. We reached a giant tree, a strangling fig. It had begun as a small creeper, and grown slowly, leaning upon and feeding from its host tree. After many years the host died and rotted, the fig now totally self-supporting with a void where once its victim lived. Something similar is happening in human culture today, as we are losing our maturity to forces which, mercifully, it still remains in our power to overcome.

This work is a development arising from my `Eudaimonia: Happiness is not Enough`, published in October 2011 by Troubadour/Matador, which was produced in some haste, as I was becoming incapacitated with a recurring heart condition. I am now privileged to have received an Implantable Cardioverter Defibrillator, and so the work proceeds with less haste! My lasting thanks go to the team at Dorset County Hospital for giving me new life!

I hope the only sign of decrepitude to be found is my use of two acronyms – LEAs and LDAs, for Life Enhancing and Life Diminishing Activities.

I remain forever indebted to those daughters, friends and strangers who have drawn attention to the qualities, errors and ambiguities in `Eudaimonia...`, who have reduced any lingering vestiges of self-importance and who have encouraged me. I also thank Hilary Power for the cover photo and Meg Breckon for permission to include an image of her late husband Don's painting. I thank Dr. Stephan Kemperdick of the Staatliche Museum of Berlin for permission to include van der Weyden's 1435 portrait, and the National Gallery of America for the artist's 1460 portrait. (These really must be viewed in full colour on the Web).

I am also highly indebted to Richard and James Fitt and staff of Authors Online for their hard work and patient good humour in delivering this offspring of mine. Should it `fall stillborn from the press` it would not be down to them.

My books simply had to be written as the climax of a life dominated by the unseen struggle to make sense of it all. Authoring these leaves me open to foolish accusations of arrogance and vanity, all of which I would reject. These are the contribution of one who has a desire to share his treasures with others. I now feel life's struggle has led to a place of joy and inner peace, not needing hope beyond the grave.

> `How mature is the one`, you might well ask, `who dares to write this stuff?` I have learned from a story I first heard on the BBC Home Service in the early nineteen fifties, when I was a mere lad. An old Rabbi was addressing the young at a bar mitzvah. `When I was young,` he said, `I determined that one day I would convert the whole world to the faith. But when I was older, I hoped that I might at least convert some people. Now I am an old man, I have but one aim - to convert myself.`

If you know me, you'll know that this remains `work in progress`, but there is a vision here that has to be shared.

Mike Newby
Dorchester England 2013

INTRODUCTION: The Pervasiveness of the Superficial in Contemporary Life

With aching hands and bleeding feet
We dig and heap, lay stone on stone;
We bear the burden and the heat
Of the long day and wish 't were done.
Not till the hours of light return
All we have built do we discern.
                 -"Morality", Matthew Arnold (1852)

The most unperceived yet destructive force amongst so-called developed societies at the present time is not itself the pollution they cause, neither is it the ruthless consumption of resources, nor prejudice and hatred, and not even the inexcusable social inequalities, crippling though these may be. Underlying them all is the relentless spread of superficiality amongst peoples of the developed world. In societies boasting universal education, the deep and most important issues of our lives are rarely taken with any serious urgency and certainly make little difference to us even when attention is given to them. 'Developed' humanity appears to be giving up on them. This is a powerful mark of our continued immaturity as adults. Superficiality easily strangles whatever education we might have received, showing us to be lovers of ease, pleasure, money, excitement and popularity, all without knowing, or at least caring much, what we are about as we dwell on the planet. In turn the development of our children is suffering. This may be, on balance, too dark a picture, for hopes remain that we may extricate ourselves both personally, communally, and as a global society. Without personal change, the community has less hope, and without communal change, the world has less hope. The key to change for the better begins with family and school life. In short, when we think carefully, it is too often for self-interested reasons, without concern for the widest and longest term effects of our choices

Such empty living largely develops at times of ease and affluence, when even the poor can sleep in their own beds, watch TV and have free health care, and the rich can acquire the endless purchase of 'must-haves' and stack spare capital in investment accounts. As the senses are seduced so the mind atrophies and thinking is only seriously applied to financial security, social status, self-image and (if we're decent folk) to the prosperity and pleasure of loved ones. Markets being successful, the economy prospers and jobs are plentiful. Taxes pay for services, child education can be free and university education largely funded by the state.

That is how things were in the UK until recent years, but costs would exceed the acceptable if such were to be continued, since political parties know how unpopular it is to increase direct taxes. Even purchase taxes have a ceiling of acceptability, so a policy of 'rationalization' comes to the fore. Public service professions are forced to make efficiency savings to the extent that the quality of their work suffers. Health, security and educational quality become leading victims of such policies. Midwifery almost disappears; patients wait unduly long times for operations; policemen hardly walk the streets; teachers are made to rely on untrained assistants in order to manage large groups, and 'non-essential' subjects are sidelined from the school curriculum or taught by amateurs. Perhaps most significantly, yet of less concern to the average voter, is the slow strangulation of higher education. All these trends point to a loss of focus and perspective.

It follows that our personal development becomes measured more by sense of security, personal health, wealth and basic freedoms, and less by development of learning and qualities of character. So long as we are kept clear of poverty, deprivation, disease and danger, we have learned to be contented enough never to think of protesting, and may even consider that we could wish for nothing more. Nevertheless, we may not have grasped the meaning of growing up. It means a lot more than being full-size or of full age. The following examples represent a selection of some of the less-obvious yet far-reaching forces driving contemporary life.

• **Hi-tech personal communication devices have dramatically usurped vital aspects of human relationship**. The vast success of so-called `social networking` sites, chiefly `Facebook` and `Twitter` has led, unnecessarily, but inevitably, to widespread cultural loss. Perhaps it is the popular demand for `publicity` and fame that motivates obsessive users, who depart from extended conversation, and cultivate cliché in language, unwise and destructive messages, and brevity without qualification. This last often borrows witty `sound bites` with no space or time for clarification or evidence where such might be needed. Thinking becomes abbreviated and stereotypical, without progression of idea and argument, and without genuine information.

The art of letter writing is now becoming rare, leaving nothing lasting for recipients to reflect upon, treasure or pass on to the future. The threat to true conversation is compounded by our ability to achieve some false sense of belonging as we widen our circle of `friends` – of which it is easy to obtain thousands – and reduce our messages to brief `tweets`. Great pleasure is derived from positive responses to such things: if a hundred users `Like` the message or picture, one's sense of self-worth is enhanced. The sharing of substantial conversation is made unlikely, just as our passion for such activities reduces our chances of devoting ourselves to any substantial learning. Personal intimacy, mutual respect and loyalty become distorted in meaning as the friend ceases to be a true presence: their demise is not the passing of a living person, but the loss of a virtual being, easily deleted and replaced.

(These sites are not *per se* destructive since they can be used constructively, amongst genuine friends and business contacts, for the spreading of information and important messages which haste matters, but this is all too rare. They exacerbate the `dumbing down`[1] of society, but are not its cause).

Recent research has also confirmed that the more people use Facebook, the more dissatisfied they become with life. This first longitudinal study shows how mood change occurs after each of a long sequence of Facebook visits. Visits cause envy after reading the oft-exaggerated

---

1 `dumbing down` is a term introduced first by USA filmmakers in 1933 and has appeared in the title of several recent works, notably Charles J.Sykes, Charlotte T. Iserbyt, Glen L. Murray.

accounts of peers` achievements and their (oft-doctored) photographs![1]

The potential of the iPhone has, at the same time as Facebook steals people`s quality of life, given rise to worldwide obsession with a multitude of useless messages (`hits`) which their owners cannot, it seems, manage to open less than fifty times a day. Finger sliding on small screens takes away any continuity and depth that might have been encountered through reading material of length and value, or pursuing conversation requiring uninterrupted thinking and intelligible ideas. Similar things might also be said of `zapping` (or `zero-consciousness`), flashing through a hundred TV channels, seeking one knows not what so long as it grips one`s attention for a moment or two.[2]

Such preoccupations, generating as they do a beguiling world for young people, are without a doubt major factors in contributing to poor educational standards in the UK. Students in other European and Oriental societies may also enjoy this false world, but a more traditional family life, in the control of parents who want the best for their children`s future, ensures that schoolwork comes first. It is, of course, as bad to force the young to study for 15 hrs or more a day as to let them loose in their bedrooms with computer toys from the moment they get home!

An implication that should not be drawn from the foregoing is that people should keep away from high tech devices! These are not just entertaining, but indispensible as tools for learning in school and in the home. However, they are simply tools, and should not, as I argue below, become a new curriculum subject for the under 16s.

•   Superficiality is apparent in the **preference of most for sound, film and television**, even on those occasions when wanting to educate themselves. The effectiveness of audiovisual teaching in gaining learners` attention is offset by the near impossibility, in the absence of guided follow-up, of their accurately recording, recalling and transcending what might have been learned.[3]

---

1   For precise research sources see Economist Aug.17th 2013 p.67
2   For zapping see Appignasesi, R. & Tarrrant, C. (1995)
3   See Foley, M. ch. 9, op.cit

Reading, by contrast, requires quiet concentration and reflection, for unhurried thinking starts in solitude and quiet. Reading rewards us with the facility of choosing the duration of the activity, of returning to specific pages and sections, of recording accurately what has been said and discussing it meaningfully, saving ideas for future use. The shelf life of a book is indefinite – great-grandchildren can read it. The book is a capsule of knowledge and a mine of ideas that can be located, bookmarked, easily opened, moved and treasured. Whether an `e-book` or CD-ROM can function in such ways, let alone a DVD, remains a moot point. (One can also think of what learning a foreign language by such methods does not give the learner.) Quality learning comes best from a combination of audiovisual, enactive and printed sources: these together are a key to lasting growth.

Genuine learning is revealed in the learner`s ability to speak, write and apply ideas to solve problems. This is not likely to be achieved through merely watching, hearing and playing. Thousands are losing their ability to truly read and write, and most of our supposedly educated young will never achieve it: self-discipline and practice are required. There is more to literacy than being able to read the label on a tin or the content of a manual. What counts is not simply that we are able to read, but that we come to prize content, to understand, assimilate and appraise. In the absence of such, any overt ability to read words cannot be literacy. Just imagine the importance to a mature mind of enrichment of the senses as ideas multiply through vocabulary gained by listening, talking and reading, these giving new perceptions.

The richest food for the mind of the child comes from projects of listening, beholding, making, and doing. This is, in infancy and early childhood, activity shared with whoever is beloved of the child, be it parent, grandparent, teacher or older sibling. This takes time, but offers spontaneity, the unrehearsed sharing of something precious in the adult`s eyes! (Children become easily disenchanted when their fun is limited to the ready-made and skill-depriving luxuries on offer.) Through such intimacies, often before bedtime at home, and in the afternoon at school, when tougher activities of the morning are past, children learn to reflect and enact. Such things do, of course, have to be regular, frequent, and pleasurable. They make for a memorable childhood and, in adult life, an interesting parent. Computers can help in this context, but they are to serve, not dominate or wean the child off human interactions.

There is nothing new under the Sun, especially in education (I)

> "What is more, even Grammar, the basis of all education, baffles the brains of the younger generation today. For, if you take note, there is not a single modern schoolboy who can compose verses or write a decent letter. I doubt too whether one in a hundred can read a Latin author, or decipher a word in a foreign language – and, no wonder, at every level of our educational system you'll find Humbug in charge, and his colleague Flattery tagging along behind him. - William Langland 14th cent. [1]

- The preference of the masses for visual and auditory stimulation over text, especially long and detailed text, is reflected in **the dumbing down of books and magazines**, even of so-called educational publications.

> One bestseller of recent decades has been the `Guinness Book of Records`. In the days when I knew and loved it, text appeared on white pages, with relevant pictures. It was ordered into clear chapters, the headings relating to matters of historical, sporting, scientific, social and geographical importance more than casual amusement. The 2013 edition almost completely ignores the historical, and reduces what at first sight appears to be geographical to a kaleidoscope of weird facts and pictures from each continent. Whilst the book deals with extremes by definition, in the past not any extremes would suffice for entry, but now the parameters have been extended to the pointless and ridiculous. (Just look at the chapter on Human Achievement, and its three sections on Food!) Printed material appears in small bites, often with a background colour, making it hard to read. This is a book by adults who know what children like, but who care little for teaching anything really worth knowing about the world. `Bits` of information and sensational

---

1   Jenny Willan in The Week 2/11/2013 citing Piers the Ploughman xv.

pictures do nothing for mental growth. Coherent wholes of meaning, the content having enlightening interconnections, enable retention and thought that can itself grow onward. Ah, but the book sells!

From its outset in 1888, the USA's *National Geographic* magazine included just a few black and white pictures, but consisted almost entirely of textual detail. In the early post-war years, when I read it as a boy, text took up at least half of each article, with some important photographs. Now the same journal is dominated by large, often stunning, pictures, and simple text. The reader is supposed to be riveted by colour and scale. Detailed diagrams and charts have become highly simplified and scarce, although when they do appear they are useful as an easy *aide-memoire*. Any scientific detail is kept to a minimum and sentences are short.[1] Such changes strengthen the magazine's circulation: it makes for a pretty item to thumb through in the waiting room.

- **The rejection of vital authority roles in home and beyond has harmed parenting and hindered children's growth.** In the home, we find parents refusing to resort, when disobeyed, to demanding obedience by threatening an ultimate sanction. It is all too common to see all punishment refused, partly as this is confused with the infliction of physical pain, never an option nowadays. The need to be in authority is confused with authoritarianism.

(Even the toddler is merely requested to obey, with a 'please', or perhaps distracted by a more attractive reward than obeying, such as the demanded snack or TV programme. Thus friction is avoided, but also the issue. The parent is ceasing to be the ultimate authority, having

---

1   As I write, I have just received my order for the 2012 Olympic Games Programme, a souvenir book. It is a large glossy magazine with little text, just a few pages being devoted to earlier games, the vast majority of the work consisting of large photographic pictures of famous participants, invariably in flowing action. The photography is technically clever. There is, however, no schedule of events in the book! Over 70%, at a guess, of the space is colour illustration, much of which offers us nothing that we might learn. 25% is taken up with colour advertisements.

no final sanction, confusing such with cruelty because the child does not willingly agree to it. The use of one's voice in a demanding and dominating way is increasingly rejected by parents as a path to pursue because it grates against the memories of home life they imagine the child will retain in later years. All this is not in the best interests of the child, who depends on beloved authority figures in order to grow personally and socially. 'Please' does not belong to the unavoidable confrontation with a disobedient child.)

Ultimate sanctions, unwelcome to the child, yet humane, positive (as in requiring tidying up, dressing or homework to be done before any desired task), and explained, are essential. The wilful, demanding and overbearing child (usually aged two in my experience!) will be put in its room (for example) until it agrees to quieten and can return without disturbing siblings. In such a case, the child will know how to get released, and will learn obedience. Such known routines enable children to avoid certain behaviours and adopt those they know to be pleasing! (We hope!) Parenting must require submission to authority on the child's part, not the parent's. From the anarchy of infancy, with its powerful yet wayward desires, the parent brings the child to follow rules and routines, to find standards of behaviour, some of which will be beyond its power of reason at the time.

> Have we lost the point of making our young behave in ways that do not come easily? *Must we always strive to meet their preferences about what they possess and how they spend their time?* Do we have to feel bad when we say 'no' to our children? Dr. Theresa Belton, a noted educationalist, claims that children need regular times when the parent makes them go and pursue their own creative activity. *True as this certainly is, without narrative, received in rhyme, song or story, the creative imagination has little to feed on.* On the basis of narrative comes the time for imaginative play, including writing, drawing and making, as well as shared activities with each other. In narrative-making, children develop the seeds of inspiration given them through narrative-taking. [1] It's not good enough just to send children off to 'play' with unfed minds.

1   http://www.bbc.co.uk/news/education-21895704 23rd March 2013.

• The same dread of becoming authoritarian is to be seen amongst those in power. For example, in the UK and much of Europe, **citizens and politicians fail to perceive the harm done by refusing censorship**, at least until they are forced to accept the obvious connection between pornographic sex and violence, and serious crime. More than the emotional stability of the very young is threatened by easily accessible scenes of violence and sexual perversion. A proportion of people, largely males, come to believe they have the right to act with force and deceit in order to live out such scenes. The perception of romance, courtship and love is cheapened into sexual possessiveness and conquest. It is hardly a coincidence that so many young adults cohabit or marry on the basis of intense, fleeting physical passion, a force that outshines other more lasting criteria for living together. One foundation of civilized living slowly crumbles as basic instincts escape from frameworks of meaning and control in the name of a false freedom.

Any person not subject to parental controls only has to type `sex videos` into a search engine and sexual activity of every imaginable kind appears. It is not just children who are harmed. The dignity of persons is at stake here. For the viewer of such material, men and women become judged according to physical appearance, and `sexiness` (an elusive criterion, now also being applied to government reports and cars!). It remains apparent that, upon reflection, human dignity is being eroded in the name of freedom to do what we prefer. Any connection between a man`s strip-club membership, which is taken to be his affair alone, the corruption of his own mind, and the degradation of woman, let alone any implications for his self-esteem, is unperceived. Little effort is being made on the part of those in power to render general pornography illegal. To do so would be seen as judging adults to be incapable of making grown-up decisions, and in any case, not worth the cost of enforcement.

• One might not consider superficiality to have entered the very forefront of learning, **the world of academic teaching and research.** However this is not so. Education, taken to be the development of knowledge and understanding for its own sake, has become corrupted with the notion that its institutions must compete in the national arena with each other through quantifiable achievements. Attainment targets reached, examination results, and number of research publications, are all criteria used to distinguish good and bad institutions. Whilst this may seem vital to an improvement in actual learning, its damaging force lies in bringing false focus to what education at all levels is really about. It is about the development of mind, whether at infant level or that of senior researchers in universities. The stress on quantity of published results in schools at all levels has undoubtedly detracted from their quality. The tendency is for learning to become instrumental to reaching levels of formal result in a set period of time. Teachers are to cover the ground and to prime learners. The path is defined as is the speed at which it must be travelled. Out goes the possibility of omitting certain material for the sake of in-depth pursuit of preferred and profound topics. Thus learning has less chance of transforming learners by becoming precious. The current obsession with competing leads to an overvaluing of formal assessment using rigid criteria. In a better world the best questions to ask are about what knowledge learners value and how they understand and apply it to solve problems and ask new questions. Motivation and enthusiasm cannot themselves be quantitative measurements, but are at the core of educational success.

That also applies at the highest levels. The university teacher finds it exhausting to fulfil required roles of researcher and teacher when also charged with producing a plethora of published papers and books in order to enable the institution to achieve higher rank in funding. Better one work of high quality, being insightful, corrigible, thorough and significant in its field of enquiry than a hundred works that meet other criteria thrust upon their originators. The Economist has published a leading article 'How Science Goes Wrong'.[1] It argues that: "Too many of the findings that fill the academic ether are the result of shoddy experiments or poor analysis... last year researchers at one biotech firm, Amgen, found they could reproduce just six of 53 "landmark" studies in cancer research... In 2000-10 roughly 80,000 patients took part in clinical trials based on research that was later retracted because of mistakes..." "The obligation to publish or perish has come to rule over academic life." Competitive pressures for employment and advancement have led to the exaggeration of findings and their significance, thus making work more attractive to publishers. Work involving verification of earlier claims is unattractive due to an apparent lack of originality, but verification is precisely what

---

1   Economist "How Science goes Wrong" 19/10/2013

claims to new knowledge require. [1]

• The **language of economics** has become dominant in the news media, especially in publications regarded as serving the public interest. Economic growth, not just stability, has become the goal of the nation, not just the goal of the economy! The productivity of citizens through their employment is made central: thousands lose their jobs because the profits of their international employer are best earned elsewhere, current labour costs being cheaper. Clearly the insatiability of the financially-successful company board ensures that many workers lose their security of employment. The greed of the successful has fuelled the decline of long-established industrial economies. The pursuit of `growth` has led to exhaustion and myopia. The UK now looks to its financial services as the last refuge against economic calamity. Most important is the effect of this dominance upon the quality of people's education, and the development of our culture as a result.

Richard Smith writes of **"a totalitarian capitalism,** an uncontrolled or barely regulated market economy in which only one language can be spoken…"[2], and this is in contrast with the whole point of education, which exists to broaden and deepen the human mind, to deliver it from slavery to the immediate, the tangible and the quantifiable. He cites Michael Oakeshott's phrase "the conversations of mankind"[3] as the focal concern of university education. To enslave the mind to economic concerns is to deprive it of so much in life that not only furnishes alternatives, but enables deeper understandings, rich interests, true enjoyment, the possibility of good conversation, becoming more interesting, effective mental self-discipline, and so on. To understand history, geography, the sciences, literature, world cultures, music, is to become more fully human. It is to be more alert, less preoccupied with the

---

1 See also `Trouble at the Lab` on the poor quality of much scientific research, pp20-23 in same issue.
2 `University Futures` in <u>Journal of Philosophy of Education</u> vol.46.4   Nov.2012 p.655
3 Oakeshott, M. 1962 `<u>Rationalism on Politics</u> London` Methuen

mundane and, above all to develop towards maturity. It gives a person other languages than that of economics with which to think, speak and live.[1] Without such, the mind atrophies and the thought life becomes enslaved to whatever it is that the eyes see and want, what taste demands, and what top people possess.[2] Whilst it may appear that universities have multiplied in the UK, they are not, for the greater part, true universities at all, but renamed polytechnics and further education colleges whose key focus is on career development. Whilst such are sorely needed to counteract the high unemployment rate suffered by the under 25s throughout the UK and much of Europe, the erosion of higher education stunts growth, not just for the most intelligent, but for all citizens.[3]

Behind such trends lies loss of faith in traditions of culture. These are dismissed as outmoded tools for controlling humanity, each being rooted in the neuroses of their patriarchal founders. By contrast, moderns are assumed to have become educated, perceptive and autonomous beings, able to define their own cultures. Such is, however not the case. Individualism has taken centre stage in opposition to the collectivism of traditions now outmoded. The roots of this lie ultimately in European history, movements towards individualism at the expense of community life, and towards scepticism at the expense of faith. Thus, without an education having the power to generate maturity, its members are open to all the evils of the past. The now-lost traditions fuelled a sense of community, through which the individual learned how to live aright, having rules, roles, meanings, a sense of proportion, and sanctions (now largely accursed) against disobedience.

---

1   Readers of the excellent `Economist' weekly journal, can have nothing but praise for the breadth and depth of its subject matter, for its concern with the human present and future, calling upon historical, cultural, scientific literary and philosophical thought as they address the language of economies.

2   Perceived long ago in the Christian Bible: 1 John ch.2 vv15-17. The writer of these epistles succeeds more than any other Biblical authors to show how faith works at the everyday level, such is his understanding of the way of love.

3   Dilemmas abound here for policymakers, some inroads into such being offered in Chapter 8.

Some Hints on Growing Up

Of course there are cultures that strongly resist such manifestations of folly. Cultures building upon age-old ideals live on in the present world as alternative voices. Here follow a few exemplars, each giving strong hints that the road to maturity is yet open. They suggest that we do not have to persist in the obsession with capitalistic measures of human progress, that we can restore the loss of virtue in contemporary relationships, and that we can learn to stop seeing other people and cultures as alien others, as rivals and enemies.

Gross National Happiness in Bhutan

The assessment of gross national happiness (GNH) was designed in an attempt to define an indicator that measures quality of life or social progress in more holistic and psychological terms than the economic indicator of gross national product (GNP). The term "gross national happiness" was coined in 1972 by Bhutan's fourth Dragon King, Jigme Singye Wangchuck, who opened Bhutan to the age of modernization.

Beneficial development of human society takes place when material and spiritual development occur side by side to complement and reinforce each other, according to the Buddhist culture of Bhutan. The four pillars of GNH are the promotion of sustainable development, preservation and promotion of cultural values, conservation of the natural environment, and establishment of good governance. At this level of generality, the concept of GNH is transcultural—a nation need not be Buddhist to value sustainable development, cultural integrity, ecosystem conservation, and good governance. Through collaboration with an international group of scholars and empirical researchers the **Centre for Bhutan Studies** further defined these four pillars with greater specificity into eight general contributors to happiness—physical, mental and spiritual health; time-balance; social and community vitality; cultural vitality; education; living standards; good governance; and ecological vitality.[1]

---

1   Guardian Weekly 1/12/12 also 29/3/12 but see Economist 6/7/13 for a less happy prospect for Bhutan

A second-generation GNH concept, treating happiness as a socio-economic development measure, was proposed in 2006 by the International Institute of Management. Socio-economic development is here assessed by tracking seven development areas including the nation's mental and emotional health. GNH value is proposed to be the average of these measures:

1. Economic Wellness: Indicated via direct survey and statistical measurement of economic metrics such as consumer debt, average income to consumer price index ratio and income distribution
2. Environmental Wellness: Indicated via direct survey and statistical measurement of environmental metrics such as pollution, noise and traffic
3. Physical Wellness: Indicated via statistical measurement of physical health metrics such as severe illnesses
4. Mental Wellness: Indicated via direct survey and statistical measurement of mental health metrics such as usage of antidepressants and number of psychotherapy patients
5. Workplace Wellness: Indicated via direct survey and statistical measurement of labour metrics such as jobless claims, job change, workplace complaints and lawsuits
6. Social Wellness: Indicated via direct survey and statistical measurement of social metrics such as discrimination, safety, divorce rates, complaints of domestic conflicts and family lawsuits, public lawsuits, crime rates
7. Political Wellness: Indicated via direct survey and statistical measurement of political metrics such as the quality of local democracy, individual freedom, and foreign conflicts

Certainly this looks like a great advance on GNP as a measure of national development. It takes into account other factors in society to indicate more fulfilled lives. However, no interest is shown in the quality and spread of personal growth through education, for example, even though all in Bhutan receive a free education. A narrow educational experience, focusing largely upon training for work, maintaining good health, respecting the law, getting on with others, aspects of citizenship and care for the environment are all implicit in the Bhutan GNH. However, education of a non-pragmatic kind which would enhance the love of life beyond conventional roles and statuses as citizens and workers is ignored.

Critical awareness and the enjoyment of activities chosen for the love of them appear to be of little interest here. In other words, the broader and deeper aspects of a person's development are ignored. The authoritarian, pragmatic state looms too large, threatening our lives with deep gloom.

Seeking Wisdom in Ancient Traditions

We write the story of our lives as we live from day-to-day, and remain responsible citizens as we keep the law, care for the family and, if possible, keep providing for it. Being educated, we might also heed the lessons of science by reducing our polluting effects on the world to a reasonable minimum. Being upright, we are honest in dealings and true to contracts. But is something missing here? Perhaps there is a third story, the power of which the amenable conditions of life have caused us to forget. The loss of literalistic belief and of true religious devotion may not mean religion should now be without influence. Outmoded theologies have been discarded through history, only for the faith to rise again in purer form. It has been a slow process, but is one which remains. "How long," asked Ernst Renan a long time ago, "can we live on the perfume of an empty vase?"[1]

Before embarking on a more explicit account of the importance of the religious narrative, the supernatural elements of which this author firmly regards as irrelevant to true faith, we can illustrate the continued significance of the Bible story for our relationships by reference to insights from a renowned Jewish leader and writer. Jonathan Sacks makes the crucial distinction between covenantal relationships and contractual relationships.[2] Both are seen as vital to the healthy society. He finds the concept of a covenantal relationship to have its origins in the ancient world, especially the Hebrew Bible. Without an understanding of covenant, the whole biblical collection would remain a mystery to the reader. What's more, its cultural influence would be lost, and is becoming so today.

The **contractual relationship** is a binding contract, as in financial and commercial agreements. For these to function well,

1 `Vie de Jésus` (1863)
2 Jonathan Sacks (2002) ch8. The author has been Chief Rabbi in the UK.

virtues such as honesty are required, as well as professional skills. Political philosophers from Hobbes to Rousseau saw government as answerable to a 'Social Contract', whether explicitly formulated or tacit. What matters about this form of relationship is that, once it is broken, the relationship ends and some form of justice will be sought by the offended party. Sacks sees modern life as becoming dominated by contractual relationships which, nevertheless, only work well if honoured, thus being dependent on the inner qualities of participants. Sacks distinguishes these from **covenantal relationships**. On these the long-term success of contractual business in society depends. The covenantal relationship is one of intimate bonds, as in family, friendship and marriage. Should any members act falsely to the relationship, they are not to be written off and the covenant ended. Forgiveness, patience, and reconciliation will be sought. Should the last fail, that will not imply that bonds no longer exist. The father never forsakes his prodigal son. The decline of the covenantal sense has led to the erosion of those very virtues that made both forms of relationship enduring and stable. Business is, notes Sacks, conducted impersonally and at a distance. No bond develops between parties to contracts. Thus the covenantal undergirding which might have made for honour and persistence in contractual relationships has diminished. Loyalty no longer matters: 10000 workers can be dismissed at a stroke because a cheaper contract beckons.

Where have things gone wrong? Since the 17th century, philosophy of politics, ethics and mind has become preoccupied with human individuality, focussing upon issues of rights and freedoms more than upon culture and community. The era known as the Enlightenment underlined relationships in the contractual sense, but in truth, our individuality only means something as we have relationships, not simply of justice, but of loyalty and friendship. As Sacks perceives, our individuality is an abstraction[1], and the more so as we grow towards maturity.

---

1   Ibid. p.150

Where else have things gone wrong? There is a malaise that so often passes unnoticed, and to which Sacks draws eloquent attention. It is the failure to listen to deep lessons coming from the living traditions of faith in the world. The metaphor of ancient story, formative of specific ways of life across the planet, was the birthplace of wisdom. However, when we take such to be *literally and universally* full of truths about life, its origins, purpose and paths to paradise beyond the grave, it easily becomes a tool for division, oppression and destruction. This is because we are failing to understand the supreme importance to our developing minds of metaphor, poetry, paradigm, allegory and myth. Such forms alone make and express truth that is to be felt with passion, and which delivers us from the all-invading post-Enlightenment literalism of modern life. These are sensed and felt, rather than hammered out into a conceptual system of beliefs. Their truth is *found rather than made* and makes us what we are. And its expression is more in demeanour, attitude and action than in words.

Such inner transformation of our living cannot occur as we simply align to the required beliefs of a local religious community without being touched by its demands on the everyday manner of living. In the parable, the Pharisee and Levite passed by, distancing themselves from the helpless, mugged victim. The despised foreigner, the outsider, the unclean man, had compassion on him.

Our sacrosanct individuality itself has evolved from the traditions of the world. As thought moves on and such traditions become weakened through criticism, so their power becomes less apparent to the point of decay. We have come to live within another story, the global story unfolding today through scientific narrative. That also calls us, for it shows how we as a species might survive together and save the natural world.

We, therefore, need to live according to three realms of story, our developing personal life narrative, that of the traditional community in which we live, and the revelatory narratives of the global story. Our relation to each defines us as individuals, members of communities and beings in the natural world. In the absence of these features a life cannot be called adult, at least in the developed world, in anything but a superficial sense.

Teachers cannot really understand their role unless they see it in terms of a vision of the growth of children, not simply as autonomous selves (able to think and choose independently of internal and external pressures), but as historically members of communities of living truth (not dead stuff, like beliefs), the metaphors of which shape their growth. As an integral part of their education, older pupils need to understand the contribution made by the great traditions, from Chinese to Christian, to the global conversation. It is this dynamic that must complement scientific learning, working with it to negate the power of superficiality, thus enabling us to outgrow the immaturity of the present.

Conciliation Ousting Division

Sir David Cannadine's latest work[1] is reckoned by reviewers to be of major significance for our understanding of international and community relations, as well as relationships at all levels in the shrinking world. His contention is that we need to grasp what it is that we all have in common as human beings, thus countering the long-standing tendency to assume differences and oppositions. Such differences are all too easily seen in religions, civilizations, nations, classes, races, and sexes. It is not so natural to look for shared outlooks and values.

> "Where previously our history has been characterized by a plundering of the past, to separate and differentiate us, our future now holds the optimistic possibility that...we will revisit the past more comfortably and find...elements of kinship deliberately neglected, of connections deliberately overlooked..."[2]

Cannadine's view of history is that it exemplifies, not simply division and conflict, but also collaboration between groups at all levels. The great key to this lies in readiness to learn through conversation, thus countering destructive attitudes and actions. We must be prepared to put aside suspicion of the strange ways other communities live to find common purposes in mutual customs and rituals. We should never readily dismiss such things as ancestor worship amongst Oriental cultures

---

1 `The Undivided Past: History beyond our Differences` (2012)
2 Mary McCaleese, cited in Cannadine's Frontispiece

without imagining qualities of reverence that we may no longer sense for ourselves. Cannadine`s is not a lonely voice, for many have sought to bring traditions towards mutual respect and discovery of shared ideals. Martin Luther King, Betty Friedan and Nelson Mandela are cited as examples of those who sought, not the supremacy of any group, but the equal status of all in rights and freedoms.

Later in this work, we focus upon the work of Joachim Habermas, a contemporary European writer whose analysis of the qualities required if we are to converse effectively with anyone else has improved public debate in Europe. Habermas has done so much to reveal the imprisonment of our thought and talk by media, business and political institutions. Assumptions of division and conflict are invariably assumed.

The `best` news, these days, has become, for the popularist press, about conflict, evildoing, scandal and celebrity, picturing endless, pointless struggles happily read about from a safe distance. What a distance all this dark, divisive material is from faith and hope, neither of which will ever be overcome. Whilst our shared struggle as human beings rarely draws us together – exceptions do give hope, even if it takes tragedy, such as the Philippine typhoon of 2013, to awaken our love. We must not condemn civilization outright.

> "When I despair, I remember that all through history the way of truth and love has always won. There have been tyrants and murderers and for a time they seem invincible, but in the end, they always fall — think of it, always."
>
> (Gandhi from `The Story of My Experiments with Truth` 1940)

CHAPTER 1: WHAT IS HUMAN MATURITY?

"It is not beyond the sea, that you should say `Who will go over the sea for us and bring it to us that we may hear it and do it?` But the word is very near you; it is in your mouth and in your heart, so that you can do it. " Deuteronomy ch.30 vv.13-14 (ca. 700-500 B.C.E.)

"The unexamined life is not worth living" Socrates, cited in Plato`s `Apologia` ca.335 B.C.E.

"But what is well-being (eudaimonia)? If we consider what the function of man is, we find that well-being is a virtuous activity of the soul" Aristotle `Nicomachean Ethics` Bk.1 (B.C.E.350)

"Fortune can only snatch away what she has given; but she does not give virtue, and therefore she cannot take it away" Seneca (ca. C.E 60.)

Education as Learning to Contemplate

For Aristotle, writing so long ago, contemplation is the highest activity of human beings. It follows from the fact that our mental powers are our highest faculty and define our humanity.[1] Thinking, for which we need an education giving us tools to think with and subject matter to think about, is the supreme activity of man:

> "Contemplation would seem to be the only activity that is appreciated for its own sake, because nothing is gained from it except the act of contemplation, whereas from practical activities we expect to gain something more or less over and above the action."[2]

---

1   Nicomachean Ethics Bk Ten parag. vii
2   Ibid.

Today, this insight is held to be nonsensical: contemplation does little to change our lives. Invention, hard work and determined action are needed. Thinking matters, of course, but is no more than a tool for use in performing more effectively as we face life's pressures. *There is something vital we are missing here.* Contemplation is a special kind of thinking, in contrast to calculative, or practical, thinking (see below, ch.3). It enables a clear perspective, so we can understand more the things that interest us, learn the languages of knowledge like mathematics, history and music, get our priorities right, and make sure we have not gone seriously astray. Its end product is understanding, which builds a stronger self. As children grow, so both aspects of thinking, contemplative and calculative, need, of course, to be encouraged. Nevertheless, in this work I argue that the contemplative must have priority in our lives as children and teenagers: practical reasoning and skill may perhaps come to predominate for the time that many train for a specific career. That remains, however, an unfortunate and dangerous necessity of practical life, and will do so until total automation delivers humanity from the need to work for a living. The question we try to answer in this book is 'what to do then?'

We do well to question the wisdom of developing calculative, or practical, thinking as the ultimate aim of the curriculum for the under 16s. Our general education is *primarily* for the development of our minds and bodies, not *primarily* for the achievement of practical skills. We must first learn to think and to understand, developing a degree of autonomy across the broad scope of language, mathematics, sciences and arts. *This is designed, not in order to fit some special role in life such as engineer or nurse, but to develop the love of learning for itself.*

Practical and Contemplative Development in Compulsory Schooling.

If children are given problems like calculating times of arrival of railway trains travelling at given speeds over given distances, how to sell marbles in a pretend shop, or how to make a strong structure using minimal supports, such tasks are not given in order to train them to be timetablers, shopkeepers or engineers, but to develop mathematical and scientific concepts, using them imaginatively. Practical problem-solving for children is simply a tool for the development of the mind. Thus contemplation is the ultimate aim of compulsory education. The acquisition of such knowledge and understanding for its own sake then gives children the hope of lifelong development of mind, for the love of learning can permeate their whole life.

Successful education stays throughout learners' lives and continues to enrich their being, delivering them, *given the chance,* from the exhaustion of having to work for money in ways they might not choose. The focus on practical thinking such as skill development for job preparation truly belongs to post-compulsory learning. This can be adapted to employers' needs. All too often, practical learning is taken to be the true measure of an education system that functions effectively. It is certainly tempting to enthrone successful training for work at the expense of deep and broad knowledge and understanding.

At the same time, the teaching of abstract concepts in sciences and arts must respect the insights of modern pedagogy, of which Jerome Bruner is an acknowledged founder (see ch.8). Not only must teachers promote interest in subjects (topics or themes) with exciting activities, they must organize and sequence such in a progressive manner to match the developmental needs of the learner. This requires great skill, insight and commitment probably equal to that of surgeons, musicians and scientists and surpassing that of politicians, bankers and athletes.

Teachers, therefore, need philosophical understanding in order to see the big picture of what counts as education and its ultimate aims. They need developmental psychology to understand children as individuals and social beings. They need to understand cultural traditions if they are to enable children to understand human communality and respect differences. A substantial period of professional learning and practice is required. A housewife or an accountant cannot simply be transferred to teaching by virtue of their relevant experience, a short course of induction being all that is required of them. No shortcut to enlarging the profession can make a teacher.

Teachers have more opportunity than anyone else, even most parents, to set children on the path to a fulfilling life. In fact, some schools have found themselves forced by the pressure of local social circumstances to make learning more appealing to the less academic under-16s by responding to the requirements of employers. Whilst courses in technology and computer skills appear to usurp the principles of pure education, being tools for employment rather than for the development of mind, they can also mediate powerful ideas, being, to a large extent potential Brunerian means to icons and symbols (see below, ch.8). If we really want slow learners to make progress, we must begin with whatever can motivate them and build their confidence, but we must not forget why we are doing so.[1]

Parents and teachers are the closest equivalent to the priests of the past, for they are entrusted with the `sacraments`, the holy food, of life. They feed the minds and senses of their children, born to love and be loved, to wonder at the world, to have nourishment for mind as well as body. Without effective upbringing and education, citizens cannot understand enough to live wisely. They cannot distinguish between the Cave of Myopia and true adulthood, marked out by those virtues which enable one to practise a life of love.

The way of deliverance from cave-living begins with the stimulation of the senses of the infant, with his own beloved symbols (such as cuddly toys and blankets, that fill the vacuum of `the space between` that is neither himself nor his mother[2].) It is through the tough but exciting paths of learning that the child finds his joy, thought, speech, conversation, games, fun, wonder and reverence – those things which enable true communion with others and love of the world. Such communion and love are surely what our lives are for. And how might this come to pass? Our one central task is to take the first major practical steps to maturity for all. We need, as a first priority, education that knows where

---

1   In the 1980s it was Seymour Papert who first focused our attention on the power of computers to enable children and terrified adults to master powerful ideas.
2   See Winnicott D.W. (1971)

it should be going and why. To this vital matter we shall constantly return.

Awareness of our true fulfilment as humans is not the fruit of modern science or philosophy, for it is not found as a result of the forward march of empirical knowledge – it has been with us in our consciousness from ancient times. It is the defining feature of personhood and can be lost. There is no guarantee of attainment to maturity. The human mind is as capable of devolution as it is of evolution. What is unique to us humans is that maturity is spiritual in a way that animal maturity appears not to be. The salvation of the planet and the life upon it all hinges upon whether we learn, think, see, feel, and change the world of our own lives. At the present time, should mankind die out, the animals would have a greater chance of living on. Without the revival of our contemplative faculties, we will press on, unconcerned that our insatiability threatens everything.

Well-being and Maturity

`Maturity ` is a term I will employ throughout this book. It is the *telos,* the shared goal of our lives as human beings. It is synonymous with whatever makes the difference, at the end of a life, between the incomplete and the complete life. We can speak of the `well-being` of humanity at large and of the world itself, with its myriad beings. It is not possible to isolate personal maturity from these. *I cannot own true well-being if I diminish that of others and the wider world itself.* The well-being of other people, nations, fauna, flora and the planet itself is protected and enhanced through my own maturity, and diminished, if only by some small amount, without it. It is my maturity of being that saves the world, if only to the smallest degree. It is `up to me` before I can say it is `up to them`. Any use of the term `well-being` that simply equates with the meeting of mere functional needs and freedom to fulfil ones ambitions in life falls short of equating with human maturity rooted in the human spirit and its virtues. There is more to life than survival, safety and outward prosperity. These may not even be necessary to human maturity of being, as examples cited later in this work will reveal.

Therefore, difficulties arise for the use of 'well-being' in this work. I find it perfectly suitable as used in the previous paragraph, but the well-being of persons cannot be restricted to popular notions of the term. These are insufficient, even though they should never be ignored. Professor **John White's** work on well-being through education[1] faces up to these shortcomings, questioning the relevance of wealth acquisition, fame and status, and stressing the importance of healthy living, consideration for others, and the pursuit of worthwhile interests. He, nevertheless, sees success as an important ingredient, and luck as a relevant factor. He is almost bound to do so, for he is honestly considering the best schooling a child should have, the well-being of children its ultimate aim.

Success, however, is an ambiguous concept as many will be considered failures by conventional measures who, upon a deeper look, may not be so. The **Skidelskys'** excellent work on human well-being focuses upon how we can deliver ourselves from the insatiability that dominates modern life by being weaned off it through 'non-coercive paternalism' on the part of good government. This would encourage education, more leisure and less working hours, reduce extreme differences in earnings, advance freedom to develop a fulfilling life and cultivate friendship.[2] There can be no objection to this, but is it a complete picture? What meaning is left for the life of failure, suffering, and oppression? There remains, we must understand, hope for an unmentioned and supreme prize in life that may never be lost.

The emphasis here is upon inner, or spiritual well-being, that is true maturity, an aspect of human development in which luck and success (in the conventional sense) have no essential place. Human maturity overcomes deprivation in basic goods, it outdoes poverty, physical handicap, loneliness, injustice, being not *destroyed*, but

1   White. J (2011)
2   Skidelsky R & E (2012)

even potentially *enhanced* by such things. It is not, for example, luck and success that make a person virtuous; they might well become obstacles to it. Maturity, the result of lifelong learning, signifies deep and permanent changes in our lives, advances that must be made if there is ever to be any progress in curing humanity of its folly. Mature persons may never succeed in the great projects of their lives, may have no luck in any normal sense of the term, and may even know a life dominated by suffering and poverty. They are not destroyed, but rather gain strength thereby.

Without the attainment of such, we become lost in hard times because we have had no vision, or an inadequate one, of the meaning of our lives. It is clear that any attempts to change the human world for good, ridding it of the domination of greed and cruelty, must begin with oneself. That goes for presidents, prime ministers, business executives, parents, and the rest of us. Unless the inner person is changed, everything will go on as before, at least in the long term. Also, our presumption that luck, wealth, paid work and success are essential to living worthwhile lives must be at least tempered. Even in times of extreme hardship and suffering, it is our maturity of spirit that accentuates the positive, retains dignity and preserves hope. Inspirational lives often tend to be achieved more commonly in the midst of troubles than in times of ease.

In White`s work on well-being and education, the concern is with changing educational systems and teaching methods. Such things as reducing the power of politicians to dictate how education is organized, and transforming the curriculum, are also seen to be central. Nevertheless, there remains a degree of incompleteness to the work because it has no vision of humanity in its maturity. Therefore White presents no *telos*, no ultimate yardstick for what education is all about. The truth remains that we must look for what it is that makes our lives worthwhile *whatever* our success (or failure) by conventional measures, and *whatever* our health or the injustices we suffer. To fail to do so is to make the life of suffering and deprivation itself void of meaningful potential. What is it that makes people victors in life`s struggle despite poor showing on conventional measures of well-being? How can they grow enough to handle, and even gain from, suffering, failure and deprivation?

Without knowing the answer, we cannot perceive the shortcomings of defining true 'well-being' in terms solely of functional success. Having succeeded in attaining such well-being for all, should that ever be imagined, how do we then live meaningfully and in a way that advances the quality of life for ourselves and the world? If we have some idea of what mature human living might be like, we can see beyond the pragmatism of the present. Our maturity as autonomous, reflective and loving beings is surely one supreme, if invariably tacit, aim of all education. That aim is not likely to be fulfilled in our youth, for learning to live, through formal or incidental education, is a lifelong process. Normally, it is in our adulthood, if at all, that we can be called mature. Sadly, millions of sane people die in old age having lived in some semi-dormant state all their adult lives, devoid of any sense of the privilege of having lived or for what purpose beyond meeting their needs of the present.

For Aristotle, *eudaimonia* is the "Highest Good", valued for its own sake, and to which the virtues lead[1]. To possess the virtues is to possess *eudaimonia*. For him, the development of virtues is an activity of the soul. We can learn much from this odd-sounding position. Aristotle identified at least nine virtues[2], the most important of which was wisdom, which consisted of *sophia* (theoretical wisdom) and *phronesis* (practical wisdom). Others included prudence, justice, fortitude, courage, liberality, magnificence[3], magnanimity, and temperance. He also added wit or good humour! Each virtue involves the avoidance of extremes of behaviour, and reflects wise self-control. Self-control involves giving authority to the faculty of reason over that of the passions. For Aristotle, this does

---

1 'Eudaimonia', the term used by Aristotle, is translated as 'happiness' by such influential writers as J.A.K.Thompson. The choice is defended in his Introduction, which should be read. This is not, for my purposes, at all helpful. Although popular usage of the term 'happiness' refers to a state of mind related to joy or pleasure, ("well, it's OK by me... so long as you're both happy..."), 'eudaimonia' rarely had such connotations, and the less subjective "human flourishing" is often preferred. It is not necessarily 'happiness', but 'well-being', a term I used to prefer to 'human flourishing' (see Newby 2011). But now, it appears that the term 'well-being' will not do for my purposes because it is now used by an influential writer on education in a manner which requires wealth, success and luck as integral features. (See White J. 2011). I settle upon 'maturity of being'.

2 Thompson.p.104 includes a range of virtues, each shown to be a mean between excess and deficiency

3 (Nichomachean Ethics Book IV pt.2) see ch8 below

not mean that passions are to be eradicated: they are to be encouraged through the guiding power of rational wisdom. (When we don't have time to think before we must act, our instinctive passions certainly take over: the issue remains whether such reflect wisdom, good habits of thought having refined their path.)

It is clear to many that such virtues are being submerged in unthinking pragmatism and materialistic values. If greed in its many forms has dominated human history from time immemorial, there have also been countless people who have seen its emptiness and learned to overcome it. Prejudicial hatred and fear of the stranger has created enmity between peoples since the dawn of history, but countless people have seen beyond and learned to transcend it. Maturity is possible, and not just as a special gift to exceptional individuals, but for us all. And how dare we live and die in peace without attaining it? It is "not beyond the sea".

When we do so, our lives have not been in vain whatever we have suffered and whatever our list of failures. Conversely, when we do not, all the wealth, popularity, power and experience that has come our way amount to little of enduring worth for the good of the world we are shortly to leave behind. Even in the Jewish Bible, the Old Testament of Christianity, these insights are interwoven with the primitive, and reach the surface in the poetic books, such as the Psalms, Proverbs and Ecclesiastes. We have known so much since early civilizations without truly living the lessons, but this is no cause for despair: humankind advances just a little when individuals change.

Christians have employed the term 'blessedness' to refer to life's supreme goal, a state of approval by God.[1] But is there such a state of being making sense in the large arena of ideas and intermingling traditions of today's world? Can its defining features be expressed? Once expressed, is the result of any use? This work is a positive response. 'Blessedness', in the Christian tradition, draws attention to a quality that is not happiness, although it may include it. It is a quality of human living which is not about feeling-states, but focused upon

---

1   This is not far removed from the ancient Greek word for well-being, for 'eudaimonia' consists of the word "*eu*" ("good" or "well-being") and "*daimōn*" ("spirit" or "minor deity", used to mean one's lot or fortune). 'My gods smile upon me!'

reverence for the spheres in which we live. This is a state of being, and is revealed in the way we think, what we seek, how we respond to our world and our life within it. It differs crucially, if a little, from Aristotle's `eudaimonia` insofar as one may be poor in the extreme, yet still in a state of blessedness. Maturing people, in either tradition, and in all the great traditions of faith, may have varied emotional states of mind. They may not feel happy. The hardships and misfortunes of life may grieve them, and they may know suffering and the failure of their projects. They may feel fear, grief, or disappointment, but will not be dominated by such. And they will rarely know confusion regarding what their lives are about: they can take refuge in this foundation. They will not feel their existence is a matter of insignificance, of pointlessness and final shame. They will not close their minds to the world and simply pursue their own fancies.

A vital question to ask myself, I am claiming, is whether my life is lived to express and promote love of myself, mankind and the world, whether in matters large or small. *Whatever I may endure and fail to achieve, my life is not then vain or wasted.* Neither is it foolish, for I make well-being my possession by virtue of the wisdom gained from reflective thought and conversation. Consideration of how we might love ourselves, others, and nature itself, forms the heart of this work. We should remember that love without wisdom is folly[1].

At this time, the prospects for humanity and the Earth as a living planet are under threat, and this is so to the extent that careful reflection on hard data can too easily lead to despair. Now is not the time to despair, but to act and to find hope – but not before we think. Reflection and an examination of attitude come first. It is also the time to find encouragement wherever we can. And it is important to realize that there has to be more to human well-being than saving the planet. When it is saved, what then? What is the *telos*, the end state for which humanity lives?

---

1   I am reminded of C.S. Lewis's comment in a footnote to his `*Problem of Pain*`: "She has devoted her life to caring for others. You can recognize the others by the haunted look on their faces."

Global Criteria for Appraising Ways of Life

But what might be the criteria for recognizing a life of wisdom? On the surface, it seems that these might be as varied as the traditions in which lives are lived, and no criteria can possibly be found to give anything but answers special to each. We might ask ourselves whether there are shared criteria for a life of wisdom irrespective of any system of ideas peculiar to each tradition. Should such be found a basis exists for dialogue, and a basis for such things as combined campaigns against corruption in society. People with many differences can unite in a common cause. Furthermore, change is no doubt occurring at pace with the spread of human communication throughout world cultures. Those oppressed by dictatorial and corrupt regimes are feeling deliverance and the chance of a better life for all. It is no longer plausible to claim the relativism of ideas of maturity in cultures. Even through bloodshed, whole communities are prepared to resist and rethink the dogmas that restrict their roles and status in life. Women want to be educated; adults want a vote that counts; almost all want freedom from fighting over issues that matter only to extremist men.

The search for such criteria requires an ability to listen to and learn from each other, whether or not we belong to a clearly defined tradition.

Many of us no longer associate ourselves closely with the Christian tradition partly as a result of at least two shortcomings. The first is that few of us tend to subscribe to any supernatural beliefs such as life beyond death and the divinity of Christ: the force of such beliefs is felt to lie in the comfort they give, not in any evidence in their favour. The second is that most thinking people do not see prayer as asking for God to change things for the better: horrific events remain once prayers are said.

This does not mean that we have no `life of the spirit`. We may remain as deeply concerned to fulfil our responsibilities, to see our lives as a temporal gift of fortune, to make the most of our faculties, and to seek `peace at the last` through having been true to ourselves and our fellows. As I claim throughout this work, tools are needed if we are to come to a deeper understanding of ourselves and the direction of our lives, tools to be found in the narratives of the sciences, of literature, of drama, of film, and through the revealing power of music and art. Nothing here implies that the holy books of mankind should be demoted to a dusty shelf, for, amongst some primitive nonsense, timeless wisdom is to be found. The symbolic language of religion feeds all these narratives.

The transcultural criteria serving as shared `common denominators` in our shrinking world express opposition to cruelty and oppression. They look to maximizing opportunities for living a life of one`s choosing which promotes the good of others as well as oneself. Thus homosexuality (or any sexuality!) becomes wrong when it is cruel, but not when it is self-fulfilling for participants, for example. We know what cruelty is in such contexts. Wearing the `burkha` is harmful when it is oppressive, but it is a legitimate right when it is both self-fulfilling for the wearers and does not justifiably create fear in outsiders.[1] Every lifestyle demands a rationale convincing to an ever-growing audience.

If there are transcultural criteria for appraising specific beliefs and customs, traditional upbringing must stand the test of criticism employing them. Today such principles are key foundations of liberal education, which is the form of education found in state schools in much, if not most, of the world. In a liberal education, there is no matter of importance to the learner that should not be raised in the classroom[2]. The principles of honesty, justice and fairness, the duty to listen to all without prejudice, respect for persons, their freedom to think and speak for themselves, and equality of opportunity, together these serve to identify the open and humane society. Whilst such principles continue to have their problematic sides, the extremism that denounces them as absurd or degenerate has simply given up on them: they have swept under the carpet of resignation the best hopes of humanity.[3]

The mutilation of a female child`s genitalia, whether voluntary or not, is repugnant to outsiders because it is the imposition of both pain and

---

1   All the wearer might reasonably be asked to do is to remove a face covering when passing through a security check or entering a bank or post office. The same requirement applies to wearers of crash helmets.
2   At an appropriate stage of the child`s physical, social and emotional development.
3   Michael Foley does so, quite unintentionally, in his important work `The Age of Absurdity` (2010)

permanent restriction of a life on grounds of custom or dogma. It is repugnant on the basis of a movement in human cultural growth that denounces the rationale offered in support of the practice. It does so because it is based on values that no longer have credibility in the wider world such as the subjugation of women, (who may have no sexual pleasure) and the superior rights of the male of the species (who may have sexual pleasure). This is a battle not yet over.

Values that remain once cultures have encountered each other and learned from each other may serve powerfully to expose the parochial nature of some customs and beliefs. These become as a result downgraded as superstitious. Change occurs because a way of life appears that asks powerful questions of the old ways, meets common basic needs more effectively, enhances human dignity and opens up new dimensions of practical knowledge. Force, however, must have no place here, except in extreme circumstances: values cannot be changed from any outside power, but from within the society itself. Change has to result from its own struggle. Democracies cannot be imposed by invasion, however subtly it may be defended.

That renowned philosopher, Alasdair MacIntyre, appears to somewhat dampen optimism about the hope for a global world community sharing humane values. In his `After Virtue` and later works he insists that moralities are rooted in the traditions of communities.

"Morality which is no particular society's morality is to be found nowhere" [1]

A universally acceptable, reasoned support for a moral position requires a shared agreement on the good for human beings in the same way that reasoned arguments in the sciences rely on shared agreement about what counts as scientific definition and practice. This agreement about the good for human beings does not exist in the modern world, claims MacIntyre, and so any attempt at reasoned argument about value-related or moral issues is doomed to fail. Therefore, the only solution, he claims,

1   After Virtue pp. 265-266

is for people to revive small community living within a cultural tradition.

Importantly, a strong evidential case for MacIntyre's plea for a return to small communities can be made. Gladwell[1] cites the likely cause of longevity of individuals in **Roseto, a small town of Italian immigrants in Pennsylvania**, as their community life. This gives them stability, identity, meaningful roles, cooperative attitudes, relative disinterest in wealth-differences, and shared celebrations through their Christian tradition. We can surely appreciate the value of living in a small community in which we share friendships and cultural events together, and in which our interests overlap, whilst remaining personal to each. How then can we say, at the same time, that a world community is developing with shared ambitions values and means of communicating them to each other?

The same communal quality is found in small schools of less than 500 pupils: they can meet together, pastoral care can be more personal, the cultural life can be shared by the whole school, and almost everyone can get to know each other. This is not so in large schools, especially those of 2000 or more, as can be found in the UK.

MacIntyre's scepticism does, nevertheless, somewhat disregard the globalism of the present. He appears to ignore the influence of modern communications. This global perspective helps disseminate the view, for example, that women have rights equal to men, that children should not be deprived of education, that racial groups have equal basic rights and that cultural traditions should be respectfully acknowledged. It tends to define forms of cruelty that the world is coming to accept as such. Perpetrators of cruelty in non-religious societies, even the worst dictators, tend not to challenge the values and principles of humane morality when they attempt to defend themselves, but simply focus on the facts. They make up excuses for their actions which, if accepted, would win them sympathy from other states. Global awareness can serve to awaken in societies new sensitivity to the cruelty they may be inflicting on the helpless. Voluntary international cooperation to help the abandoned children of Eastern European countries enlightens those communities that previously saw

---

1   Gladwell M. (2009)

no cause for shame. Examples abound of such work in the neediest parts of the world through which global bonds are encouraged. If this is accurate, as I think it is, that sense of mutual dependence found in small communities is also to be found, to a growing extent, internationally. *The plea for a return to small communities is important, but it is equally vital that such communities also share the benefits and responsibilities of the global society. As local communal life is to be conserved and enhanced by outside support, so such communities must contribute to the well-being of the world at large.*

That there are cognitive principles of a universally (i.e. cross-culturally) binding nature is emphasized by, for example, Jurgen Habermas, the celebrated philosopher whose work has been of major influence in Europe. These principles are tools for appraising behaviours which entail controversial claims involving rules and human rights.[1] There is, to say the least, no easy conciliation between liberal humanism and religious views of life, even though we attempt something of the sort in this volume. Where words fail to reconcile, deeds might succeed, and the language of religion, in its parables and sayings, is the very source in the West of its vaunted liberal humanism. All is not lost, however, for less dogmatic forms of religion, open to less rigidly orthodox interpretations and with a greater emphasis on the symbolic as opposed to the literal, can inspire the outsider with a deep sense of the profound and thus become vehicles of reverence.

Whilst the ancient books must be subject to thoughtful criticism if they are not to be swallowed whole, thus resurrecting the troubles of history, we should also recognize the importance of traditional sources, with their origins in the deep past, as repositories of wisdom. We listen to Christianity, Islam, Buddhism, etc., not because any way is the one true way, but because their teaching is a source for humanizing and world-respecting criteria. They are, despite their ancient world view, rich in truth to be inwardly grasped, and by which we may live. It is also undoubtedly the case that careful reflection on these time-honoured texts can expose a sterile superficiality in our own thinking! They can convey and engender

---

1   For Habermas, See ch.7 & Bibliog. This leaves him having to face conservatism in religions head-on, an issue he has recently addressed in `An Awareness of What is Missing: Faith and Reason in a Post-Secular Age`.(2010)

a sense of reverence transcending words.

The loss of reverence is the beginning of the path to decadence. The local community, a small group of families, workers, and their children, settled in a much-loved place, gathered around a centre of sacred significance to them, links them to the ages, bestows a rich identity on the newborn and gives them a home for life. There they learn language and generate image, idea, and vision. From it they venture out and to it they return. Today the young generations are inescapably becoming citizens of two worlds – the local and the global. They turn their back on either and lose themselves, or live for both and find themselves. Or is this optimism completely mistaken? Has their local world of rite and symbol been obliterated and the global world of rivalries and opposing lifestyles pre-empted the possibility of world community?

The Interdependence of Humanity

Egocentricity is not acceptable. `Goodness`, `wisdom` and `quality` are not private notions – ideas that I make for myself, answerable only to me. Why not? Criteria of quality are socially developed – we ignore that and nobody can understand what we are trying to say, so that we cannot find common ground for communication with others. We are in a world of our own which even we cannot understand! There is no quality worth having if it cannot ever be appreciated by anyone else but myself. For the human species, understanding oneself is impossible without the use of concepts expressed in language. Language and thought cannot be my own private creation. Were it so, it would be gibberish. If I have a brilliant insight and cannot express it in words, music or visual art, I do not yet have one. To communicate, I must first communicate to myself. Having succeeded, I require a pretty good reason for keeping it secret.

This applies to music and the arts, so long as we remember that the language of these forms of culture is not verbal, except perhaps in a metaphorical sense. Any verbal interpretation of a work of art will not exhaust its potential meanings for the beholder or hearer. It may yet have more to say or be understood in a different light. What does matter is that it conveys something with some degree of power that goes beyond any form of words it may employ, as in a poem or drama. In the case of musical works, paintings or sculptures, if nothing could be said in terms of their meaning, they most likely have none. A work of genius, however, creates new departures from the norm, as did that of impressionists, abstract artists and composers. Such transcending must be verbally debateable, but cannot be reduced to such interpretations without loss.

> For example... ...in London's Royal Academy Summer Exhibition, a warning notice advised those of a nervous disposition to avoid entering the display area of **Damien Hirst's** work: he was shown in a photograph, greatly enlarged, grinning beside the head of a beheaded convict. This is for me the supreme expression of man's loss of tradition, the loss of all civilized values. Nothing remains to shock or shame. The world is gripped by anarchy and nihilism. If it is a warning, perhaps it has some meaning. But if it is enjoyed for its notoriety, it is but a revival of that desire to be horrified, but with immunity, from the ringside seat, much enjoyed in the Colosseum of Rome or a horror film. Is mankind becoming resigned to its own primitivity?

We need to call upon the thoughts of those considered to be luminaries, and also to get help in our reflection upon their work. The naïve assumption that past thinkers are less advanced than ourselves has to be rejected. *The opposite might well be true* – modern people have become preoccupied with material, commercial and technological advancement. Locally they tend to live for their enterprises and a small circle of loved ones. Rivalry has so often replaced comradeship. It is an open question whether they can regain what has been lost, and what might contribute to salvation from the false light – the darkness – of the present. Once freedom to think and act for ourselves in a society is realised, human evolution is threatened with devolution as wisdom is lost and we, willing victims of popular entertainment and advertising, live mainly for projects and pleasures not truly chosen by us.[1]

---

1   Such matters are powerfully addressed in Skidelsky (2012) and others. Skidelsky makes the important distinction between pleasure-seeking and leisure: the latter is a means of growth.

We need, especially in this shrinking world, to understand versions of the good life that do not emanate from the West. Middle and Far Eastern philosophers and reformers have much to say in critique of current lifestyles, and a dialogue between them is developing so that each can learn from the other. Material wealth and freedom from oppression have always seen us humans put off guard. Our abundant freedom, particularly in the so-called 'developed' world, so readily leaves us living thoughtless and aimless lives. Our brains have developed superb specialized functions, leaving whole areas of the mind a wasteland. Such lies in contrast to the Muslim world of ordinary folk – not that of the political extremist or Middle Eastern elites – in which devotion to Allah, contentment, hard work, helping the poor and welcoming the stranger stand in contrast to western secular materialism. Likewise there is great contrast with the Buddhist traditions, which emphasize simplicity of living, meditation, opposition to pleasure-seeking, living the Noble Eightfold Path[1] and the Four Immeasurables.[2] As Third World nations become part of the global society, their cultures will serve to combat the ruthlessness of present living, perhaps inspiring and empowering people against the forces of decadence. The ancient traditions of humanity serve, with hardly an exception, to do battle with empty materialism and individualism.

> Deep in the lesser-known regions of the Jewish scriptures, **the book of Judges** teaches relentlessly that there is a cycle of history. It's an old story of cyclic sequence:- prosperity, ease, pleasure, corruption, weakness, defeat and slavery, deliverance, a return to prosperity, ease... and so on. Cycles of 'boom and bust' are at least 3000 years old. Boom is, in the long term, bad for us, bust is good. How very odd! Our darker selves have invariably thrived during peace and prosperity. We begin to doubt if enduring stability will ever be realized. Now there are at least some signs that the human species is beginning to pull itself together even if that seems to occur only during its darker times. One day we may learn to keep our guard up once we

---

1   See quotation at end of this chapter
2   Brahmavihāras i.e. four Buddhist virtues of loving kindness, compassion, empathic joy, and equanimity

think we are winning. Only wise parenting and a liberal and lifelong education have the power to enable that.

Maturity, Inwardness and Partying

When I ask 'How can my quality of life be improved?' I cannot possibly ignore my inner self, the state of my being. There are too many bulls in the china shop of the world, and bolting horses...

> 'He who has not understanding,
> Whose mind is not constantly held firm -
> His senses are uncontrolled,
> Like the vicious horses of a chariot driver'[1]

This brings to mind the similar analogy, borrowed also from the Hindu tradition, of the driver and the elephant. The elephant, a powerful, dominant beast, is our 'automatic system', our instincts and intuitions, our unrestrained desires to do and have NOW. But the elephant needs to be controlled if it is not to get us into difficulties, and most elephants are quite amenable to careful training. This is the role of the driver, the controlled system of our reasoned plans, who reflects and directs. Notice, however, that

"...the rider is an advisor or servant, not a king, president or charioteer with a firm grip on the reins...the rider is conscious, controlled thought."[2]

There is a difference between elephant driving and chariot driving. The elephant driver may be wiser, see further, and gather vital information – but he cannot force the elephant to do anything. The controlled system within us has to become in charge of the automatic system by learning from experience, restraining reflex responses by self-persuasion, distracting desires from the powerful yet foolish goal, etc. It takes a long time, watching and listening to others, reading, conversing, reflecting, practising, before steady control of our instincts and emotions can be

---

1   Katha Upanishad 3.5
2   Haidt 'The Happiness Hypothesis p.17 I am indebted to Haidt for this interpretation of the elephant analogy

gained. Passion struggles hard before it yields to reason. Fortunately, we have a very influential aid to self-control, namely, social conditioning.

This begins in the home and accelerates in the school. Our instinctive passions will be restrained by those whom they offend, and encouraged by those they please. That`s fine, so long as we mix in the right circles and also bear in mind that other people are all driving elephants. The Socratic philosophers, Socrates, Plato and Aristotle, placed great emphasis on the pivotal role in the path towards *eudaimonia* of the role of reason, or reflection, to check and direct the passions. Socrates, calling upon the analogy of a two-horsepower chariot, also speaks in practical terms of the way we find ourselves led astray by unbridled passion, how we should learn to rein in this wayward horse that drags our chariot to dark places, and how the good horse must be encouraged to play a greater role in resisting the wayward stallion.[1] For Plato, self-restraint, sometimes translated as `balance`, `temperance` or `self-control` (*sophrōsuné*) is "the agreement of the passions that reason should rule"[2], a virtue essential to personal growth.

A vital path in all this is that of **deferring gratification** – of being prepared to plan for the long term by foregoing in the present. How many couples can resist the offer to buy furniture and not begin to pay for it until the following year? How many vehicles are acquired on the basis that, in three years` time, a large payment will ensure possession? How many homes are acquired through loans requiring interest-only payments? How many couples bind themselves to each other informally or through quick weddings because the sex is good, but before each knows the other?

Preschoolers whose mothers have been responsive and supportive during particularly stressful times of self-regulation when the child was a toddler develop a greater capacity to delay gratification. Using attentional strategies during highly demanding times indicates that maternal (less often, paternal) responsiveness is crucial for the development of self-regulation, self-control and emotional competency.[3] Loving one`s child

---

1 `Phaedrus` pp. 29- and pp. 40-
2 Plato`s Republic Bk.IV e.g. par.441-2
3 See Rodriguez M.L. et al. In Social Development vol.14 no.1 2005

will require some tough refusal to yield to its persistent demands – for the child's sake. Discipline, in the form of persistent requirements by the parent during eating, toileting, bedtime, etc., enable the child to control impulse. Many adults are pretty hopeless at this one. Our society today makes it increasingly easy to receive instant gratification.

"We have devalued the time we spend alone just thinking, but it's that time for reflection that leads to the big ideas...Multi-tasking is espoused and almost glorified in the United States, but it is dehumanizing us and making us less creative." [1]

In addition to self-awareness and control, we cannot afford not to examine the effects of others on ourselves. For example, these days the influence of the popular press and entertainment media in the West tends to reinforce the presumption that wealth is the supreme mark of personal fulfilment. Mass communication is a worldwide business that frequently tends to have little interest in what is good for us: it usually confirms what we find easy to accept. It all too often panders to our weakest selves and is frequently willing to harm us as much as is financially profitable to it. Its interest in bettering the human lot is put aside for the sake of things the masses want to hear and read. Only certain newspapers, tending to have a smaller circulation, at least in the United Kingdom, endeavour to stand for the general good.

Our newspapers and entertainments also reflect those two horses powering the chariots of our lives and that of society at large. The calm, responsive, obedient horse is like those media that seek to convey true reports upon matters in the public interest with a view to promoting knowledge, understanding and humane values. The wayward stallion can be likened to those that seek to give the masses an easy, exciting, biased and titillating read about matters that are usually irrelevant to, or conflict with, the public interest, requiring little thinking and offering subjects for gossip. Public media of communication, information and entertainment form a large part of the cultural diet, and have a mighty influence on people's inner life. The effect of the sensationalist press on its readers is to increase their ignorance, pervert their outlook on life, and decrease their self-understanding. By contrast, the aim of the responsible

---

1   Alsop, Ronald J. (2011) 'Gotta have it, right now'. Notre Dame Magazine.

to the loss of mutuality and intimacy. Once upon a time, the table was laid, the plates arranged, the meal begun and shared together, hands having been washed. Cutlery was used, unlike in junk food outlets, and clearing the table and washing up was a shared task. The routine of family mealtimes bonds members together and enables informal talk during which children can express themselves and parents can enlighten, enjoy or guide them – a haven from the hustle and bustle of the wider world. The memory of these times can be taken into the future – not so with a trip to KFC or McDonald's, eating out of cartons on white plastic tables, or, worse still, in the car whilst travelling. Routines and continuities in the home are vital to upbringing, respect for parents and, of course, deferred gratification.

So, if you must buy the stuff, take it to the prepared meal table at home, and get it no more than once a month!

My references to Socrates, by contrast, can give the impression that our maturity requires formal education at a high level as well as so-called middle-class customs. Learning comes from many activities that are an informal aspect of the life lived and its struggle. That is how the formally uneducated can become wise and strong, although this achievement tends normally to have its roots in strong bonds with wise and thoughtful parents.

To illustrate how varied and wide our concept of maturity might be, here are three examples of fulfilled lives. Joey Deacon[1] was a cerebral palsy victim from childhood whose whole adult life was spent in an institution. Not until his old age did others learn that he had a full understanding of the world around him. One fellow 'patient', also handicapped, though able to speak, found out how to 'read' Joey's noise and movements. Another patient possessed a typewriter. At a painfully slow pace, Joey's autobiography was thus written. Miraculously, with the help of a perceptive

---

1   24 May 1920 - 3 December 1981

consultant and devoted friends, Joey published his life story[1]. He was never wealthy, had no sex life, was hardly famous, and died within a few years of his success. With his royalties, Joey purchased a bungalow in the grounds of St. Lawrence's Hospital Caterham, and lived there with his friends who were also disabled. He overcame his worst handicap, retained his courage and determination, and inspired others. Joey fits few of the popularized versions of the fulfilled life, yet he developed his mind, and loved life and other living beings. Little else matters, and nothing matters more.

Freda, who lives near me, and of whom I have no picture, spent her life as a housewife and teacher until she decided, late in life, to volunteer to teach in South Africa amongst the poor country folk. Her two years there enabled her to find a new kind of fulfilment enabling young people to learn, and, as things turned out, to help them protect themselves against the scourge of Aids. Now, having completed her assignment, she enjoys retirement, using some of her time helping others who are volunteering with VSO. Hers is an unremarkable life, viewed from the perspective of seekers after fame, but it is a life finding itself in the joy of others.

Lilian did this. In her old age, Lilian, my step-grandmother, inherited £300 from a woman to whom she was unrelated but of whom she was the only known friend. She had never possessed money like this. After some investigative research she found ten other people who could have an equal claim on the money, and sent £30 to each. Lilian enjoyed company and conversation – she enjoyed people. She cared nothing for material wealth, and I don't think she ever had, or even wanted, a holiday.

Ludwig Wittgenstein, the great philosopher, was the son of one of the richest men in the world, the steel magnate, Karl Wittgenstein, and inherited, with his siblings, the vast fortune, but in 1919, when only 30

---

1   'Tongue-Tied' - see Bibliography. I recall a chance meeting with Joey in Coulsdon, Surrey, High St., and having a conversation with him through his friend. Unforgettable!

years old, he insisted that he receive nothing. He preferred to hand his wealth to the rich rather than the poor. The former would be unaffected by it, the latter corrupted! Wittgenstein saw clearly the value of owning as little as possible.

More impressive for me was the centenarian who appeared on the `Terry Wogan` chat show on BBC television some years ago. `How do you manage to keep smiling at your age?` he asked. `I find my happiness in the happiness of others`, she replied. Such a source of delight cannot be summoned up from nothing: it is the climax of a life story in which one`s self-oriented cares slowly but surely fade into the background. If we fail to attain that, we may, as the years advance, lose the love of living.

To Lose or Find Oneself?

Whatever else we may find obscure about Martin Heidegger`s thought, one insight must surely be of vital importance, namely that *the most distinctive feature of human being is to be found in its ability to find or lose itself.* The nation, race, and species can find or lose its soul[1]. Man is in the world without being of it. That is, he can become worthy of his humanity or not. For example, a person loses himself as he blindly follows tasks without reflection on their significance. He can lose himself as he only sees people and things as useful aids to making things and controlling his world. He can find himself as he learns also to contemplate his life, to listen to the signs and signals coming to him from the spheres in which he exists, and to respond as he draws from the myriad pools of excellence. He is a `Being-in-the-world`, a term Heidegger used as the most distinctive feature of the human being. As such he can ask `What is my true life?`, and his response can deepen his relationship to his world. Heidegger gave few clear and simple indications of an answer to this question. That is because his answer might otherwise be taken as a

---

1   `Being and Time` p.76 Of course, Heidegger was probably inspired by the passage from St. Matthew`s gospel `If any man will come after me let him take up his cross and follow me....what shall it a profit a man if he gain the whole world and lose his own self?` (ch.10 vv.38-9). But how can I cite this in full without giving the false impression that the life of love cannot be pursued unless we take a myth literally? Too many who seek comfort through a life beyond the grave fail to see and live the message.

formula to be borrowed: the answer has to be truly one's own. However, he did, in his later works, emphasize the importance of the meditative, a faculty in man that has become crowded out by concern with practical ambition. Meditative thought opens up reality in a completely different, even mystical way. Powerfully structured though our bodies and brains may be through our genetic inheritance, we live in the world as potentially autonomous beings, and have a long way to go before we actualize the possibility. We make changes as a result of considered thought: we can initiate, innovate and decide one way or another about a matter, *so that not even an omniscient God could predict for sure what we might think or do because it is our creation.* That is our nature as maturing selves. That belongs to our spirituality. We mature into living agents for change towards good.

> Various thinkers from Kierkegaard to Dostoevsky, Nietzsche and Sartre have been labelled `Existentialist`. Heidegger has also, at least in his early thought, been included. Their concern has been to focus upon the living self as a subject, rather than with ideas of what may or may not exist in the external world. The concern is with the dynamic of living in the world and how we might do so authentically as opposed to being victims of fashionable ideas and attitudes. Such thinkers may more accurately be called `Phenomenalist`. Like the founder of Phenomenalism, Edmund Husserl, each claims to see beyond and behind everyday assumptions. They seek to transcend the conventions that cloud our understanding of what it is to be human and to find a path to deliverance from mental oppression through authentic living. Thus the path one chooses in vital aspects of living becomes truly one's own. Clearly insights about oneself and one's relationships lead to a more critical attitude to everyday living. The chief difficulty that remains relates to whether we can think and choose for ourselves without submitting to the influence of the past and of others.

Thought feeds on culture. There can be thought that is inauthentic because it is not truly our own, and there can be thought coming to us from a conversation, book or drama that becomes authentic because it has been made truly ours. Thus we have to understand ourselves in a way that goes beyond the biological and scientific. We are more than the sum of our parts. We are dangerously powerful beings, the development of whose minds is our own responsibility. We have to learn to take charge of our ways if we are to avoid the status of vermin on the planet. We are pivotal to the future of life in the world, with no predetermined guarantee of success.

All of us have a calling to family, society, species and the natural world. This is not a dogma of the humanist. It is a requirement of meaningful communication with each other. To seek the truth without prejudice is to listen to all who claim to speak it. If we grunt at the world and its cultures, its problems and its unfinished business, walk away to solitude or to join a group of non-participants in the life of wider society, we have failed ourselves and our fellows. There is more to life than being left alone, or in a huddle, to waste it.

(This also implies that we must learn to listen to those we love but ordinarily regard as strange in their way of life, to grandparent, son-in-law, child, aunt, even father and mother, just as we should expect them to listen to us!)

There is a relationship with the world of nature itself, both living and inanimate. Our being extends to this. It inspires us, gives us common joys, teaches us, sharpens our perception, and helps us keep things in perspective. This oneness with the world is a primal and vital dimension of being which is under threat from our world of objects made, bought, possessed and dumped. In the world of culture, of the arts and sciences, in film, book and play we find powerful symbols of life's light and darkness. They are there to shake us out of our unconscious state, to see what we have done to ourselves and how we might enhance our inner life. They are there to point the way to abundance. They give life to our inner selves. It is in our infancy, in our private encounters with other beings and scenes that we freely begin to feel the life of the world, to find joy and excitement in the encounter. That is the beginning of growth. It cannot come simply from systematic programming by adults. That tends to yield counterproductive results[1].

Why do so many of us lose our childhood joy and sense of the awesome nature of life? Why is it that our faculty for laughter diminishes as we grow older? It is not because life is tough: for most it is too easy. It is because we have lost our way and have no place to refresh our spirits. Of course all this talk really matters. It matters more than religion simply because religion, in its widespread institutional forms, tends to settle all the important issues of life and marks out a narrow path for our minds, not for their creative imagination, but for their control.

Our emphasis on maturity also contrasts sharply with the growing number of books on `happiness`. Such regard happiness is the ultimate goal of all, so that once we attain a level of stable and long-term happiness, our lives are fulfilled. The least profound of these works simply show what makes people happy and what makes them sad and offer data suggesting paths to help us cheer up in life[2]. They do little to ask wherein lie self-fulfilment and maturity of being. Happiness is not enough, and it should not be the focus of our striving. Parents may find that children bring grief which itself does lasting damage to their health. I know a lady whose son is mentally sick: she has done all she can over many years, but no improvement is seen. She will ever love him and would die, if it helped, to help him. That is because she is his mother. Even her son`s happiness is not her goal: he might be happy doing the most destructive things. She lives for her son`s well-being, his finding himself, in some way at least. This is a magnificent aspect of her attainment as a mature human being. She has reached a height not perceived by those who think in worldly terms of wealth, public recognition and pleasure. She has gained the right to live and die in peace.

---

1   This is the urgent message of `Too Much Too Soon: Early Learning and the Erosion of Childhood` (2011) a seminal publication whose contributors cite the powerful international research that has led some European nations such as Finland, a world leader in educational success, to reject systematic goal-focused preschool learning in favour of play, music and story bases for infant activities.
2   See for example Powdthavee, D. (2010)

George Mallory and the Mould-breakers

As one might suspect in the light of the foregoing, I found myself challenged by the virtual canonization of people like Mallory and Irvine, the early mountaineers who died on Everest. Each personified the heroic ideal pervading public school education in the early years of 20th century Britain. I considered that Mallory had a wife and children whilst at the same leaving teaching to repeatedly travel on dangerous expeditions. The 1924 Everest tragedy reflected, we might think, a lack of *sophrosune* (practical wisdom) on George Mallory's part, not to mention a lack of parental love.[1] Whilst the climbing of a mountain provides a prime metaphor for facing and overcoming difficulty, initial doubt about it as enhancing the path to maturity may remain because the participant is putting his or her life at risk for the sake of an achievement of questionable value. One might also think of anyone who wants to `push the limits` of life-risking achievement from depth-diving to trans-Antarctic walk and ski treks. There lives in people, it seems, especially in the male of the species, an apparently irresistible urge to outperform and to be a pioneer. That, however, may well be vital to human advance, even in the modern age. Even crazy achievements, like skydiving from space, may expand the frontiers of civilization. (How I know not.)

Mountaineering, like exploring unknown places, feeds mind and spirit. The doing of it is not necessarily for some extraneous end. The task becomes an irresistible vision. The mountaineer understands how this can be life-enhancing and profound. Nothing else can prove himself to himself, and to others, in quite the same way. The heroic explorer or mountaineer certainly develops great inner strength and becomes an inspiration to others: the desire to conquer a height, to scale a near vertical rock face, sometimes without any tools apart from the hands and feet, is a magnificent generator of virtue. It develops courage, self-belief, almost superhuman skill, and inspires wonderment in others. Whether it is also vain self-seeking is known only to the climber. Perhaps our heroes should enjoy their fame without seeking it.

I might accommodate such people to my idea of maturity by saying that the mature life is not always simple to define. For most of us, the path of

---

1   See Gillman's book, `The Wildest Dream` (2000) on Mallory's life.

practical wisdom and love, with consideration for the long-term results of our manner of life, must be paramount. But here we find an irresistible passion, a channel for energy not to be left aside. It was present from early childhood[1]. That man had to climb Everest or die in the attempt. It defined his *telos,* but surely cannot be taken as an excuse for others to venture on such a momentous task in a foolhardy (to us here and now) fashion. We may then allow that exceptional people may live short lives because they possess a kind of overwhelming vision, and cannot but pursue goals deemed foolish by the wise, the success of which has but an outside chance. The romantic hero inspires for years to follow. Oates, Matthew Webb and Amelia Earhart did not die in vain: the moral luck of becoming an immortal was, in the long term, on their side.

I have to allow that degree of maturity is not the only yardstick of greatness or *telos* for every life. I may choose not to claim maturity of spirit for such as Mallory, or Guy Gibson[2], who became addicted to dangers that predictably cost him his life. They behaved idiotically, one might say, pushing their luck that bit too far. In times of peace, the few generate in the living a vision of humanity at its greatest. My courage to face up to possible pain under medical treatment is strengthened by thoughts of Yeo-Thomas, `the bravest of the brave`. Mine is a pinprick by comparison.

Maturity is not, then, the be-all and end-all of human existence, but if the majority fail to approach it, even in their old age, communal life has a poor future. Neither is maturity likely to be a *consciously* chosen goal; it's far too general a concept for that. Nevertheless it requires thinking time if we are to have any critical tool for taking stock of our direction in life. Without such a steering mechanism, we may wander wherever our fancies draw us.

To What Goal?

That human growth, whether as maturity of spirit or stability of communal life, will not be achieved through the endless pursuit of economic growth,

---

1   Gillman`s biography tells us that he climbed roofs and walls from childhood, compulsively and with innate expertise.

2   Guy Gibson VC, British WWII hero.

particularly in the developed world, has long been known:

> "In contemplating any progressive movement, not in its nature unlimited, the mind is not satisfied with merely tracing the laws of the movement; it cannot but ask the further question, to what goal? Towards what ultimate point is society tending by its industrial progress? When the progress ceases, in what condition are we to expect that it will leave mankind? It must always have been seen, more or less distinctly, by political economists, that the increase of wealth is not boundless: that at the end of what they term the progressive state lies the stationary state, that all progress in wealth is but a postponement of this, and that each step in advance is an approach to it." John Stuart Mill (1848)

Whilst the phenomena of modern technology and wealth creation weaken Mill's view, since new technologies may reduce the consumption of materials, indeed, wealth creation may not always involve visible goods at all, the point remains as to what else progress is about than quantifiable wealth production. At the present time, this very wealth production is itself being diverted to the new super-rich, benefiting from global finance, whose self-interest diverts wealth from its truest goals – the transformation of the human lot through education, meaningful work and health provision for all.[1]

Assuming that such corruption will one day be rectified and wealth become a benefit to all according to their deserts, the question remains: what is to be the source of fulfilment for the people? Undoubtedly, when all the pains of living that could be eased are eased, when none are deprived of their basic rights, none suffer birth defects, none live in danger from others, when the race lives in peace and plenty, what is to be our life?

There will be then, surely, time for leisure as 'play' that is spontaneous and freely done. But then, our play, if requiring nothing of our characters

---

1   See Will Hutton 'The world is actually stagnating' in UK Guardian Weekly 18th Feb.2011.p21.

in terms of skill of mind and body, will leave us without growth benefits. We then reinforce our emptiness. The cycle of boom and bust returns. By contrast, play must be understood, not as a trivial aside to real living, but as an aspect of our fulfilment as humans. We grow through play.

Our vision will be one in which the inner life of the self is as important as outward prosperity. Indeed it is <u>more</u> important, since it can, for example, enable a meaningful life within hardship. Our tendency to greed can only be defeated through the growth of unquantifiable values like friendship, learning, and the pursuit of excellence. The post-materialist age needs bringing forward, both for each of us now, and for society. This focus brings us to the need for, and means to, finding depth and shared direction despite the demise of the master stories of Christianity in ordinary life. Indeed, `direction` is only half the story, for, as we shall see `direction` is not everything. It is a good metaphor, but, like all metaphors, incomplete and potentially distorting. `Destinations` are just as important. Our fulfilment consists in getting places worth arriving at along the way.

That said, we should strive for economic productivity within the context of sustainability. We have no other choice if we are to preserve our communities. However, economic values tend so readily to usurp the life of the mind and the fostering of virtue which are of far more telling value than production. These enable us to attain a perspective on wealth, its uses and dangers. Ultimately, we may regain the vision of St. Francis, Wittgenstein and my grandmother, that of the joy of owning as little as possible.

Conserving the wisdom of the past is no less important than moving forward into the future. The good life for mankind will take on many traditional forms and involve myriad practices, but is one in its deepest meanings. Its kaleidoscopic forms all add to the wealth in the world. The most enduring and promising forms of wealth are not material, but are expressions of the enjoyment of life, of the profound in the everyday, of the lasting in the passing, of the bonds of love. Our passions are to be kindled, but kindled through considered choice of their object. Thus they are focused upon worthy goals which *are* their own reward.

We now perceive that our upbringing and education, beginning as it should, with play, creates for us playing of increasingly sophisticated form. Our schooling, leading to a lifelong education, is to focus upon play, not simply in the childhood sense of pretending in an imaginary world, but in an adult sense of pursuing interests that fascinate and are precious for what they are in themselves and not simply for what they might lead to. A successful school education gives learners precious pursuits for life, whether or not they also provide for their material needs.

In this world of high stress work, ladders of promotion up which we are expecting to climb, productivity targets, the pressure to update, and criterion-based scrutiny, we may cease to play altogether. We can easily forget the pleasure of unplanned conversation about whatever pleases, strolling in relaxed fashion, reading for pleasure, observing nature, constructing something simply because we want to, playing sports for the love of them (as opposed to meeting the social expectations of others), enriching one`s senses so that one notices things (perhaps by painting, perhaps by observing creatures). Ultimately, there is no goal for mankind beyond growth into wisdom, love and understanding. Our education is for these. Jobs, schedules, contracts, and production are all subservient to the former. When we grasp that, wealth creation may also trouble us less.

"I saw an ancient path, an ancient road, travelled by the Rightly Self-awakened Ones of former times. And what is that ancient path, that ancient road, travelled by the Rightly Self-awakened Ones of former times? Just this Noble Eightfold Path: right view, right aspiration, right speech, right action, right livelihood, right effort, right mindfulness, right concentration...I followed that path. Following it, I came to direct knowledge of aging & death, direct knowledge of the origination of aging & death, direct knowledge of the cessation of aging & death, direct knowledge of the path leading to the cessation of aging & death..."

(from the Nagara Sutta, the teaching of Buddha)

"Enter by the narrow gate; for the gate is wide and the way is easy, that leads to destruction, and those that enter by it are many. For the gate is narrow and the way is hard, that leads to life, and those who find it are few."

(St. Matthew ch.7 vv.13-14 RSV)

CHAPTER 2: IN SUPPORT OF THE SPIRIT

"The sea of Faith
Was once, too, at the full, and round earth`s shore
Lay like the folds of a bright girdle furl`d.
But now I only hear
Its melancholy long, withdrawing roar,
Retreating to the breath
Of the night-wind, down the vast edges drear
And naked shingles of the world."
- Matthew Arnold `Dover Beach` (1867)

"What is truly great is accessible to all"
- Kierkegaard , Fear and Trembling (published 1843)

In the contemporary context, religious identity, which was once synonymous with spiritual identity, is fast fading from view amongst developed nations and only seems to get attention when it has a political face. Whether this becomes increasingly so depends upon how religions themselves face up to the most pressing issues of the present. The being of our soul (or `psyche` of the ancient Greeks) is, in our secular world, no longer seen to be related to a supernatural cosmos watched over by the Supreme Ruler and Saviour. There is now, in this secular world, no majority worship or fear of the Almighty. We have, associated with this, a loss of concern about how to live a righteous life. Indeed, the very notion of `righteousness` belongs to past centuries. The superstructure[1] of creed, dogma, belief in miracle, resurrection, judgment day, etc., can readily be understood as a system giving meaning to our existence, guiding our behaviour in rigid directions, and giving specific identity to the divine. It gives the institution, such as the Christian Church, its authoritative message to believers and enables them to know how to

---

1   My late university supervisor, Dr.Terence McLaughlin, made this helpful distinction between the `foundations` of religion and its `superstructure`.

live. The `foundations`, on the other hand, are those sensibilities which have given force to such superstructures. These may include a sense of mystery, awe and wonderment at life, inner awareness of good and evil and our standing in relation to them, of our tendency to destroy and fall short, of guilt and the need for forgiveness and restitution, of the preciousness of life and the immense value we place on the life of those we love. These foundational awarenesses are not themselves religious in the sense that they are system dependent. They remain at the heart of our devotion to the well-being of the world, people and nature.

Such foundations, enhanced through the traditional teaching of our upbringing, tend to become lost once we reject the beliefs and practices of the religious superstructure. Thus, to question the Crucifixion and Resurrection of Christ as the way of salvation so readily leads to the loss of a sense of our own corruption and the possibility of repentance and deliverance: but this should not be so. The foundational sense of life`s momentousness for me can remain whatever my beliefs: we may shake free from the bonds of religious realism without losing the virtues it engendered within us. We can still wonder at the miracle of evolution, experience shame at our failure to become what we know we should, whether or not the judge of all the earth records it, and learn to know the joy and pain of loving without expecting reward of any kind. The soul can live on.

However, through the traditions of faith, our sense of the preciousness of the lives of people, creatures and the cosmos has been generated and fostered throughout history. From their rituals, stories, celebrations and sayings, our sensibility to the precious calling of our lives towards thankfulness, wonderment, and the path of wisdom is brought to consciousness. We cannot understand education or human maturity without understanding this. From cradle to grave, the powerful symbols we encounter feed our spirit. Traditional religious stories, parables and sayings are archetypes of such, and deserve to be conserved and revisited throughout our lives as belonging to those powerful symbols that can awaken us to the largest issues of our lives. There is, of course, no need to hallow such stories as divine, and their insights can be learned equally well through the wealth of modern fiction. Lifelong education to maturity is founded upon such symbolism, fuelling our sense of life`s mysterious, precious yet temporary nature. This awareness empowers parent and teacher, and its growth in the learner is perhaps the supreme mark of an effective education.

> The view that life is sacred need not leave us once we reject the dogma of religion. We may no longer take literally those miraculous events in the life of Christ, but that does not mean we must lose our sense of the mystery of life and of the supreme miracle, that of humanity itself. We need not look outside the miracle for a divine explanation. The chance-laden evolution that has led to ourselves is itself cause for wonderment. Life certainly comes from almost nothing. We might, therefore, see no need to `go outside` for explanations.
>
> We may not, however, view this `naturalism` as complete. There remains, for example, a gulf between scientific understanding and the autonomy, the freedom, and the individuality of the living person. I am me: the whole is more than the sum of its parts. Mystery returns. A gulf remains between the world of DNA, genes, cells and neurons and the living person. Somehow a sense of awe clings on. We then think we see as through a glass, darkly[1]. Once we sense the extent of our darkness, we know our ignorance and find ourselves on the way to sharing the visions of others.
>
> Perhaps that is why religion, in some form, will live as long as Humankind.

One of the central factors in this departure from religion has been the decline of theism and the absence of ideas of the divine to surpass it. `A-theism` need not imply the loss of a sense of the miraculous and

---

1   1 Corinthians ch13.v 12

mysterious in our being alive.[1] It certainly implies loss of acceptance of ideas of a God who foreknows our thoughts and deeds, even determining them in order to enact His will, as well as intervening in natural processes to show His love. Such is theism, which survives more through its emotive attractiveness than its coherence. But this loss of traditional theological loyalty need not necessarily imply the denial of the transcendent in our existence, or the power of love to change the world. The spiritual forces that drive humankind for good and evil are no less powerful for not being turned into gods and angels, for they are our inner selves, our *psyches.*

Here are words I often see on an 18th century tombstone as I pass it:

> `Keep innocency and take heed to that which is right,
> For that shall bring a man peace at the last.` [2]

I first saw this in 1985, when it was clearly legible. Now the words are fast disappearing from view and can only be read clearly when the low sun shines upon them on a winter`s day. Just because the divine world has lost credibility, that does not mean we have to forget our inner selves, the meaning of true maturity for us and the well-being of the world at large, for both are indivisibly connected. Having lived what has become a life of truth to ourselves gives strength as we approach the end of our lives. Can we find a path to follow together beyond that we individually tread out? With the loss of a master story directing our lives do we have a path to follow at all?

Consider the spirituality of religious believers. Mary Seacole forsook a life of ease and affluence and a life of married domestic normality for the dark and painful places of this world and she transformed them. Did she do so on the strength of her belief that her reward was to be found in heaven? If her eternal destiny were the explanation, we would think far less of her than if it were that she cared about the suffering of the sick and

---

1   Theism might be superseded by other ideas of God in Christianity known as `panentheism` and ` process theology`. Key proponents of such were Teilhard de Chardin, A.N.Whitehead and Charles Hartshorne, this last being the least unreadable. Rem Edwards (1972-) writes clearly on this subject
2   Thomas Palmer (d.1779) Psalm 37 v.38 at St. Edith`s Church, Kemsing, Kent.

wounded. The imagined eternal reward carries little weight. The hope of it could give no stamina of the sort required to persist against enduring long odds and would fall short of unconditional loving. So the master story may inspire to love, but only as scaffolding supports a building in a temporary way. The story creates virtue that stands independently.

Mary Seacole amazes me even more than Florence Nightingale. A Creole from Jamaica, she spent years gaining traditional medical experience whilst helping American soldiers in Panama before unsuccessfully applying to offer her nursing services in the Crimean War[1]. Her fame spread amongst British and other soldiers for her medical skills and hospitality. She built the `British Hotel` from driftwood and old building rubble and fed and housed the sick. She treated them with traditional poultices and herbal methods learned from her mother. Her unremitting compassionate love for the men in need was, in later years, celebrated throughout Britain, and funds were established to gain her release from bankruptcy. She had spent all her inheritance on her work. She was not known to be a devout person in any religious sense, although she was a Roman Catholic by birth. Her love enabled her to understand the needs of the men, which included humour and good cheer. She also sold them liquor. Needless to say, much unfounded gossip and scandal followed her, probably because she could not have contrasted more clearly with the high-born Miss Nightingale, who, for some years, warned of the disreputable nature of Seacole`s work. Here are two people whose love transcended their formal religious beliefs. Propagating such beliefs amongst the suffering men, would inevitably have led to the questioning of their genuineness!

---

1   Mary Seacole (2005)

Understood as myth, to have a reward in heaven is to have no earthly or popular recognition, but to know that the life of devotion to the well-being of the world is an aspect of one's own full growth. The reward, if any there is to be, is inner wealth, the fulfilment of life. Nightingale and Seacole's stamina came from the single-minded vision, compassion, self-confidence, intellectual assurance, and refusal to be silenced, of extraordinary women. That was their spiritual life. The master narrative of the life of Christ to be found in the Bible was undoubtedly one, possibly the only, source of the value they placed upon the life of love, *but the value transcends the story.* As fiction, a story can inspire such love just as if it were known fact, perhaps more so: it can then yield truth that cannot easily be threatened. This is not to dismiss the master story, but to place greater value on the importance of myth in our spiritual development than beliefs in supernatural historical events so central to the theistic religions. Myth is not nonsense: myth can carry truth to the ages ahead.

Thus we can now reclaim human spiritual development from its institutional invader. The great religious organizations of the world, with their articles of faith, criteria of orthodoxy, requirements for salvation, entry qualifications for paradise, their version of history and the end of the world, have come to imprison the human spirit. Their grip is loosening (or perhaps becoming more desperate) year by year as the world becomes smaller and minds are opened to freedom. Religious observance is not to be our master but, at best, our servant. It has to be understood in a new way. The myriad symbols of story, ritual and custom may evoke a sense of life's fragility and momentousness, and may themselves generate new insights. We cannot, and do not, live without its language, as I hope to show, but to mature, to be a blessed spirit, we need not be 'religious', at least in the sense that we need a supernatural edifice that comforts our sorrows and explains our existence. Supernatural beliefs have had their day, the love their stories and sayings created, lives on. We have indeed 'come of age'.

In the secure and prosperous English-speaking world, at some distance from the forces of natural and human evil, the sacred story is hardly taken seriously. Initiation into the kingdom of the saved becomes, for most, no more than the celebration of a new life at baptism, and the rites of religion no more than the occasional expression of a sense of dissatisfaction with the mundane. It is quite unsurprising that the hopes of humanity have focused upon the improvement of earthly existence, especially when the tokens of traditional faith, such as the design evident in nature, the act of creation, and miracles of divine intervention have become sidelined through the growth of new ways of seeing the world.

But here begins the great tragedy of the present. Throwing out the master stories of the faiths is not simply to deny their basis in fact. It has become also to deny their basis in fiction, and *without fiction, we simply do not live, but merely exist*. We look at the language in the old stories, that of temptation, of losing our innocence, learning greed and hatred, of punishment for wickedness, of wandering in exile from home, of awesome power and mystery, of being saved by the skin of the teeth, of sacrifice, of forgiveness, of constant love, of dreams and visions. We need be mindful of such language habitually. It forms our being and comes from the depths of the past. True fiction, in a thousand stories, has conveyed it to us through the years. The master stories were the first in, and the most formative of, our cultural landscape.

All spiritual development, which is primarily the development of psychic self-identity, involves the personal composition of a coherent and creative life narrative. In what follows, I will consider those shared elements in the values, beliefs and attitudes of citizens in a humane culture, and show how the embodiment of such in narrative forms helps children and adults in the composition of their own life narratives.

Out of this common cultural ethos criteria for personal maturity become necessary:

These criteria are important because an idea of maturity as the state of being to be reached is an important prerequisite to any notion of development.

This is not maturity of body, but of mind, the centre of our being.

The Development of Mind Towards Maturity:

To develop we have to know where we are going. Unless teachers and parents focus their minds upon human maturity as the ultimate goal they are seeking to advance, they will be unlikely to progress much towards truly effective practice because they will have an inadequate vision of what it is they are trying, in the final analysis, to achieve for the learner.

To be mature in the depths of our being is not `happiness`, although its possession may bring a peace and assurance that people might call `happiness`. Neither is it prosperity in material things. Sometimes its possession may bring sorrow, poverty jealousy and fear.

In order to grow as individuals living within the whole world of beings, we need to share a master story, a global vision in which we all live and to the conclusion of which we all contribute. Otherwise our traditional communities may pull in opposing directions.

Once we share the global master story for today, namely the saving of the life of our planet from the destructive forces for which we are largely responsible, we grow through the power of symbolism energized through learning the arts and sciences. These are food for mind and heart and make us bearers of living meanings. They form the serious conversation of our communal life, furthering thought and action.

The creation and sharing of meanings, needing no point beyond themselves in terms of wealth creation, health enhancement, celebrity or social status, is the `Holy Grail` of our lives today. Some might want to say that the internet is a God-given tool to help us find it: they`d have a point.

Expressing our Deepest Responses to Being in the World

Therefore, the secular approach to the quest for maturity need not imply the demise of the sacred story, but rather its mythic role in the development of selfhood, as the work of Egan and others discussed below, supports. The major role of religious education surely lies, not in the inculcation of a religious view of life, at least as commonly understood, but in the development of knowledge, understanding and sensitivity to the messages of world traditions. By means of such, individuals can enhance their vision of a personal life narrative. The sacred stories and festivals of the world may now be seen as mediators of pivotal images and metaphors which serve as societal foundations to many peoples. If such stories are powerful in the secular world of today they find their power in their *expressive* role, rather than as historical and philosophical sources of truth. Their archetypal nature preserves their authority beyond their demise as literal history and as accounts of the forces controlling everything. They show people paths towards inner transformation of spirit.

The movement in theology towards *expressivism*[1], as opposed to *theological realism*, develops this interpretation. The expressivist view is, in essence, that religious forms of language and activity cannot be transposed into literal propositions about the way things are in the external world without distortion and loss, and without slipping into the status of authoritarian dogma. Therefore it is a misunderstanding to see them as rigidly assertive of what exists and how the world works.

Religious practice is irreducibly symbolic: it does not attempt to describe, but, at its most profound, to express deeply-held feelings about life as wondrous, as mysterious, as full of hope even in dark times, of life as a special gift to be lived wisely, as fragile, and as triumphant, even when all the signs seem to say otherwise. It is also intrinsically mysterious, the language and symbolism is itself an indication that the devotee's understanding is but dark.

As an unbeliever, I enter an old church. I think at this time of **St. Catherine's on the Hill** at Abbotsbury in Dorset, built in the 15th century. It is but a monument these days, empty, and with an earthen floor. It overlooks the world below. To be there is for me to leave the mundane, to be thankful

---

1   e.g.; Cupitt D, 1989; Fawcett T. 1970; Hick J. 1977; Keighley A. 1976; Phillips D.Z.,1971; Spong R, 1994

 for living, to know the shortness of my time on Earth, to be aware that I know almost nothing, and that, in the final analysis, my worries and fears cannot harm the wonder of living. I feel, when inside, at one with a thousand who have climbed the hill to this age-old place. That means no less for my lack of belief in traditional doctrines. I would not, as would many visitors to St. Catherine's, leave a prayer on paper in a niche. Such things signify the genuineness of those who climb the hill: they bring their lives to their God. It would be a violation to destroy them.

Sadly, this is resisted by the conservative wings of religious movements, who make great emphasis upon being a 'believer', all too easily forgetting the darkness in faith. The colloquial distinction between being a believer and being an unbeliever belongs to that corruption of thought which sees religious language and practice as based upon a list of indubitable assertions and experiences. The early Church, influenced by Greek philosophy, is the originator of this turning of faith into dotting the 'i's and crossing the 't's of a creed. Christians thus became defined, not by their love, but by their creed.

By contrast, the post-traditional age is one in which fiction is no longer rated as a poor second to fact as mediator of truths-to-live-by.[1] Under an expressivist umbrella, rich dialogue between traditions can become possible. It offers the likelihood that religion need no more be a cultural remnant in the open society, and that its language, rituals and stories live again. It is such symbolism that conveys a sense of life's precious fragility, of its mystery, of its coming to us as a gift, not to be taken for granted or abused, but to be enhanced through our living. It evokes reverence, wonderment, humility and sensitivity in the depths of our being. You cannot straitjacket what it means to be regenerate.

---

1   Cupitt 1991 p. xi

Education as the Development of the Human Spirit

If our common national culture is not religious, and the planned development of children into maturity should not be religious in any schools that are not specifically faith schools, why might we continue to speak of spiritual development at all? There are at least four reasons:

The spiritual self is the inner person, the self as existing behind its *persona*, its mask of appearances. This has as its goal self-understanding, which seeks to uncover the self as a product of the expectations of others and of its own unrealistic fantasies about itself, and to discover insights and outlooks that one can truly make one's own. Thus one can come to find oneself as a creative agent, developing in directions which one can truly underwrite and understand. The autonomous self will learn, reflect and choose, ultimately, on its own. As an autonomous self, one's life will neither be dominated by the conventions of the day, even though one may often choose to follow them, nor by inner impulsive whims based upon long-held unexamined biases.

This aspect of development is not the same as moral development, although one's morality will be affected by it. Such development is more fundamental than moral development, for it concerns one's attitude towards oneself and others, one's key values and ambitions and one's perspective on life. *It is about who one is, not simply what one does.* Virtues and vices may not declare themselves simply in deeds, for they lie deeper than actions performed in the field of human society. Good-looking deeds may come from a devious source. Conversely, deeds that appear harmful may have their source in foresight and concern for the best interests of those affected. Actions may not always signify what appears on the surface. Deeper in the psyche lie those powers which explain chosen actions.

The self seeks to be integrated and coherent. Whilst I may seem to be one person, judged in terms of my name, dwelling, roles, and biography, deeper analysis may reveal a fragmented existence, in which I take on a variety of lifestyles, perhaps contradictory in aim, having no coherent theme and, therefore, no unified meaning. I might be a different self, two or more sorts of person, in different places. It is one thing to have a variety of pursuits in life, another to have a variety of conflicting pursuits, entailing inconsistent loyalties, values and viewpoints. Spirituality includes, then, the movement towards becoming an integrated person, clearing out the inconsistencies in our lives and making sense of what we stand for.

> We may recall famous writers from the past who could not achieve this, men like **Dickens**, flying against his respectable self with his young mistress, his friends **Wilkie Collins** and the painter **Frith**, both of whom had two simultaneous families. They split their lives in two for the sake of powerful uncontrolled passion for women who adored them. (Secrets, especially sexual ones, have a mysterious way of invariably coming out.)
>
> We may have little doubt but that such brilliant people perverted their talent: they could always tell themselves a story to explain their deviance. The double life is destructive of one's integrity because it is a breach of trust. It might only be lived justifiably for the sake of the greater good of mankind, as with some secret agents in wartime: it is this greater cause which might deliver the self from integrity loss.[1]

At the heart of enduring relationships lies trust, which itself implies that we believe in the personal integrity of each other. That is not a superficial or pragmatic matter, but one that goes deep: hypocrisy, duplicity, dishonesty are vices at deep levels of the self: they are matters of the spirit, darknesses at the heart of our lives. They can only be erased through and with love. There is no other way: exposure, punishment, indoctrination, even conditioning can never change people irrevocably. They only find themselves through the discovery that they are respected and cared about, even when the path they must tread is hard and long. Such is the power of love.

---

1   Klaus Fuchs is perhaps an example. He lived a double life, working for the UK and USA on nuclear physics in the 1940s, yet also serving as a spy for Communist Russia. His overriding cause was the right of Russia to possess nuclear knowledge. This might, upon reflection, have saved the world from the use of such weapons in the Korean and Vietnam wars.

Inner development is progress from ill-being to well-being, that is, growth towards maturity. It is the unfolding of one`s most enduring and overriding commitments. Such commitments may, in some contexts, require resistance to conventional views for the sake of personal integrity, but, even should this be so, they will not be egocentric. It would not seem to be necessary to waste time arguing against a self-indulgent style of life. The self-indulgent, wilful or not, have become immune to the demands of humanity upon them, treat their existence as if it were of no significance for the future beyond it, and have no time for reflection. Their deepest thought is that `life sucks`, and the resultant strategy is to make the most of its opportunities in terms of survival and pleasure. This is a form of what I describe in the next chapter as `living in the cave`. The distinction is to be made between wilful, inconsiderate resistance to the norm, and resistance that comes from careful thought, undermining only those *unexamined* assumptions about maturity as conformity with convention.

Human development tends towards love as it grows. Indeed, spiritual maturity cannot, in the open, liberal society be religious in the old realist sense. If my life is based upon assent to beliefs given me by the founders of the faith, I cannot break these bonds in the name of love. They have become chains. I cannot truly learn from outsiders, nor respect their views, for my belief system is inviolable. How dare I continue to imagine that they simply do not understand because the divine light has not shone in their hearts? Such supernaturalist beliefs imprison me because I refuse to revere those who live in darkness. Once I was shocked to learn of a Christian charity, `Christian Aid`, building a mosque in a Muslim country for the local community.

The expressivist position gains further support from the insight, which originates in Freud, especially in his essay `The Future Of An Illusion` (1928), that the preciousness of religious beliefs tends to relate to their nature as comforters and motivators rather than their resistance to critical thought. They all too often reflect the `wish-fulfilment` motivation[1], in which people believe out of need for hope and security rather than on the basis of what `reality orientation` offers them. Freud also subscribed to the view that religious interpretations have a *de facto* indispensability

---

1   "fulfilment of the oldest, strongest, and most urgent wishes of mankind" (Standard Edition Ch. 6 pg.38).

to the well-being of most people. If this is still the case, the process of initiation into the values underlying secular education will threaten the protective cocoon of beliefs into which people tend to retreat at times of crisis. Nevertheless it can also have the effect of enabling self-awareness and self-criticism, through which growth out of this dependency can begin. Furthermore, as we pursue the way of love, so we can identify with suffering and death to the extent that we accept this for ourselves as Christians have always done for lesser creatures. Thus we can become more at one with other species.

Life comes to be seen as a gift made more precious and wonderful because of its very brevity and fragility. Once we become freed from our desperate wish that it should go on forever, we can focus all our capacity for wonderment upon the here and now, and upon all forms of life without having to feel sad that they will not go to heaven![1] *Religious meanings can be understood anew in a manner freed from their mundane association with `beliefs`.* It is time for the foolish distinction often made between believer, agnostic and atheist to be put aside on the grounds that it is founded on a failure to understand human spirituality. If there has to be a distinction it may be between merely existing and living abundantly.

Just a Few Marks of Personal Maturity

I've retained the term `spiritual` in order to show that our personal maturity lies deep within us. It serves to draw attention to the `underlying` *psyche* in who we truly are and which reveals what we wish to do with our lives. I now want to suggest that the mature person displays such qualities as those following, whether or not she identifies herself as a religious person in a traditional sense. The ten marks of maturity selected here (deferring gratification, altruism, mental enrichment, self-control, overcoming, growth through narrative, acceptance of life's brevity,

---

1   I consider the wonder that I exist at all. Billions did not even come to conception, let alone birth and survival: how dare I hope for immortality! To be here rather than nowhere, to have this life! But would I feel no need for immortality if life were for me and my beloved ones suffering and starvation? Religious hope will remain until all life-threatening suffering is no more.

commitment to the future, wise communication, enduring capacity for wonderment) are not to be taken as exhaustive.

1. **The mature person will be able to defer gratification.** Such people will recognize those forms of immediate desire fulfilment which lead to future loss. Their self-fulfilment will hardly be determined solely by forces of the present, whether within themselves or from outside, and will involve foregoing present satisfactions where these might lead to long-term frustration. They will, for example, be acutely aware of the dangers and limitations of the natural appetites, for, unchecked, these are a threat to their being.

Impulse, the sort of driving force that generates our worst follies, should not be entirely dismissed. Sudden intuitive decisions can also save the day, free the spirit and offer fresh understanding. But this is dangerous talk: it's unlikely that intuitions and impulses will open up life-enhancing territory unless they are themselves cultivated and sharpened through learning and experience. The teacher and parent foster deferral of gratification in children through rule keeping, and stimulating thought about the consequences of actions.

2. This entails, therefore, **commitment to others' fulfilment as much as one's own.** That does not mean we cease to look after ourselves: the best way to look after ourselves is to devote ourselves to tasks that serve others also. Such involves devotion to family and friends, caring for the needy, but also pursuing activities that have merit and attraction, thus enhancing thought and shared conversation. This attitude speeds the decline of anxiety about ageing, wealth, and one's own standing in the world. Constant anxiety about our past errors is certainly bad for us. Nevertheless, it is equally foolish to dismiss our past and enjoy the present ignoring the lessons we should have learned[1]. That can only come as we learn to value others as our friends, and deepen as we mix with them, talk with them and learn to share our lives together. Thus covenantal relationships

---

1   Such a view stands in strong opposition to unashamed hedonists like Flocker, who teaches that the only way to look after yourself is to maximize your pleasures by enjoying whatever you fancy, not taking life too seriously and not trying too hard. Surely living is a serious business: it is *my own* standing and success that can be taken too seriously. Only in this last point is he right. Flocker, M (2004) `The Hedonism Handbook`

come to reign supreme over contractual[1]: our world of family, locality, and friendship takes precedence, and defines our lives.

> If you are the regular supporter of a Third World charity, for example, and you have the opportunity to visit a place in Africa or India, you will no doubt admire the joy, friendship and community spirit, even in deprivation, of local people. As many of us as possible need to take up the opportunity to see how joy is to be found amongst the poor and unwesternized communities of the Third World. If we cannot do so directly, we should watch a video on the subject. See, for example, www.marysmeals.org.uk, a remarkable organization founded by a schoolgirl from Scotland to help young people in Malawi.

3. Spiritual maturity is marked by a person's **love of activities which promote quality of life in the mind.** It is quite natural for the human being to pursue material wealth, fame, and social standing, for doing so is pretty instinctive. On the other hand, the will to possession, acclaim, freedom and power cannot take pride of place in harmonious society, and cannot dominate the harmonious psyche. Whilst the desire to get rich and create an influence appears to be a common aspect of human nature, the question that should be asked is, surely, 'To what end?'. Mature persons will have answers, for their focus is not ultimately upon these, but upon the myriad objects of valuing which are loved for what they are in themselves, from fun with friends to sport, to group projects, making works of art and craft, dance and drama, or making and hearing music. They find a love of life in matters great and small in many places and through many pursuits. Such a love has no goal beyond itself.

> As I write during the 2012 London Olympics, greatness is measured in terms of sporting achievement. Sporting prowess is an activity which can develop great inner strength. The qualities possessed by young champions like Bradley Wiggins and Jessica Ennis are not simply physical, such as endurance, technique and control, but also include virtues such as persistence, self-belief, courage, honesty,

---

1   See Sacks cited above.

 self-discipline and mindfulness. 'Mindfulness' here, includes 'keeping a sense of proportion'. For example, success is often accompanied by fame and wealth. These can be a great barrier to growth unless the recipient has the ability to keep them in proportion and use them for the common good. Champions are an example and a model, and are, by virtue of their success, endowed with great power and responsibility. Last year, Bradley Wiggins won the Tour de France, a towering achievement. He has declared: "There are other things in my life that mean more to me than this. But in a sporting sense it's my greatest achievement. I've just won the Tour. What else is bigger than that?"

To maintain a sense of proportion in that context is truly an achievement!

4. **Self-control is a quality to accompany self-understanding.** This requires, as the Buddhists teach, a good foundation in the maintenance of an overall perspective on what is important in life and what is not. Hasty actions based upon the passions of the moment do not rule the mature personality. Passions have their place, of course, but, like horses, should only be left to run in a well-fenced field. That fence is experience, past learning and reflection upon it. In our decision-making, we often have no time to think. Love moves us, and in the virtuous person, habits will tend to promote a wise response.

Miracle in the Potomac Disaster, Winter 1982 – no time to think

An airliner carrying 78 passengers crashed into the river Potomac in Washington D.C. in very bad weather. Two people emerged as heroes during the rescue: Arland Williams and Lenny Skutnik. Known as the "sixth passenger," Williams survived the crash, and passed lifelines on to others rather than take one for himself. He ended up being the only plane passenger to die from drowning. When one of the survivors to whom Williams had passed a lifeline was unable to hold on to it, Skutnik, who was watching the unfolding tragedy, jumped into the freezing water and swam to rescue her.

5. **Overcoming is a hallmark of the mature self**. This is not the same as being successful in the conventional sense. One attribute central to inner strength is the ability to accept the adverse circumstances in which we find ourselves and endeavour to exploit them to the furtherance of our own and others` well-being. The truly great are often people who have overcome the apparent restrictions of bad fortune, employing it as a foundation upon which to build for the future. Even the limbless, deaf or poverty-stricken are enjoined not to curse their lot. In some way, unknown at the start, they can overcome.

To fail to reach the heights, in sport or anything else, can also enable us to mature. Oliver Burkeman makes a strong case for not overdoing the so-called "power of positive thinking" so successfully advocated by Norman Vincent Peale in the1950s[1]. It can be more effective and less destructive of the self to focus upon worst-case scenarios and degrees of failure as we embark on projects in life rather than to think only of succeeding. What matters is to `give the project our all` without deceiving ourselves into believing we shall inevitably succeed. Not only does it make success a surprise, it also enables us to cope more easily with failure. *Overcomers learn from failure, even if they never succeed as they would like.* Overcoming in the spiritual sense is not closely linked with outward success or failure. The self transcends either or falls a victim to either. The weaker self does not cope well either with success or failure.

Afghan athlete Tahmina Kohistani[2] knew from the start of her international career that it would be, in athletic terms, a fiasco. She was by far the slowest runner in the Olympic women`s 100 metres at London 2012. She was a true pioneer, hoping to inspire other

1   Burkemann in Guardian weekly 06/07/12 and his 2012 book (see bibliog.)
2   `Sprinter sounds clarion call to Afghan women` Guardian Friday 3/8/2012

women to assert their human rights. The only woman athlete from her war-ravaged country to compete in the Olympics, Kohistani had encountered fierce opposition from conservatives in Kabul but called on other Afghan women to follow her lead. Overcoming does not require success. Sometimes originality, forethought, and courage, will do!

Pervasive hindrances to maturity to be faced and overcome in the mature person include those vices and misconceptions that underlie our avid consumerism[1]. Sheer avarice, the want for things that enable us to appear sophisticated, or that make us appear ahead of the masses, and the general equating of wants with needs, become exposed for what they are – destructive of the inner growth of society. Advertising can be exposed for what it is.

And what subtle inner forces there are to overcome as we grow old and our course is largely run! Grumpiness about the state of the world and the loss of the past is one of our last hurdles. This can readily be neutralized as we know people who rekindle our faith in humanity, especially in the young, a regular target. I will keep grumpiness to a minimum in what follows.[2]

6. **Maturity of spirit thrives upon narrative.** The great variety of narrative may include myths, parables, fables, legends, sayings, novels, poetry, anything that stimulates the mind, to examine, in order to stimulate mind and heart. Narratives are vital, for they present values, explanations and forms of heroism. Story is not an optional extra in human development: it is our spiritual food. It gives form and direction to our progress, thus encouraging our growth as persons.

Shared stories enable the hearer to become strengthened as a member

---

1   See Skidelsky R & E ch.1 `Keynes` Mistake` The Skidelsky`s give a revealing analysis of insatiability and its social promotion in their 2012 book.
2   To transcend the grumpiness habit, read the grumpiest book I know! It turns Scottish dark wit into an art form and will have you laughing with inverted misery. See `The Wee Book of Calvin` (2004) Bill Duncan Penguin books. It is sad to see Michael Foley`s highly amusing and encyclopaedic `Age of Absurdity` (2010) marred by such depressing grumpiness, but the title does warn the reader.

of local, national and global society. Such vicarious experiences are not an option, to be left to the child. They have always served to shape the very being of societies.[1] As it is not possible to speak without a language, so it is not possible to grow without narrative that enriches the mind by offering new images, new tasks for the spirit, new ways to transcend the present, new ways of understanding people, and that reveals unnoticed virtues and qualities in things. Stories enable one to see life's obstacles and a way through them. Stories can penetrate to the inner person because, rather than directly point and give the answer, they reveal it only to the ready mind. Without them, people do not mature. They remain conscious of little but the set tasks of life, and the given relationships, and have nothing much to reflect with. Without a place in narratives new-found ideas are quickly forgotten. And stories make life fun.

It is within our being to seek a life narrative that is integrated, telling of *one* character, not several with incompatible lifestyles who cannot be understood or trusted. Where that story splits into sections, having endings and new beginnings, the uniting element is the insight that rejects past follies, or perhaps finds new ways of using skills learned, or finds depth in a new vision, task, and goal. As we grow, so we change, consolidating values, sidelining spent ideas, embracing new relationships and projects, but the story makes, however slowly, for continuity, a narrative of our growth towards maturity. (If I cannot see the story of my life, learn from its past, move on, and envisage its future with hope, I am in trouble with myself. Work is needed, of an inner sort.)

Listening to stories which come from the master narratives of world traditions enables us to imaginatively indwell their truth, their light and darkness, for ourselves. Wittgenstein distinguished between the 'surface' and the 'depth' grammar of stories. On the surface, they are largely not believable. Perhaps the first tellers knew that well, so hearers would feel the image and find the metaphor. Beneath the litcralism of a superficial interpretation, with its magic, its darkness at noon and its bloody Sun, awaits the power of symbol to fascinate, to inspire and to quicken the

---

1   It is also, surely, important that the child hears, reads and tells these. It is doubtful whether the visual experience of TV allows a return to the experience and recall of its narrative in the way that telling can. The voice on screen is not a living person here with me!

human spirit.

John Bunyan put it thus:

> "Am I afraid to say that holy writ,
> Which for its style and phrase puts down all wit,
> Is everywhere so full of all these things –
> Dark figures, allegories? Yet there springs
> From that same book that lustre, and those rays
> Of light, that turn our darkest nights to days."[1]

That is how we are able to perceive the drama in human life and grow within it. Let us notice also that, just as stories furnish rich symbolism, so also can places and objects. The one who reveres an object or place finds himself quickened by its inexhaustible meanings, unlike an idolater, who calls upon its magical powers. In the former, his mind is enlivened, in the latter, his mind is surrendered. The power of the printed story accelerated its long march of enriching the European mind during the 18th century. Such greats as Defoe, Swift, Fielding, Goldsmith, not to mention Continental playwrights and novelists, did not write merely to entertain. They wrote to quicken vitality, to sharpen perception, to bring fresh insight and hope to lives. Spiritually, such writing transformed minds in ways that the ancient master story, its reputation tarnished through being placed in the same canonical volume as the doctrines of St. Paul, no longer could.

Thus, deep and lasting spiritual transformation lies, not in the Evangelical Revivals of the past, important to the working classes though they were, but in the rise of deep fiction. Such work has had no axe to grind against new philosophy and science, and marches on, finding its appeal not in the yearnings of the heart for a paradise beyond the grave but in understanding and enriching our brief earthly lives.

7. The mature person lives contentedly in the knowledge of his own ageing and death.

The escape of the mind from the fact of its death is almost ensured in

---

1   Bunyan J. `The Author`s Apology for His Book` Pilgrim`s Progress 1678.

our society by our own abstract systems, which serve to "sequestrate experience"[1], so that ultimate questions about the meaning of our lives are only asked in times of extreme crisis, often when it is far too late. Knowing the transience of our lives helps us think again about what we seek to achieve whilst here. This awareness of the brevity of life is balanced with the perception that one's contribution to the human colonization of the future far outweighs the duration of one's own existence, and that this generates a sense of responsibility which will serve as a tool for considering the effects of present actions. Can I have contentment about my coming demise if I see much of my past life as one big mess after another? The consolation of penitence comes to us through the great stories of the past. When these are forgotten, hope dies. Penitence need not carry the implication that we think the Judgment Day will come. Penitence enables us to forgive ourselves now. We own up, we regret, we rebuke ourselves, we learn, we press on with life, not looking back.

8. By no means the least of these criteria for human maturity is **commitment to the well-being of the world beyond the local and the present.**

> `No man is an island, entire of itself...any man's death
> diminishes me because I am involved in Mankind;
> And, therefore never send to know for whom the bell tolls;
> it tolls for thee.`
> John Donne Meditation XVII.

How can we fulfil our humanity if we neglect the well-being of our species and the world over which we have so much influence and potential control? This implies that we live as political beings, deeply involved in issues of how money is spent, how justice can be achieved, how we can least harm the natural world, and how the young can be given exciting `life chances`.[2] It takes great strength of will to rise above excuse and indifference, especially when the giving of time and wealth is not praised or even noticed, yet how can a person be fulfilled if his life gives nothing to the world?

---

1   Giddens 1991, ch.5
2   Term also from Anthony Giddens` works.

Commitment to the well-being of the world also embraces resistance to overconsumption of its resources. One not-so-obvious example is that of the borrowing culture. Banks are said to exist largely to lend money for expansion of production and personal need-fulfilment. That is why they make money from savings and loan repayments as well as more speculative ventures. Therefore, when society is in recession there comes a cry for more lending in order to climb out. This is normal, but surely it is odd? Why should a person or company need to borrow in order to survive or expand? What has happened to the profits of the years of plenty? People have not saved their profits. Companies have not built-up capital reserves. Commitment has focused upon present consumption alone. Company directors have kept the profits: private earners have spent their spare earnings. It is wrong to allow a tradition of borrowing to dominate society. Greed is at the heart of things. Its far-reaching consequences should be foreseen. The mature person does not let material acquisition rule his life: he foregoes, for the sake of the future, self-indulgence. It`s as simple as Aesop`s fable of the ant and the grasshopper.

9. A further criterion of maturity lies in a person`s **ability to communicate openly with bearers of opposing viewpoints**. Debate becomes a matter of presenting the case on the basis of what one knows, and for reasons that are not hidden in deceit. It involves hearing and appraising the new without the influence of underlying self-interest and prejudice. The rare skills of listening and weighing up the results are developed. Self-awareness and understanding are obvious prerequisites, as is the willingness to consider the need for a change in one`s own ideas and actions. (We consider such qualities and their absence in Chapter 7.) Dogmatism inhibits communication. Confidence enhances it, as Gordon Allport wrote, "we can be sure without being cocksure"[1]. Furthermore, we would do well to recall Chesterton`s wise remark:

> "You cannot take the region called the unknown and calmly say that, though you know nothing about it, you know that all its gates are locked."[2]

---

1   Perhaps that is one reason Gordon Allport included the `Heuristic Character of the Mature Sentiment` in his criteria of maturity in religious belief. See `The Individual and His Religion` pp.81-

2   `William Blake` (1910) p.74, cited in Aidan Nichols (2009) p.10

We are nowadays being called away from the assumption, inbred since the early days of science and philosophy, that truth is one, at least in any simple sense such as `If I am right, you must be wrong`[1]. As cultural traditions meet, each has something to say, for each represents the accumulated wisdom of centuries. Fresh insights may instruct and enlighten us. I have in mind, for example, the Chinese view, coming from ages past, that the mature individual is devoted to the well-being of the whole community because his being *is* that of the community. It follows that the wisdom of time-honoured sages will always be greater than an individual`s leanings. For traditional Chinese, personal autonomy, with its free choice and uninhibited expression, is not personal maturity, but an aberration from the path. That view sits badly with democracy, of course, but we have also learned that democracy sits badly with inequalities in society. Human growth will always depend in part on mindfulness of the ancient lessons conveyed in cultural traditions. In the global world, these lessons meet, and should converse rather than resort to unexamined resistance to each other.

10. Spiritual maturity displays those **enduring capacities for wondering at life**, with which one is first endowed as a child. In this there is deep joy, delight and celebration. These generate the love of arts and sciences as gatherings from the otherwise inexpressible worlds of our lives. My wondering at the fact of my existence will inevitably lead me to a far-reaching insight; that my very being here on Earth was the most unlikely event. It took a billion events that might not have occurred, deep in the past evolution of humanity, and right into the recent past, for me to be here. There was, in the recent past, the fact that my father and mother met, made love, that one egg was fertilized by a certain sperm, and that the resulting foetus grew to be born and to survive until now. (`How dare I sigh for immortality?`, I wonder. I am a finite miracle. Now that we live in material abundance and peace, has the hope for immortality become redundant?)

Life comes to be seen as a gift made more precious and wonderful because of its very brevity and fragility. Once we become freed from our desperate wish that it should go on forever, we can focus all our capacity for wonderment upon the here and now, and upon all forms of

---

1   I am indebted to Sacks, J. (2002) pp.18- for this insight.

life without having to feel sad that they will not go to heaven! *Religious meanings can be understood anew in a manner freed from their mundane association with 'beliefs'.* It is time for the foolish distinction often made between believer, agnostic and atheist to be put aside on the grounds that it is founded on a failure to understand human spirituality. If there has to be a new distinction it may be between merely existing and living abundantly. In essence, the whole underlying point behind systems of religious practice and doctrine is that they are not essentially about the world out-there, but about the world in-here. If taking the identity of a tradition does not involve the transformation of one's life in such ways as the above, it counts for little.

"Let knowledge grow from more to more,
But more of reverence in us dwell;
That mind and soul, according well,
May make one music as before."

-Tennyson, 'In Memoriam A.H.H.' 1849

CHAPTER 3: SEEING ONLY SHADOWS ON THE WALL

`Life is not one damn thing after another: it`s the same damn thing over and over again`
(Mae West 1938)

`The utter servility of the masses comes out in their preference for a bovine existence`
(Aristotle c.330 BCE)

`God created the angels from intellect without sensuality, the beasts from sensuality without intellect, and humanity from both intellect and sensuality. So when a person`s intellect overcomes his sensuality, he is better than the angels, but when his sensuality overcomes his intellect, he is lower than the beasts` (Hadith – sayings of Mohammed C.750 CE)

The Cave of Myopia[1]

Many human beings live their lives as spiritual troglodytes, shut in from the light of the real world in which they might live, hardly perceiving their own lives or the world in which they find themselves. Such people might not even be described as `resigned` to something: they did not resign because they never signed up. In the *Republic,* Plato used an analogy in which he sees the ignorant person as one who lives, chained, in a cave.[2] Such people`s sole conscious awareness consists in perceiving images which they take to be real, but are only projected shadows on the cave wall. Their progression out of this cave into the real world is, for Plato, movement from illusion towards real objects, thence towards socially-derived opinions and thence towards true knowledge, reached when entering the world outside the cave of ignorance. The final state,

---

1 The Concise Oxford Dictionary gives a second meaning for myopia as "lack of imagination or intellectual insight". It is this mental condition rather than the physical condition of eyesight which is our focus.
2 The Republic Bk VII .514a-520a. (380 BC) diagram to be found in Wikipedia, if that helps!

called the vision of the "Form of the Good" is exit into the sunlight of true wisdom.

I take this imagery as an analogy. It reminds us that true wisdom cannot be attained unless we learn to think, and once we think, we are on our way, even if, unlike in his interpretation, the final goal is never reached. Only the philosopher might reach the later stages of departure from the cave: there is truth here, for the philosopher is in us all.

The analogy, or something like it, has force today. In a reasonably affluent and liberal society it is likely that a large number of people will either fail to develop in spirit from childhood or return to such a state of darkness through self-loss. Plato's cave immediately reminds me of a modern-day cinema, which might be misleading unless I put the matter with care.[1] Cinemas are very attractive, but a cinema is no place in which to live, even were our needs to be met by kindly friends passing food through the doors. Our understanding of life, our view of ourselves, and our place in this 'world' would come solely from films. To glean our images of happiness, success and greatness solely from things we watched on the big and little screens of public media would be to live in a myopic cave of imprisonment within the film or programme maker's version of life and maturity.

The cave has to be left in order that we may get out into the daylight of knowledge and understanding, reflecting, comparing, distinguishing mere desires from real needs, truths from delusions and wise actions from impulsive folly. It also has to be left if we are to experience profound joy beyond easy delights that leave us no wiser or stronger. Film fiction, just like reading printed stories, is not direct personal experience, it is vicarious. We can only enter the cinema, turn on the TV, or read a novel safely if we take with us insights that protect us from the unrealism of much that is offered there. That we cannot do if we have no real life away from the screen or page. The screens become our world.

The darkening powers that lead us back into the cave are resisted and exposed as we develop rich experience through conversation, books,

---

1   Please do not misunderstand the analogy of the cinema cave: film can be deeply artistic and symbolic for us, so long as we have minds receptive and alert.

films, TV… Oh dear, that advice is of no help at all, for it was just these things that distorted our view of life in the first place!

To find our best chance of genuine and lasting deliverance from a cave-bound life only *education* will do. This anchors us on to the wisdom of the ages and enables us to draw from it. How? Teachers, who include parents, are the key, for they must be the experts who know a good film, a good book, good television, good subjects for learning ideas and skills. Without teachers of integrity and skill the circle of darkness is not likely to be broken, nor the wisdom of ages passed on. Even if we become largely self-taught, we have to be directed initially to the best images and words that humankind can offer. Good teaching and good learning content are of equal importance. Good content will furnish essential knowledge, rich and far-reaching ideas, and solutions to problems of importance, all in the context of enabling human beings to understand themselves and their world.[1]

Teachers, after parents, hold the key to human growth towards maturity. They have to be equipped with great knowledge, skill and wisdom. The population fails to understand that teachers play a pivotal role in our future in a less obvious manner than medical experts yet which is every bit as crucial: they are agents in the development of mind. This shapes the future for each child and the community. The schoolteacher is not, however, the first and most significant person to teach us how to grow. Parents teach the child, from birth and onwards, the power of love, enabling the awakening of senses, of trust and hope in life. When this fails, the whole world view and expectations of the child are threatened, potentially for life.

All this is vital for the learner, but it can itself become a harmful shaping of their being. Passions to do a wide range of things that don`t fit the conventional may sometimes be allowed to run free! This world`s eccentrics, inventors, pioneers, and highest achievers need space to do the seemingly crazy things they love as children. More on this later! Eating and drinking, being entertained, buying stuff, sexual activity,

---

1   How then might the quality of teaching and status of the teacher be improved? I
    focus on this, being the most immediately practical solution to the current cultural
    decadence, in ch.8

travelling – all these valid and even vital things commonly become the dominant content of a person`s freely chosen activity. They tend to define the leisure activities of the masses – Aristotle`s "bovine existence".

> This is `**deep cave dwelling**`, a condition which pervades Western societies at the present time amongst the rich and the poor. What do such pursuits have in common?
>
> If successful they get immediate results. Any planning and reflection are harnessed to these immediate goals, and do not focus upon the long-term effects on oneself, others and the world.
>
> Also, these activities tend, by and large, to be cyclical. You have to take a break from them or they become boring and dissatisfying, and, with shopping and sex at least, exhausting. The physical needs of our lives have to be met, but they also have to be surpassed.
>
> They are not good in themselves. When we promote them as end goals, we lower our being to that of the lower beasts, stunting our mental life, emptying our minds of thought and conversation that enriches humanity.
>
> Such activities are not true `*teloi*` (ends or goals) for humanity, but serve merely as means. They promote survival at best, not life abundant. Basic needs met, we must focus beyond if we are to live in ways that distinguish humans from other species in a way that transcends the physical.

People who are born into wealth, or who suddenly come into it, may, nevertheless, find no attraction in the reflective or meditative (athletic, scientific, literary, musical, dramatic or artistic) aspects of life, and obtain their *divertissement* easily and, for the large part, pleasurably, caring for nothing much outside their social concerns. One measure of this is the inability to converse without cliché and to discuss anything beyond financial and other trivialities.

Culture as the Medium for Growth

What is this cultural world in which we do the things we do, and which fills our brains with the stuff that gives us our prejudices, assumptions, ambitions, etc.? Do many of us actually live only within this nearest-at-hand world, doing what we do simply because it is what the demands of our particular place in the world require? All too often this may be so. We need to step back from time to time to appraise how we have come to our present state of affairs, and whether we are making fair assumptions about the way things are going for us. Are we in charge? What dominates our minds? Do we notice causes for joy and contentment, or have we let the darkness take over? Is our dissatisfaction insatiable? Where did we get our ideas from? Do we care?

For many of us, mental hibernation can invade far too much of our waking time. Alertness of mind does not come automatically. Nurture, training and education are not optional add-ons: they fuel our consciousness. Unfortunately, these three can also hinder its development.! Sadly, this is achieved through such things as teaching in a planned and systematic way before a child is ready, putting pressure on him or her by focussing upon systematic progress. The mistake here lies in teaching how to do such things as read, write, spell, count, etc., at a time when what the child hungers to do is engage the world in its own way through play and self-initiated fascination. What damage we can do to the young child who is systematically put in harness to a programme of premature disciplined teaching! Even if it appears to handle such a regime, it is deprived of that more spontaneous and lasting love of the world cultivated in a caring and stimulative environment.[1]

One important lesson to be emphasized is that the human mind *is* its culture. There is no such thing as mind without culture. *Mind without culture is not mind: it is brain.* Symbols of meaning that enable a person

---

1   There is also much research to indicate that early teaching programmes such as are foisted upon nursery teachers in the UK Government's EYFS programme give no benefit in the long term. Indeed, Germany demands no systematic learning until the start of school age at seven years, two years later than in the UK, having found there to be no benefit arising for the child. See 'Viewing the Long-term Effects of Early Reading with an Open Eye' by S.P.Suggate in House et al (2011)

to represent actions, images, looks and gestures are all fundamental items in culture – a tradition of expressions and roles made by humans in order for them to develop mentally and interact socially. These carry the communal language, with words and word structures, gestures, and a multitude of symbolic forms. So, we can't understand ourselves until we understand the cultural influences upon us as well as the cultural influences we have upon others. We need to learn our society's own language, ideas, images, stories, parables, customs and ideals, for these convey its past, present and hoped-for future.[1] Unless this is achieved to at least a minimal extent, we lack communicable consciousness. *But for many of us, mental hibernation can invade far too much of our waking time.* Alertness of mind does not, then, come automatically. Nurture, training and education are not optional add-ons: they fuel our consciousness. Unfortunately, these can also hinder development as they switch out our lights. Sadly, this is achieved through such things as:

- teaching in a planned and systematic way before the children are ready for it;

- putting pressure on them by focussing upon their limitations and degree of progress;

- teaching how to do such things as read, write, spell, count, etc., at a time when what they longed to do was to engage the world through play, story and exploration.

Once such lights are lit, children can develop chosen attachments to the shared world.

Culture – Low and High

An aspect to be perceived all around us in the developed world, and particularly in Britain, is fashion, fashion that changes quickly but

---

1 "The destruction of the past is one of the most characteristic and eerie phenomena of the 20th century. Most young men and women …grow up in a sort of permanent present lacking any organic relation to the public past of the times they live in." -Eric Hobsbawn (2002)

may not last more than a decade at most. At the present time it is for tattoos which tend often to mimic Polynesian designs and, for men, the shaven head. (These will become *passé* in no time at all – the time to get into business as a tattoo remover.) Another aspect of low culture which one fears may last far longer is the ownership of motor vehicles representing imagined status and wealth, irrespective of any effects on the environment or functional relevance to the owners' practical needs. Such are known as positional goods[1]. Low culture is also reflected in popular entertainments such as soap operas, regularly watched by as much as two-thirds of the British population. These form a large slice of the subjects of informal conversation at home, work and 'pub', and tend to emphasize the darker side of human interactions, which appear far more interesting than happy events.[2] The subject matter of the popular press abounds in gossip about the lives of celebrities, extended accounts of shocking crimes, and pictures of semi-naked females. Low culture is popular culture. 'White-van-man' requires a good supply of sandwiches, a flask of coffee and a copy of the 'Mirror' or 'Sun', without which the day's work can hardly commence. That does not exhaust the forms of low culture by any means: mass devotion, even on an intercontinental scale, to massively over-financed football teams provides a crowning example. A season ticket will stretch family resources almost to breaking point, but without it a man can feel left behind.[3]

Herbert Marcuse wrote of "one-dimensional man" as humanity imprisoned in lifestyles thrust upon it by mass media, depriving it of any higher-level thought, especially of critical skills which might have offered deliverance.[4] But is low culture really bad for us? It can be insofar as it promotes loyalties and models to emulate which are stereotypical and not thought out. The forces that bind people to such are the desire for attachment and acceptance within the group, membership of which requires shared subjects for casual chat. Their long-term effects are not considered, especially regarding health, the development of mind in terms

---

1 Skidelsky pp 34- The richer people get, the more they tend to seek more expensive 'positional' goods.

2 Low culture can also deal with profound matters, such as aided suicide as did 'the UK's 'Coronation Street' in |Jan. 2014

3 Ibid. These are examples of 'bandwagon' goods, as are 4G mobile phones and up-to-date kitchens. (Kitchens get 'tired', they say.)

4 One-Dimensional Man: 1964, 1991

of knowledge, ideas, skills and attitudes, and contribution to the future of the planet and its life. This might not be harmful so long as followers can see it for what it is, and also pursue deeper meanings in life. Deeper meanings come, not simply from the disciplines of learning, but also from other paths to self-transcendence such as sport and exploration. (Marcuse would not have respect for sport as potentially offering a life transcending low culture, by contrast with the ancient Greeks.)

The route to 'high culture', and all stations between, is marked by a progression in complexity, applicability to life problems, expression of the profound in life, durability and debate-ability. High culture has its genesis in genius. Iconoclastic ideas and outlooks come from those who see in a manner transcending the common view of things, be it in literature, the sciences, mathematics, fine art, drama (including comedy), and architecture. Structures such as bridges, stadiums and office blocks will (hopefully) reflect high culture, being an expression of purity of form as imagined at the time. It is rare for high culture to pass away at great speed – although the contemporary modernist forms of structure of the mid-twentieth century are widely demolished now. They had little of benefit to say to us.

High culture is dependent for its genesis upon profound education, a process of development which alerts learners, enabling them to choose with understanding, to defend their choices, to know the significance of their lifestyles not only for themselves, but for the living world. Insofar as education fails, the student is shackled within the confines of low culture, which tend to reflect what Aristotle called "the preference of the masses for a bovine existence".

Things were not much better in the past – our impressions of a refined and relatively crime-free society in the Britain of 200 years past need to be tempered with the realization that refinement and maturity of mind were largely the possession of a small upper class from which came the literature and art of the time.[1] What is, nevertheless, tragic is widespread failure in more recent times to effectively disseminate the virtuous life through mass education. This began in the 19th and 20th centuries, but

---

1 Gilbert White`s 18th century diary makes mention of the vandalism of his prized melon plants by young lads.

reached its climax after the World Wars, with the growing cynicism of new generations, religion being the first and most significant victim.

> Here's an odd truth. **To despise `respectability` is to despise civilization.** A culture defines what is worthy of respect. Only some respectability is `empty`, the mark of which is conformity without understanding. Little is right about that. True respectability reflects the preference for conventional standards of behaviour with full awareness of the consequences of their loss and the benefits they endow. Nothing can be wrong with that. But even true respectability is questionable, especially at those times when new situations and dilemmas arise. It is not quite sacrosanct. Unconventional behaviour becomes creative and progressive as it reveals weaknesses in the conventional and opens up new paths for human development previously rejected as perverse. (We exonerate one who steals out of undeserved poverty.)

Without upbringing and education, people will have little with which to measure their lives, to measure those measures, and with which they may modify their responses. We all need to be brought up in a framework of beliefs and ideas of what is good, right, true and worthy of us; and all this needs to be instilled within the context of parental love and wisdom. That is not to claim that children always have to be told what is right and wrong behaviour, as if offering them a manual of instructions will do the job. Deeper than behaviour lie the valuing of people and things, awareness of the forces within oneself, possessing powers to help and hurt, and the qualities of character to cultivate if one is to become worthy of respect. The possession of virtues defines maturity of spirit. Such deep qualities are learned through the many forms and media of story that feed the mind, but, more importantly, they are assimilated through precious relationships with parents, teachers and friends.

> According to Michael Shermer, the following characteristics are shared by humans and other social animals, particularly the great apes: "...attachment and bonding, cooperation and mutual aid, sympathy and empathy, direct and indirect

reciprocity, altruism and reciprocal altruism, conflict resolution and peacemaking, deception and deception detection, community concern and caring about what others think about you, and awareness of and response to the social rules of the group".[1]

It appears that many more humans are seriously lacking in such qualities as a proportion of the total population than is the case with apes. Apes would not survive without the above qualities. Humans manage to survive without them, even if, in more deprived cases, they may enter care, prison or rough living. Humans can grow physically whilst failing to experience the benefits of such things as bonding, care and teaching, and this can happen from home life to schooling, later youth and in `adulthood`.

Educators have a steep uphill struggle, especially when children come face-to-face with the bestiality of adults on the media. A libertarian culture handicaps its children, and strict controls need to be set in the home simply because the state rarely legislates against corrupting the minds of the young. It follows that educators need humane standards and criteria if they are to give spiritual direction to their work. Guidance and authority roles must be revived in home, school and state policy in order to select what children feed upon mentally.

That does not simply mean preventing children from witnessing bloodshed, slaughter and pornography. In order to learn beneficially, children have to engage with what has been learned already. Other species do this by example. We go beyond that to initiating children into human ways by teaching. Nothing of spiritual worth comes from within alone. Even genius has to engage with traditions of wisdom, knowledge and skill. Newton, Mozart, Darwin, van Gogh, Freud, Einstein – all had to learn the skills, ideas, styles, strategies, theories, of what had gone before in order to extend them and take human knowledge and abilities to pastures new. It is not enough to be a `natural`. For some learning tasks, a human teacher (or coach) is essential, for others not, but a *source*

---

1   Shermer, M. (2004). "Why are we moral: The evolutionary origins of morality". In *The Science of Good and Evil*. New York: Times Books.

of learning, be it the voice of another, the printed page or a screen, is necessary to all. Accompanying this, guidance and selection is essential in order to select appropriate material, good tasks, and a good match to the needs of the learner at that time.

Even if people grow up into a specific, named, cultural tradition, like Christian Catholicism or Sunni Islam, do they have any *independent* criteria by which such a tradition can be appraised? A large number of people do not have any means of appraising the measures which they assume to be ones by which the satisfactoriness of their lives can be judged. For them, if the sacred book or holy man says it, it is right and true. We consider ourselves, especially if we acknowledge no religious way of life, to have outgrown the need to submit to an authority simply because it claims authority. Authority becomes something that has to be *earned*, not by magic, but by relevance, descriptive power, coherence with agreed truths, truth to life, etc. We can no longer be ruled by powers that make declarations and execrations. Well in the past our forefathers submitted, for it was better than punishment, and safer not to air doubts, but now we have learned to see through the dictates of those who refuse to be questioned. Charisma, presence, oratory and miracle working earned authority for millennia, but now the sources of our beliefs and hopes gain authority based upon sensibilities which stand independently of hallowed traditions, even if they had their birth in them.

It is important to remember that there are times and places when and where authoritarian cultural regimes are vital to human progress. Humanity has to pass through such times, and even return to them where necessary. After the relative anarchy of tribalism, centralized authority maintained respect through ideological systems which defined all knowledge, gave rules for living and promised a glorious end state for mankind. The Roman Emperor-god, Christian Papacy, Muslim Sultan, Mogul emperor, Hindu Swami, and Buddhist Abbott, held society together, and thus it remains in many parts of the world. These traditional forms were all historically vital, but are now becoming viewed under a fresh perspective. Such have not, until now, possessed a global perspective on themselves, a perspective having liberal and humane criteria for appraising local ways. For example the emergent global community commends respect for persons of any age, sex, race, or creed and rejects cruelty in all its forms. Whilst we also know that the idea of what is good and what is cruel is culturally influenced, most of us humans now perceive, whatever our culture, that cannibalism, enforced silence, slavery, torture, imprisonment of the innocent and mutilation are abhorrent. Progress is being made. Whilst it is not always simple to apply such criteria to the task of appraising cultural practices, it is the only way forward – and it yields powerful results.

That this is so is not because reason is a faculty in our minds that can give closed answers to questions about ultimate forces directing the cosmos and ourselves, but because reason makes sense as a tool of communication for all peoples, a tool which is a fundamental prerequisite for intercultural dialogue to work[1]. There are principles of effective communication and shared human values that transcend any one traditional culture, and these infiltrate a billion minds as they read the World Wide Web, which is, potentially and, we hope, predominantly, a force for good in the world.

Some ways to become less boring and more interesting:

I must accept the theory, however questionable, that my listeners may know more than me about the subject at hand. This should give me a better chance of listening and learning.

This will hopefully make me a better listener, thus multiplying my conversational attractiveness.

Beyond mere words, I need to be informed, having ideas and webs of knowledge arising from my interests.

Through music, art and literature I will be furnished with scenarios and symbols. Thus I sense more, perceive more, question myself more. This includes watching TV and film as well as reading.

This gets me to know more about the past, to enjoy and understand the present, and to envisage the future I want

---

1   see the work of Jurgen Habermas in ch.7

to see and the future I want to help prevent.

Cautionary points:

Don`t tell jokes, as wit, if you must attempt it, must be unrehearsed and spontaneous; amusing true stories, if brief, might be risked, occasionally.

Don`t think ahead about what the informal chat shall contain; let your relaxed, easy self, come out.

Silence is golden. If you find this unpalatable, just imagine – it might make you a mystery to others, someone to ask about...

Of course, the self-discipline involved in acquiring knowledge, understanding and skill is also hard. I think, for example, of the strain, even pain, that comes with the very thought of seeking solitude, expressing ideas to others, becoming physically fit for demanding tasks, reading carefully, listening to a teacher, trying to solve a problem or to master an idea. I also think of the ease with which I shy away towards more immediately pleasurable things. However, at the end of such a day I sleep more peacefully for having been in charge of myself by using my faculties. Too often we might agree, unusually perhaps, with St. Paul:

> "...the good that I would I do not, and that
> which I would not I find myself doing..."[1]

Dwelling solely in the unreal worlds of mere entertainment and immediate pleasure does nothing for our self-confidence or sense of achievement. It is a form of engagement in life-diminishing activities. By contrast, engagement in life-enhancing activities may be tiring, and require short-term self-denial, but it gives us strength and a sense of direction. We are fortunate indeed when we find ourselves passionately immersed in a worthwhile pursuit, rather than simply doing it because it will supposedly

---

1   St. Paul`s Letter to the Romans ch.7.v.19. (1611 version) Paul has no solution in Chapter 7. He finds one in chapter 8: the solution lies in what we set our minds on.

be good for us. As children, we find ourselves loving making things, hearing and acting stories together, competing at games and sports, sharing new discoveries; it is in childhood that we first transcend the cave of myopia.

Life-diminishing and Life-enhancing Activities

Alasdair MacIntyre`s `After Virtue`[1], which has influenced this account of life-diminishing and life-enhancing activities, is widely regarded as amongst the most important contributions to understanding contemporary society and its current cultural difficulties. MacIntyre`s view is that society has lost its way and has become culturally fragmented. The traditions of living that gave us our identity in the past have lost their power in the face of post-Enlightenment presuppositions about reason and truth. Enlightenment figures such as Leibnitz, Hume, and Kant, regarded `reason`, unbound from tradition and dogma, as the authority for deciding the nature of reality and, as a result, what constitutes the good life. The so-called `Enlightenment` of the 17th and 18th centuries was a period when European thought found unfettered reason, rather than sacred tradition, to be the new path to learning.

MacIntyre sees this powerful movement in the history of thought as at the root of our cultural malaise today. As a result, people have no clear cultural identity in the secular West. They speak the language of `everywhere and nowhere`[2], using terms like `rights`, `justice`, `fairness` and `freedom` assertively to back their grievances without having any mutually-agreed means of supporting such assertions. What is obviously reasonable to one person may be irrational to another. Consequently, ideas of maturity employ fragments of past traditions, dissociating them from their context within a tradition. Thus they are confused and incompatible. For MacIntyre, one aspect of this is the loss of engagement

---

1 'After Virtue' (2nd. ed. (1990)) London, Duckworth
2 See also 'The View from Nowhere'

in `practices` and the consequent development of virtues[1] The concept of a practice has received much attention in subsequent debate, the chief problem focusing upon which activities exemplify it. The main point is that, without engagement in `practices`, the development of virtue is likely to be haphazard, even absent, in a person`s life. I have preferred to call practices `life-enhancing activities` (LEAs).

For MacIntyre:

> A social practice has a history, and has developed over a period of time.
>
> It has its own criteria of excellence and of successful engagement.
>
> It requires reflection, planning, decision and communication.
>
> A practice has enough qualities to become both attractive and fulfilling for people. Each has its own science and art. It follows that it is not pursued, at least primarily, to realize some external goal, but for its own sake.
>
> Engagement in practices strengthens the personality in certain ways which have significance beyond the practice itself. In other words, it calls forth virtues of character. Fairness, honesty, self-criticism, courage and devotion are such virtues, and are examples of `internal goods` (on which more later).
>
> The qualities, or internal goods, of a practice cannot be acquired without participation in it.

---

1   As will become clear, we need not accept his rather narrow and restrictive choice of examples of what might be included in `practices`, but we may see a rather more liberal version of them as vital to the good life. Neither need we necessarily agree with his critique of `reason`, preferring to follow the ideas of Jurgen Habermas, who sees reason as a universal tool of communication without which the race goes nowhere, an emphasis to which MacIntyre appears to give little explicit attention.

One comment on this last point is, I think, worth making. Whilst non-participants may admire and possess such virtues, acquired elsewhere, they cannot acquire them simply by being enthusiasts. Being a sports fan may inspire, but it is not likely to enrich character in the way that participation might.

To such criteria might be added the point that a practice has endless possibilities for enhancement in skills, knowledge and qualities of character. Some activities can be mastered and fully understood, such as driving, bricklaying or, probably, knitting. If so, they can hardly be called `practices` because complete mastery of them can be reached so that no more remains to be gained from them as no problems arise that beckon one towards as-yet-undiscovered dimensions of understanding... `Cooking` was once an example, at least in my childhood world, but has, I think, risen to `practice` status thanks to luminaries from Mrs. Beaton to our contemporary experts who have endowed it with aesthetic and technical possibilities and refinements. Closure is never achieved in a practice: the final book never gets written, nor the last word said. A practice opens up a world of possibilities. I may have maligned knitting here, I fear.

The Fishing Business

MacIntyre used an example taken from commercial fishing to show the effects of engagement in fishing as a practice.[1] Unlike teams of deep-sea fishermen who see the activity merely as a business to be deserted once it becomes harder to make a living, the team that grows up into the job as a way of life develops communal bonds of understanding, skills and passions for the work, mutual loyalties, comradeship and attention to the quality of their products. It becomes central to a way of life from which they cannot walk away without a sense of mighty loss. They prefer to struggle on.

(Of course, too much engagement in a particular practice might lead people to lose their sense of responsibility and fail in their domestic or

1   In Horton J & Mendus S `After MacIntyre` p.284

political roles, so that they become detached from vital concerns. It also follows that hardly any activity in life, amongst those that directly harm nobody, is *always* or *never* an LEA. For many of us, to take up surfing might become an LEA since it raises us above idleness, and focuses our lives on fine motor skills, courage and self-discipline, but total commitment to it indefinitely at the expense of other practices will likely render it a Life Diminishing Activity (LDA). More controversially, and as I write the Ryder Cup is under way, this also applies to golf. That aside, the qualities of character, or virtues, that come with success in a practice must be transferred to other areas of life if their genuineness is not to be questioned.)

How Sport Can Help Us Grow

As our societies develop away from exclusive focus upon material and economic values, so the resulting increase in leisure time gives greater emphasis to sport. Only by experiencing such a game as cricket, for example, can one begin to perceive its power for the good of individual and society. It is a cause of deep regret that the English public can no longer view test matches through the BBC television service. These became a significant part of the national identity and a symbol of fair play. Not only are personal virtues such as dedication, patience and aesthetic style enhanced, but the game has its own marvellous history, with unforgettable heroes. They have transcended past performances and inspired the young. I wish I had been present at one of the greatest cricketing moments ever, Alletson's innings.[1]

> Ted Alletson secured his place in cricket history with one record-breaking innings played against Sussex in May 1911. The innings rescued the game for Nottinghamshire and became known as **Alletson's Innings**. On Saturday, May 20, 1911, Nottinghamshire were facing defeat when Alletson came out to bat at number nine with the score 185-7. He then scored 189 runs in an amazingly fast time, breaking the pavilion clock and the club bar, which was

---

1   See John Arlott's wonderful account in his `Alletson's Innings` 1991 Epworth Press.

 filling with Sussex fans! In one over he hit 34 runs.

Such things enrich and inspire human life despite appearing initially to be of no significance in human history. The Great War soon followed: Alletson retired from cricket and was nearly forgotten, but cricket remained one of those myriad symbols of Britishness, helping to define a nation's spirit. Cricket, like golf and running the marathon, has no essential point beyond itself. The playing of games helps define humanity. Wherever forbidden, they are played in secret.

Football is a 'practice' if it involves team cooperation, a bond of loyalty towards a valued community or organization, strategic forethought, and teamwork, all in addition to the obvious motor skills. It tends to lose its potential as a practice when it is not played 'mindfully', when its aesthetic quality is disvalued or when a sense of proportion is no longer maintained in relation to other activities in life. The distortions imposed upon the game by big business and media hype have surely hindered true awareness of what should really be going on – a game between two teams of competitors who also know they have weightier matters in their lives and who love to share the enjoyment of skills. We cannot overemphasize its power to create self-transcendence in participants through the development of courage, foresight and sportsmanship. It can enrich the human world and draw races and cultures together.

Throwing the discus is a specific practice within the body of overlapping practices called athletics. In athletics, in addition to performing, specific understanding of physical culture has become an integral element. One aspect of athletics is the aesthetic. Everyone who loves a sport delights in the prowess of performers, one aspect of which is style, being a blend of science and art. Style incorporates beauty in movement, symbolized in art and music. Whilst on this subject, it may help to consider the iconic ancient statue of a discus thrower by Myron.[1] It is no surprise to learn

---

1   Myron of Eleutherae 480-460 B.C. Myron's discus thrower sculpture has been copied from early times – see the many illustrations available on the internet.

that the first Olympics, and even the early Olympic games of modern times, included the arts as well as sport, and that mindfulness and body control were seen not only to enhance results but also to be beautiful. Paralympic sport has recently gained overdue publicity through the 2012 London Games. It is, perhaps in the achievements of these athletes that we find quite incredible stories of human transcendence of handicap and low expectation of life quality.[1]

We notice how physical pursuits require the development of intellectual perception, skills and sensitivity if they are to be enriching. As practices they are as much mental as physical. Even the physical discipline of training requires sound knowledge and strong personal qualities. The worst effect of professionalism is to make participants devote their whole being to the game they play. The sporting role becomes the sole source of the participants` self-esteem in life. It fills their lives, and can easily fill the lives of spectators who derive self-esteem as they bathe in the reflected glory of the team`s success. Sport, which would normally generate personal qualities, can then distort what is really important in life. It can have such a great influence on the morale of a nation that results come to seriously affect work attendance and productivity. One effect of the professional culture and media frenzy in sport is to give children unrealistic ambitions. It easily leads also to a yearning for fame and `greatness`, a readily-assumed mark of the successful life.

> **Darts, etc...** On the other hand, it can also be the case that personal development of mind and character does not result because people engage only at a superficial, casual level in activities that offer little of lasting value. Nothing much penetrates the mind so as to stimulate the imagination or enable a rethink. Drinking with the lads, watching films, playing darts, gambling, reading the paper – these may

---

1   Martine Wright is a supreme example. When we`re feeling doomed to mediocrity or failure, we might read her story. In 2012 she was awarded the Helen Rollason Memorial Trophy for her courage and inspiration to others.

become life-diminishing activities. They so easily become 'ruts', serving as salient features of a personality. It would be rare for these things to possess meaningful content that can be life-enhancing through feeding the mind and developing real social qualities. Their only beneficial role is to enable distraction from the demands of serious living leading to inner recovery. That implies we must not let them take over our lives: they should come low on the list of things that define our being[1]. Nevertheless such trivialities matter, not only because they are fun, but also because they can deliver us from worry and stress.

We can, however, conclude that whether we are engaged in a life-diminishing activity (LDA) or a life-enhancing activity (LEA) may not be *entirely* a matter of identifying what we are doing, but more a matter of what we are getting out of it and what we are putting into it. We also have to admit that we all need a break from real life. This means that we can do what that great philosopher Wittgenstein used to do in order to take a break from reality. He would buy a meat pie, go to the Cambridge cinema, sit in the front row and watch a Western[2] – but it's worth noting that he also used the exit.

It appears, then, that exclusive involvement in an LEA can wear us out and also make us foolishly narrow in our interests, and that occasional involvement in LDAs can enable us to take a break from life's serious business. But it should be clear by now that LEAs really have to take priority in our lives if we are to grow inwardly, since these offer scope and depth for the development of mind, for it is this that is at risk. The pursuit of excellence in sport carries various health warnings, one of the less obvious but most important being implied in this observation of Eric Hobsbawm:

> "… 'youth' was not seen as a preparatory stage of adulthood but, in some sense, as the final stage of full human

---

1   The appearance of the so-called 'World Darts Championship' on TV every year is one of the multiple nadirs of programming giving people what they want rather than content that edifies.

2   Example taken from Norman Malcolm's <u>Ludwig Wittgenstein: a Memoir</u> pp.27-8

development. As in sport, the human activity in which youth is supreme, and which now defined the ambitions of more human beings than any other, life clearly went downhill after the age of thirty..."[1]

Vital myopic symptoms suggest themselves. What has happened to adult stages of human living, to marriage and family making, bringing up children, pursuing a chosen ambition worthy of long-term future devotion, aiming to live in such a way that old age becomes the climax of living, not the slow, unnoticed extinction? The vibrancy and beauty of our early adult years give us a platform on which to build a meaningful future life. But this requires a vision of education, formal or informal, as a process that continues to thrive beyond schooling and student years, enriching our lives and probably lengthening them in the process.

Mass Immaturity and the Restoration of Love

Plato's `Phaedrus` was written in the context of relationships between those who make love together. In the dialogue they are homosexual. The clever, but `dark` character is the absent Lysias who argues powerfully for the wisdom of not getting entangled in emotional bonds with one's partner.[2] The social and emotional benefits of avoiding bonding with partners are cleverly expressed at length: such relationships are easy to end, and, for example, involve little hurt from inner pain or the revenge of the rejected one; the usual brevity of such relationships will not affect a pre-existing friendship between them adversely since no exaggerated views of lovers' qualities are involved. The friendship goes on as before. In short, Lysias' view is that carefully-managed physical affairs do not involve the folly of emotional involvement.[3] Socrates, by contrast, rejects such pragmatism as an insult to true love, which itself can do no hurt, and is the growth of the "wings of the soul".

"We must realize that there are in us two ruling and

---

1   Age of Extremes (2002) p.571
2   pp.6-11 Phaedrus (Penguin 1995edn.)
3   Summed up well as "the lover is mad, the non-lover is sane" ibid.p.26

> impelling principles whose guidance we follow, a desire for pleasure, which is innate, and an acquired conviction which causes us to aim at excellence. These two principles are sometimes in agreement within us and sometimes at variance; at one moment the first, and at another, the second, prevails. The conviction that impels us towards excellence is rational, and the power by which it masters us is called self-control; the desire which drags us towards pleasure is irrational, and when it gets the upper hand in us, its dominion is called excess"[1]

Thus,

> "the soul of the lover waits upon his beloved in reverence and awe….finds himself being treated like a god and receiving all manner of service from a lover whose love is true love and no pretence, and his own nature disposes him to feel kindly towards his admirer…"[2]

Such love is itself generated in the beloved, and consummation may eventually ensue.

Two and a half thousand years ago, not only was the nature of erotic love, its dangers and abuses, discussed with deep sensitivity, but that love was understood in an ultimate scheme of existence as the wings of the soul – the medium for spiritual development. Its twin enemies were unbridled and repressed passion. Human mastery of Earth and its laws has progressed since then, but, one wonders, why has the human spirit failed dismally to master itself?

It should not be surprising, therefore, that Shakespeare's wisdom, expressed 400 years ago, might warn the wayward lover off unbridled passion. Here is a vision maintained against common evidence to the contrary and on which he stakes his entire life's work:

'Love is not time's fool, though rosy cheeks and lips within his bending sickle's compass come:

---

1 Phaedrus p.16
2 Ibid.p41

Love alters not with his brief hours and weeks, but bears it
out, e'en to the edge of doom.'
'If this be error, and upon me proved, I never writ, nor no
man ever loved'[1]

Sexual activity, at its base level, might give desirable physical sensations,
a feeling of well-being and even pride of achievement. It may also give a
sense of power and ascendancy over peers and partner. As such it carries
no force of meaning about bonding and love. At its worst, it exhibits no
more than the levels of sensation suggested by the Greek verb 'orgao'
meaning 'I swell', a term whose root has given us such terms as 'orgasm'
and 'orgy'. Without orgasm sex would lose some of its appeal, so we
must not pretend the importance of the climax away. It can, however,
bring nothing but harm to self and society in the absence of a framework
of meanings, customs and practices to which it belongs.

At baser levels, erotic love is about possessing the other, if for a brief
while, as if he or she were property. The existence of a 'partnership' is
possible because sexual and social benefits are felt to be mutual, but this
is a meaningful relationship at its most primitive and fragile level. Erotic
love, to be profound and fulfilling to the lovers, can never be the only
major ingredient of a relationship. We should not, however, dismiss the
lustful side of love, for the powerful desire for one's partner sexually is
vital to early bonding, especially when one is fit and young. Here reason
has some difficulty ruling passion. Like so much else in our lives, the
erotic must be ruled wisely by respect for the object of one's desire.

Learning from the French

One lesson often learned only too late is that intense
erotic love between partners cannot be expected to last
a lifetime. The French know this far better than English
speakers thanks to **Stendhal**, who introduced the concept
of '**crystallization**' to their language, teaching that the
experience of falling in love involves the creation of an
image of the beloved that is idealised and distorted: "in

---

1   From Sonnet 116 (ca.1595)

love, one no longer sees things as they are.."[1] People usually fall out of love, in that passionate sense of wanting the other exclusively and sexually. Often a kind of boredom and tedium sets in, so that erotic love, the only real light in the relationship, fades away. Unless true 'companionate love'[2] develops and carries enough weight to compensate for and replace erotic love, it is probable another lover will be sought. Such companionate loving is the meeting and mutual growth of minds together, and is the lasting feature of maturity in our loving. If you're still chasing your partner around the bedroom at 80, you are blessed indeed, unless of course your partner is decades younger, in which case you deserve to die, preferably naked and at once.

Erotic love will be balanced, and tamed in its authority, by a developing companionate love. The lovers need to reflect on the future of their passion, knowing that they must look beyond the passionate present. It is also of importance to note that one partner may lose his or her erotic drive for the other person before the other loses the same for them! This causes deep grief, often endured for years, before either the relationship regains equilibrium or the frustrated lover parts. In such cases, the one who loves deeply but not passionately may experience the grief of losing their truest companion, and the one who has departed may grow to realize that there were depths to the relationship never to be truly rediscovered elsewhere. It is probably never wise to separate merely over the loss of sexual passion.

It is a sad fact that sexual desire may be at its most powerful in the absence of both passionate and companionate love. This is the dominance of physical urges over the self. Sexual desire is, as humanity has always known, a dangerous gift, and civilizations have always set powerful limits to its expression... until now, when some developed societies appear to condone ruleless sex through their widespread allowance of pornographic visual media. This augurs badly for the future, as most

---

1   Stendahl (1783-1842) 'De l'amour'(1819). His thoughts on love are clearly expressed in Josephson's 1946 work, 'Stendahl: the pursuit of Happiness'
2   Berscheid and Walster – cited in Haidt J. p.124

children under 16 easily access such material on their computers[1]. This material also reinforces the idea that violence is a valid part of sexual activity, and undoubtedly empowers criminal behaviour. It is obvious to any thinking person that making such material accessible to children should be a legal offence.

**Consider some common English talk, chiefly amongst some 16 to 30`s** – `she`s gagging for it` – `he turns me on` – `It`s over. You do nothing for me any more` – `Trouble with you is you`re not getting enough.` – `I bet you won`t score with him`. Also we look at the portrayal of love in many films, TV programmes and books. This claims to reflect the real world, the `adult` (!) world. Such is not the language of civilization but the language of decadence. It is unreflective, disrespectful, pejorative and ignorant. That these attitudes have always been with us is no reason not to oppose them. We best oppose them by simply not promoting them in literature drama and pornography. Such is not likely to be enforced with laws, but by means of `coercive paternalism`[2], enabling the masses, through educative means, to eschew such creations. That does not imply keeping silent in film and novel on such corruptions of love, but ceasing to present them as the norm to be encouraged. We fail as we leave tacit the vision of a more meaningful and humane idea of true love. Adult drama may have a tragic ending, but without hope, it is best not written.

Of course we all know what goes on in many of our minds regarding lustful and cruel thoughts. Part of me might really desire a hot affair. I am a creature with creaturely urges. But I have learned that human society is destabilized when unbridled passions take over, when parenthood is merely the result of sexual desire, when partnerships are based merely on erotic fancy. Family life diminishes, and children grow up deprived of the deeper qualities needed for long-term relationships. Conversation degenerates, and spare time includes being entertained by TV programmes

---

1   Just type `free sex videos` on a search engine for proof.
2   Term borrowed from Skidelsky p. 211

that, in the name of realism, confirm this lifestyle. The unwary love to hear anything that confirms their behaviour to be `adult`: the ratings for trashy programmes and newspapers remain high. This indicates that whole swathes of the population no longer seem to have any regard to their own inner growth. The very concept has been taken away.

Sexual activity which contains no more than physical meaning hardly begins to explain what is going on in a stable relationship. In life-enhancing sex, there is mutual bonding, the growth of positive feelings for each other, and of long-term intentions of loyalty and mutual support, all strengthened and expressed in passion. And when the passion cools, the relationship need not. As an internal good, it is not about possessing anything. It is about giving, and about enriching the life of each other – once it is realized that this intention is not being fulfilled, the freedom of either partner to depart from the relationship is acknowledged. (Indeed the relationship may cease to be sexual, partners may even cease to be partners, but they can be other things to each other, as enduring, stabilizing, profound aspects of human life.)

People often revert to LDAs in the shadows of the cave when, for example, meaningful sexual relationships are breaking down. They often labour under the delusion that regular intercourse is confirmation of genuine mutual love. They become possessive or pursue other lovers. And all this shows, in any case, how we can regress when frustrated and stressed – we can go back into the depths of our caves when disappointed and upset. But it *does not have to be this way*, and, with experience, we learn, with difficulty, not to yield to such tendencies. Life is hard for us when we are under pressure, and if we regress to childhood in our behaviour, we are helping nobody, worst of all our children, who look to us for strength and wisdom. We know all about the realities of living – we need to face up to the real possibilities of getting out of the messes we make for ourselves. Knowledge is not enough.

Plato honoured love as "the wings of the soul". He reminded his friend that love is the victory of the charioteer and the good horse over the wayward beast of unbridled instinct, and that the life of love promotes the pursuit of excellence above pleasure. Love is itself the path to maturity. For the Socrates of Plato, love raised the spiritual self towards truth and the vision of `the form of the good`. Love enabled the lover to find himself. It was an integral aspect of the master story, the big picture of which every self is a part. Without such a story, our lives carve their own idiosyncratic narratives, attaining at best ends that have no known relationship with progress, for there is no vision of progress. That there is the love of romantic passion, the love of friendship, the love of caring and compassion, is all clear to us. What so often lacks clarity is love of truth, of beauty, of mystery in things great and small. These are aspects of the love of life, of wonderment and fascination which themselves cost us nothing and enrich our lives.

The Pursuit of Pleasure as a Life-diminishing Activity

Many of the pursuits in which we engage are only indirectly life-enhancing at best. When we take a break from the serious matters of life and play on the beach, watch a comedy film, or picnic in the long grass, we are perhaps doing ourselves good. Most of us have to learn to take a break regularly. There is, it appears, a whole range of activities in the grey area between LEAs and LDAs. Pursuing these a little, at the proper time, refreshes us. Pursuing them too much may diminish us. On what criteria? Take `picnicking`, for example. Should the activity enhance our social life, our conversation, our interests, we might find justification for doing it frequently, especially given a good spell of weather, but should it serve merely as an excuse for lazing in the sun, to get that tan perhaps, or to ease boredom, it becomes self-indulgent, even if not seriously so. It brings no joy that can be shared and feeds our languor.

(As I write, I am in Australia, in the heat of Queensland. The TV shouts barbeques, camping gear, trailers, sports gear, swimming pools for the garden, places for fun days out with events to enjoy, and all in a blue sky with sandy beaches backed with palms. It is no wonder that the British yearn to live there. It might satisfy all known needs. In truth, all these met, with no deeper vision of the fulfilled life, little of lasting worth can be found)

Activities that are merely instinctive and non-reflective have some or all of the following features, the presence of which serves as an indicator of `thin ice being skated upon`:

They can be pursued without much planning.

They relieve boredom, yet themselves become boring, thus requiring ever more sophisticated forms. Yet this has strictly limited potential. Dullness of spirit and a growing unattractiveness to others await the devotee.

They are finite resources – the `drives` run out, and even the money.

In themselves they offer little opportunity for enriching the mind: they do not generate resources for personal development. They use them up.

Unless moderated by the sort of principled behaviour derived from education and upbringing, they easily generate strife.

Instinctive pleasures, pursued out of any context they might have in practices, tend to have other shortcomings also. There is, first, one associated with the so-called `paradox of hedonism`:

"Those only are happy who have their minds fixed on some object other than their own happiness… Aiming thus at something else, they find happiness along the way… Ask yourself whether you are happy, and you cease to be so." (J.S.Mill`s autobiography)

"Happiness cannot be pursued; it must ensue, and it only does so as the unintended side effect of one's personal dedication to a cause greater than oneself or as the by-product of one's surrender to a person other than oneself." (Viktor Frankl in `Man`s Search for Meaning`)

Seeking pleasurable sensations, or a `buzz`, as the sole point of the experience, is counterproductive. Enrichment comes from focusing on something for which the pleasure is not the central focus. If the activity itself does not have value and significance beyond physical sensations, then the pleasure derived will be short-lived. If sexual activity is pursued just to have physical thrills, the partner's identity and the depth of the relationship being irrelevant, then the pleasure will also be short-lived, and will lead to the urge to find new forms of sexual experience, more unorthodox than the former, and new partners. It is clear where this can all lead. The pursuit of sexual thrills quickly leads to more intense and increasingly unorthodox sexual activity, some of which is likely to include humiliation, the infliction of pain and domination over the helpless, as in sadism and paedophilia. Such a path cannot, surely, be pursued without harming one's love of life-enhancing activities requiring a lively and well-equipped mind, devotion to excellence, and the virtues associated with maturity in relationships, such as honesty, loyalty, and integrity.

(So we should stop imagining that whatever we might do in private is entirely our own affair. Everything we do has its effects on us, and therefore on the outside world. Introducing aids to erotic ecstasy up every available orifice changes the thought life, rearranges desires and detracts from one's ability to see other people as anything other than worthy sexual objects, and leads one to despise them if they are not. Depravity is not confined to institutionalized members of society.[1])

A similar path can be traced both in spending and travelling. These can become habit-forming and unsatisfying. Their sole benefits are such things as parading one's goods or trumping others' claims to have been to exotic places. The world's richest and most experienced travellers have now visited outer space, thus wasting millions of dollars. What will they do next? Living in the shadows of the cave directs the attention towards sensations, physical thrills or an ever-growing list of things done, bought or seen. Such self-indulgence is the very antithesis of a meaningful life. To come out of the cave we must engage our hearts and minds. The `practices` in which we engage enable us to do this.

---

1   Foley, M gives me a good reason for not expanding on the endless techniques for intensifying sexual sensation. See his `Age of Absurdity` pp.196-200

External and Internal Goods – Will We Ever Learn?

The paradox of hedonism is closely related to another feature of life in the shadows. The values sought tend to be `external` at the expense of `internal` goods. MacIntyre, in `After Virtue`, employs the distinction, first expressed by Aristotle, between external and internal goods[1]. (By `goods` he does not mean material `stuff`, as is commonly meant, but values, whether material or abstract.) . Valuing social status, fame, wealth, or publicity, in the absence of valued ends-in-themselves for which they merely serve as means, is good only for tragicomedy. External goods, whilst they are not to be abhorred in themselves, become destructive of the self and of society when pursued without being a means to the increase of internal goods. They are dangerous, so that we must learn to keep them in their place. External goods are easily valued as final life goals, but their attainment is, in such cases, vacuous. Take, for example, material prosperity:

> "Once people have enough to meet their basic needs and are able to survive with reasonable comfort, higher levels of consumption do not tend to translate into higher levels of life satisfaction, or well-being. Instead, people tend to adapt relatively quickly to improvements in their material standard of living, and soon return to their prior level of life satisfaction."[2].

What about fame? Once that is established, whether it be for a single act, a continued talent, or the luck of a life event, a person can, for a while, bathe in the sense of glory it may bring. But, unless fame is not itself the goal, but a mere side effect of one`s life goals, living becomes aimless and empty. It is surely deeply unfulfilling to seek to be identified by what one once was or did. The only justification for admiring the famous lies in their earned authority: they have proved themselves to be worthy of an honour they perhaps did not seek. Thus we learn to see through the so-called `cult of celebrity`, honouring those of trivial talent, most of whom are concerned to keep in the limelight by almost any means.

---

1 `After Virtue` 2nd edition p.190-
2 NEF `Growth isn`t Possible p.20

But what about freedom? Should we not pursue that as a great end goal in life, especially when living under oppression? Indeed we should, but the question remains about what to do with our freedom once it is attained. If we do not see it as a means to a life of richer quality and also know what we mean by such a life, it gives us little except an exchange of chains – out of the frying pan into the fire. We must know what we seek freedom for.

The pursuit of external goods as prized ends-in-themselves is today encouraged by the media, political policies and commercial enterprise. Internal goods are hardly understood in these areas of life. Citizens are led on by leaders in politics, media and business who have become blinded by their own unexamined delight in the power they possess and the public envy of their status and wealth.

It is also important to notice how external goods are invariably in finite supply. Not everyone can be famous or of high status. Giving everyone equal power is another practical impossibility (and how could we?). To attain wealth, land, social power or possessions as goals is to hinder or prevent others from achieving them. And if people do that to each other, then rivalry will likely ensue, and in more extreme situations, strife and cruelty will follow. One might think that freedom, which is an external good since it is to be valued as a means, not as an end in itself, need not be in finite supply. We can all be free, but the qualifier remains; there is a limit on availability here. My free actions are restricted once they threaten others with oppression. Genuine freedom is always freedom for something of value in itself, a goal oppressing no others. One can always ask of an external good, `what is the purpose of pursuing it?`. Without serving as a means to an internal good, it is corrupt.

Internal goods, by contrast, are values people have through the pursuit of Life Enhancing Activities. They are not valued as a means to external goods, even when they lead to such. In the shadows of the Myopic Cave, people are not engaging in LEAs, even though they may play games, have skills, enjoy a relationship, have academic qualifications, or vote in an election. They may claim to value these things as ends-in-themselves some of the time, but it is the absence of mutual development of mind and qualities of character attained

through them that deprives them of lasting benefit. No quality of character militates against love, because it benefits oneself, others and the living world.

Internal goods can be easily crowded out when a game is played or a degree course is studied: external goods as ends-in-themselves can take pride of place and thus detract from the genuineness of one's engagement. Enjoying qualities in experiences and objects, sharing responsibility for oneself and others, being active in cultural pursuits, and, as a result, gaining inner strength, may all be missing. Imagine having a fine education and never living it, or getting a degree and forgetting what it was all about. One has just the certificate: no internal goods have survived. An internal good has the development of virtue as a vital ingredient: it is valuable in itself and an aspect of development towards maturity.

Whilst one can ask of a particular internal good 'why pursue that?', the question 'What's the point of being virtuous, and of seeking wisdom?' admits of no convincing answer to everyone simply because *the love of these qualities defines the developing human*. There may be many good answers, but they are only valid to those having the prior disposition to receive them. That disposition is acquired, or not, during the period of nurture by parent-figure. In its absence, the child could become deeply and long-term disturbed. Whilst few people live in the entire absence of valuing internal goods, many are certainly close to doing so. As the spiritual life of a society fades with the demise of religion, so the exclusion of internal goods becomes readily accepted as an aspect of realistic, ordinary, grown-up realism. By contrast we may live a life of practices, both shared and solitary, with meanings dear to us, which naturally shifts the focus of our efforts in life towards 'goods' unlimited and free. We may have precious things which are not restricted in their potential – diary-keeping, running, gardening, climbing, studying, building, conserving, restoring, playing games, making music, reading, carving, studying. All can become practices the possession of which does not deprive others of engagement in them and which promote friendships, standards and skills without limit. As such, we are, then, no longer in the shadows. We are on the way to knowing true wealth. (Yes, even the teenage lad who kindles his passion for life on the skateboard, although the dangers lurking here relate not only to falling off!)

Many of us, now culturally deprived, live simply as consumers. We seek to satisfy our wants our own way. We want pleasure, often as buzzes and thrills. Our relationships tend not to be valued for their own sake but as a means to possessing, dominating or just feeling safe. In this state of being, we may well become unhappy because our potential is not being fulfilled and we cannot be fully part of society. We want satisfaction here and now, without deferring gratification, so we borrow when we have to. Some resort to addiction and crime. We avoid long-term planning. To emerge out of this darkness we need a nurturing home, relevant education, and specific training. Our need is for the spiritual transformation of society through enabling the love of LEAs. That is one overriding aim of education, invariably missed by those in authority, and it is an aim fulfilled more effectively when the teacher promotes wherever possible what and how a child *wants* to learn in preference to the demands of a rigid programme. The goal is love of learning, in as deep and broad a manner as the child can handle. Within broad limits, the content and themes have to be influenced by the learner`s interests.

Effective results are not likely without a keen sense of the ultimate goals of education, above all the attainment of maturity of being. Towards this end, let us have a closer look at some of the ways we think. How we think and what might be the fruit of our thinking have a close relationship with how we educate and what counts as effective education. People cannot grow in an all-round way if the very manner of their thinking is narrowed.

Calculative and Meditative Thinking

That the pursuit of external goods can, however necessary, create barriers to human growth may be made clearer through a look at Heidegger`s distinction between `calculative` thinking and `meditative` thinking[1]. Both are important, but

---

1   `Discourse` pp.46, 53

> "the approaching tide of technological revolution in the
> atomic age could so captivate, bewitch, dazzle and beguile
> men that calculative thinking may someday come to be
> accepted and practised as the *only* way of thinking"[1]
> and,

> "Calculative thinking cannot be employed to appraise
> itself. It has no notion that in calculation everything
> calculable is already a whole before it starts working out
> its sums and products, a whole whose unity naturally
> belongs to the incalculable which, with its mystery, ever
> eludes the clutches of calculation."[2]

In the light of this, it is clear that calculating cannot cover the whole of
thinking. Such thought is essential in order to measure and quantify in
domestic and commercial management and technology. It will always
be important in agriculture, finance, industry, or executing almost any
plan. But there has to be a different kind of thinking, and a different kind
of truth if we are to stand back and develop a proper appraisal of what
we are up to. Only by doing so, can we be sure that our projects are not
wasteful or destructive. This we seem, all too often, not to be able to do:

> "...For nowadays we take in everything in the quickest and
> cheapest way, only to forget it just as quickly, instantly.
> Thus one gathering follows on the heels of another.
> Commemorative celebrations grow poorer and poorer in
> thought. Commemoration and thoughtlessness are found
> side by side.[3]

Calculative thinking is always a matter of the quantifiable. Quantification
can come to dominate human life, especially in the computer age.
Measures can be artificially created, even of qualities usually taken to be
unquantifiable, such as `satisfaction`, `happiness`, etc.

By contrast with calculative thinking, **meditative thinking** considers

---

1   Ibid. p.56 Heidegger`s italics.
2   Kaufmann p.262
3   Discourse p.45

`being`. To seek to effectively encounter the being of a person, a creature, a tradition of culture, or of an activity, we have to suspend our assumption about its function in terms of what we commonly do in our encounter with it, think it is for, or what might be its worth.. We are commonly "in flight from thinking", that is, from thinking of a non-calculative sort. Indeed, to exercise meditative thought is a mark of growth itself. "Meditative thinking", in which we observe, take notice, suspend prior judgments and listen, does not have restricted objects. It may focus on oneself and one's manner of life, on an animal, on the passage of time, the light on a hill, a movement or a whole work in music, a mathematical problem, a historical situation or personage, or one's future and the future of the world. The point is that it is not selected in order to use, control, reach some set target or to quantify. *It is the devotion of the mind to the object of contemplation in order to learn it in whatever way it presents itself to us.* Meditative thought is itself an internal good, an end in itself, not being undertaken primarily as a means to something else. Success here lies primarily in enhanced perceptions of qualities in things and people, perhaps expressed in painting, the sciences, literature, music or drama. The potter may want to sell pots, but, if his work is a true practice, that will not be the chief motivation for making them. All this may serve to explain why Cezanne painted Mont St. Victoire so often!

In order to practise meditative thinking, we need to

> "dwell on what lies close and meditate on what is closest;
> upon that which concerns us, each one of us, here and now;
> here, on this patch of home ground; now, in the present
> hour of history." [1]

Meditative thinking enables us to use, rather than to be dominated by, calculative thinking, otherwise we become

> "defenceless and perplexed victim(s) at the mercy of the
> irresistible superior power of technology" [2]

Probably following Buber, who is discussed below, Heidegger sees the

---

1   Ibid p.47
2   Ibid pp.52-3

loss of meditative thought as the loss of 'Being'. The world has become one of subjects and objects, of rigid language and conceptualized, logical ideas, all of which have uses for the business of getting on with things. Those who, like Heidegger, used this term 'being', often with a capital 'B', also said that nothing literal can be said about it.[1] For example, the message in a painting or work of literature such as poetry or novel gains its value from not being exhaustible: it may forever have something new to say to us, if we 'listen'. Such living language differs from mundane language in that it has power to quicken the mind, generate lasting fertile imagery, and thus stimulate the user and listener. It generates passion for whatever our senses reveal, rather than our treatment of them as, at best, useful items. In 'being', we live beyond mere 'existence'.

Meditative thinking delivers us from the restriction to practical concepts, important though they are. It enables the generation of images and deep sensibility towards the being of that with which we engage. The language we use, unlike that of calculative thought, is metaphoric, imagic, and evocative. It points, as symbols always do, away from itself to the thing symbolized without restricting its revealed message to the straitjacket of conceptual thought. It is, therefore, a nest egg of creative imagination and profound insight. Such is an integral aspect of aesthetics, which includes such activities as poetry, painting, sculpture, music, dance and drama. It not only reveals, as well as hides[2], the being of the world and of ourselves, it delivers mankind from slavery to the task of controlling production, whether of goods, services or money. He may not forsake such activities, but he may transcend them. It enables his world to become sacred again as "language event". To hold something sacred is not only to revere it, but to acknowledge that we can only know of it what is revealed through the symbol which 'speaks' it. That holds true for a person, a dog, a planet, and my own being: it cannot be wholly experienced and known.

Heidegger gives examples to explain what he calls 'language event'.

---

1   This accords, incidentally with the Hindu view that the sacred syllable 'OM', cannot be described, for it is ineffable and utterly beyond our language – only the symbolism of the faith can point us to it.

2   Discourse p.55 "That which shows itself and at the same time withdraws is the essential trait of what we call the mystery."

One is Van Gogh`s painting of a peasant woman`s shoes.[1] These speak of a world of toil, of a pervading anxiety as to having enough bread, the "wordless joy of having once more withstood want".[2] The work thus has `gathering power`, drawing together into an image the world of the peasant woman. Thus a work of art feeds our imagination, but only if we  come to it meditatively, and not just to say we have seen it, as we so often do. Whilst we do well to have some prior knowledge of its context, it is not important that we see exactly what the painter had in mind. The value of a painting is that it does not speak literal propositions, or even words at all, but has multifaceted power to bring home to us how being is. A great work of art is much bigger than the mind of the person who created it.

Thus one is no longer mentally enclosed, but taken to see anew and differently, to have a basis for knowing that life is truly vibrant and full of wonder beyond the cell walls of instrumental living. Here is a paradox, and I think we do well to learn from it. There are elements of the everyday humdrum routine in all our lives. Some of us find there is little else for us: we may be carers for our small children in all our waking hours; we may feed, clothe and toilet our old father; we may spend every day cleaning or working on a monotonous task. Surely that erodes our hope and forces us back into the cave of myopia? Surely that makes us despair of there being any real point to our lives? Not so, for such is the potential strength within us that we can find depth and joy in such routine. We must relearn to value the present, whatever it may have for us. It is the `given` in life, at least for now. The darkness is in the spirit, not the circumstance. The spirit, however, requires nourishment, most of which has to come as narrative and imagery in film, radio, conversation, stories old and new, sacred and profane.

The darkness can be dispelled by stopping to think and to take stock. In

---

1   There are a number of paintings by Van Gogh of pairs of shoes. I have in mind his earliest, the 1886 painting in Amsterdam`s Rijksmuseum.
2   Cited Thiselton p.338 from Heidegger`s `The Origin of the Work of Art`

the darkness we have forgotten. Can we remain `captains of our souls`[1]? If we know and consider the lives of others, especially those who have endured with joy, transformed their own self-understanding, and made their situation meaningful, we know how to dispel the darkness. Van Gogh saw a world in the peasant`s shoes. Helen Keller transformed her darkness and silence without ever being released from her circumstance.

It is also quite clear that music can free us in the same way. It cannot be spoken, even though it may be spoken of, any more than can a painting, and it is not intended to be of use. It stimulates our emotive life, realigns our perspective to being rather than mere existence, and delivers us from grey gloom. It `restores our souls`, even in deep grief it can restore meaning. For me, as the `Lark Ascending` of Vaughan Williams stimulates joys to be had at a local scene, so does Elgar`s `Nimrod` call forth a sense of the beauty and harmony that endures after the struggles of life. Music can leave us transfixed, speechless, mysteriously revived.[2] Such art gives us visions that survive the worst that life can throw at us, and it takes us beyond words and reawakens our spirits. What a joy it is to think that, in the last fifty years we in the modern world have been given the ability to listen to music *anywhere*![3]

The distinction between the meditative and the calculative is important for our understanding of education. The learner who has not been recruited as a trainee for work, but who learns out of interest in the focus of her learning, will be taught and hopefully inspired, to think `meditatively`. The literature, fine art, biology and mathematics learners encounter is not geared to employment. Only after they have become proficient in the subjects they learn at school and beyond, may their learning be focused upon calculative projects. They develop in the knowledge prerequisite to becoming effective at calculative tasks before they can begin to qualify as employees, or even trainees. *This means that the entire school programme up to at least 16 years is not to be focused upon projects of a specific job-related nature.* Practical projects that may appear in the

---

1   Oscar Wilde denied he had been the captain of his soul in a letter written from Reading Goal. I borrow the term.
2   Beethoven`s 4th piano concerto, the first movement, serves as a powerful example for me as I write.
3   Since the advent of the transistor radio

classroom in e.g. Year 9 mathematics are properly used as a learning aid for learning mathematical ideas and skills. To do maths in school because the learners have opted for a programme called `Retail Studies` might be functionally effective in getting them a job, but it should be a device to help unwilling learners, and is not what education is about. It may train young people in some way, but it is itself a mark of failure to educate them in numeracy. They may leave school happy, but they are not likely to leave with lasting, widely transferable skills and ideas. Only those who have come to enjoy mathematics can call upon it in the novel and varied aspects of their lives.

Politics, Goods and Educational Aims

Let`s return to MacIntyre for a moment. He believes that politics should be a practice focused upon the internal goods, or "goods of excellence", of citizens, but at the present time it only leads, at least in the UK, to external goods, or "goods of effectiveness". Some win, others lose; there is no good achieved that is good for the whole community; cheating and exploitation are frequent, and this damages the community as a whole. This is because external goods like material wealth and the gaining of power are as dangerous as they are good, and the exclusive pursuit of them is corrupting and demeaning. Michael Sandel applies this thus:

> "…we're at the end of an era, an era of market triumphalism. The last three decades were a heady, reckless time of market mania and deregulation. We had the free market fundamentalism of the Reagan-Thatcher years and then we had the market friendly Neo-Liberalism of the Clinton and Blair years, which moderated but also consolidated the faith that markets are the primary mechanism for achieving the public good. Today that faith is in doubt. Market triumphalism has given way to a new market scepticism. Almost everybody agrees that we need to improve regulation, but this moment is about more than devising new regulations. It's also a time, or so it seems to me, to rethink the role of markets in achieving the public good. There's now a widespread sense that markets have

become detached from fundamental values, that we need
to reconnect markets and values. But how?"[1]

Machiavelli, in his classic essay `The Prince`, written in 1532,
commended political attitudes to the ruling Medicis in Florence
during the Renaissance. The work has been standard fare in many
quarters as a model of practical necessity in political theory for the
last few hundred years.

> "Men have dreamed up republics and principalities which
> in truth have never been known to exist. The gulf between
> how one does live and how one should is so wide that a
> man who neglects what is actually done for what should
> be done finds the way to self-destruction rather than self-
> preservation…Therefore if a prince wants to maintain his
> rule he must learn how not to be virtuous, and to make use
> of this or not according to his needs."[2]

This implies, for example, that appearances have to be nurtured in order
to influence opponents and make the public imagine chosen policies to
be in their interest and promoted for the best of reasons. Subtle skills
of presentation and justification are developed in order to minimize
opposition and convince the public. Power is to be retained at all costs,
so long as the appearance of sincerity, disinterestedness and honesty can
be maintained. Power is maintained by those in office because it is their
raison d'être to defeat opponents, not to promote the public good at all
costs.

Isn't the world a different place today, however?
Martin Luther King lived his political life to
promote ideals. Machiavellians would say he
strengthens their case: King was not pragmatic
enough. His aims were too radical, and his world
was not ready for them. He destroyed himself.
Yet we might consider that only in the physical

1   Michael Sandel, BBC Reith Lectures, 2010 `A New Citizenship`, lecture 1 on
    Markets and Morals
2   `The Prince` section 15.

sense was King to lose. Men of honour do that . It was worth it whatever later history may tell. King`s principles were within his soul – to forsake them would have been to him inner death. The only self-destruction Machiavelli could see lay in the loss of power: the loss of integrity was, apparently, no true loss, but a gain.

A powerful democratic leader develops authority from moral strength and clear expression of the right way to proceed based upon a clear view of the public good. Such politicians are rare indeed. Maybe that is not because people of this quality are rare, but because they keep out of the dark life of politics. It is probably true that political visions are not difficult to have. Take, for example the pervasive problem of inequality between the rich and poor, and the need to promote equality in society. What is difficult is having the courage to express a vision and the strength to bring it nearer to fruition.[1]

MacIntyre`s political reflections concur. He rejects the idea that the purpose of life is to get rich and that the advancement of a society can be measured by its economic production, for these both reflect a focus on the goods of effectiveness, rather than the goods of excellence. In addition, excessive capitalism is at present undermining communities of all kinds, including the family: we need a way of life that puts the common good first. Whilst that is not itself a rejection of capitalistic systems, it strongly suggests that such systems are feeding human greed. By contrast,

> "Market relationships can only be sustained by being embedded in certain types of local nonmarket relationship, relationships of uncalculated giving and receiving, if they are to contribute to overall flourishing, rather than, as they so often in fact do, undermine and corrupt communal ties"[2]

By "embedded in", MacIntyre surely means that other human values than economic ones have proper priority. These values, relating to the good of the community, promote "flourishing". People matter more than wealth,

---

1   See, for example, Wilkinson R and Pickett K (2010) `The Spirit Level: Why Equality is Better for Everyone` Penguin. The vision is there, based on uncontroversial evidence. It would take oratory, clarity and practicality in leadership to realize it.

2   `Dependent Rational Animals` p. 117.

more than buying and selling. A fall in the value of shares in Coca-Cola can be in the best interests of people, as can the collapse of a hedge fund. The shrinkage of the economy may hurt, but it can do more good than endless expansion which all too often widens the gap between rich and poor, for it may stimulate cooperation, caring for each other, and doing things that cost little but give lasting, unquantifiable benefit.

How might the teacher promote the love of humanizing values and enable learners to both perceive the dominance of external goods in the minds of so many and also to learn to live for pursuits that are endlessly rewarding and worth sharing?

First, teachers require a deep understanding of the political and ethical state of things in society. They have the potential to open learners' eyes to the futility of those empty values assumed by so much in the mass media. Children and students cry out for stimulation of mind and heart, and inspiration enabling them to believe their lives to be a worthwhile journey, even in the absence of wealth and fame, through engagement in activities which will both enhance their individuality and their social maturity. They need to be equipped to converse in ways that do not merely mimic the languages of material gain and entertainment. Such quality of interests results from a wide and deep learning experience whilst at school and at home. Such involvement will also enhance their ability to attract and be attracted by other people. Here is but one example of a project in outline.

Advertisements: a secondary school project. This aims to teach:

How advertising has evolved from simply informing people to more subtle means of changing their wants: examining examples from various decades.

What makes an **effective** advertisement? (Foci - modifies wants, easy to remember, humorous, startling, gives sense of importance and maturity to the purchaser, simplicity, minimizing need for conscious reflection by using arresting imagery, brief and powerful narrative, use of time-honoured tricks of trade...)

What makes a **harmful** advertisement? What should not be advertised at all? Who might suffer? Advertising Standards Authority codes of practice.

What makes a **good** advertisement? How does it enhance quality of life? (e.g. gains attention to genuine needs of self and others, promotes accurate knowledge and thinking, offers source for full information, gives practical help, enhances self-esteem of purchaser...)

Goal - to create a powerful advertisement for e.g. a consumer item, healthy living product or service, how to care for the planet, keeping safe, an aid to learning.

Key text `Hey Whipple, Squeeze This: a Guide to Creating Great Ads `[1]

We have turned already to insights about the inevitable frustrations involved in pleasure-seeking and the exclusive pursuit of external goods. Also we might note here the lack of belonging to a community of like-minded people who have a shared vision and common values in common. This lack of a sense of common purpose, this drive towards individuality and away from a sense of community is just what can be expected in a global and secular society. The sense of pointlessness is dulled by avid consumerism which can enable the masses to put off that day when a reckoning has to be taken.

The dominant role for politicians in relation to external goods, especially income, is to ensure an equitable distribution amongst the public.

'It is only in the backward countries of the world that increased production is still an important object: in those most advanced, what is economically needed is a better distribution.'[2]

---

1   Sullivan L., (2012) ,Wiley
2   J.S.Mill 1848

At present we place proportionately as little value upon spiritual wealth as we place great value on economic wealth. There are a hundred practical arguments against Marx's principle - 'from each according to his ability, to each according to his needs'[1] - but not one that destroys it as an ideal. It could only be reached either through force, which is wrong, or through the transformation of attitudes towards personal possessions. Such has only ever been achieved amongst small communities of the suffering poor. It remains a goal for humanity to be relearned and not forgotten. Something vital was lost in the modern era. There is now said to be no uniting purpose leading to a manner of life held by all to be worthy, and which enhances communal life. That uniting purpose has, in the past, been expressed, but lists of ideals or state constitutions will not suffice. These remain abstract, ambiguous and impotent.

> "What we have is a cacophony of individual narratives; everyone wants to be the author of their own lives. No one wants to be relegated to a part in a bigger story; everyone wants to give their opinion; no one wants to listen. It's enchanting, it's liberating, but ultimately it's disempowering because you need a collective, not individual, narrative to achieve change." (Adam Curtis)[2]

A grand vision is needed, the sort of vision which has served to define the great cultures of the world, and which has been expressed in their 'master stories'. That vision may now be developing, and at an accelerating rate. We have global communication to thank, as well as the readiness of people virtually everywhere to depart from ignorance and resist oppression. The new master story is the great saga in which humanity lives, the end of which is uncertain but which is affected by the manner of life of every individual on the planet. It is, however, a manner of life threatened and widely possessed by the short-term magnetism of market power, greed and pleasure-seeking.

The new saga, the struggle to deliver our planet from our own destructive powers by the spread of constructive powers, lacks the rich melodrama of the master stories of the past, and will always need to be enriched by

---

1 1875 'Critique of the Gotha Programme'
2 cited in Bunting M. 'Where is the Vision to Unite Us? Guardian Weekly 23/6/09

their warnings and challenges. We, as participants in this new prophecy, receive no ticket to paradise and no immortality. Our contribution is unrecorded and unpraised, and our lives eventually forgotten. As a story it's undramatic as yet, by comparison with the old sagas of good and evil. It is, however, powerfully true for us today, and deserves to become pivotal in the design of educational programmes.

Through such we learn to rethink popularly-assumed priorities. Take, for example, the perceptive and memorable comments of leading economics experts, who appear to endorse these perceptions:

> "If you spend your time thinking that the most important objective of public policy is to get growth up from 1.9 per cent to 2 per cent and even better 2.1 per cent we're pursuing a sort of false god there. We're pursuing it first of all because if we accept that, we will do things to the climate that will be harmful, but also because all the evidence shows that beyond the sort of standard of living which Britain has now achieved, extra growth does not automatically translate into human welfare and happiness."
> Lord Adair Turner, Chair of the UK Financial Services Authority
>
> "Anyone who believes exponential growth can go on forever in a finite world is either a madman or an economist."
> Kenneth E. Boulding Economist and co-founder of General Systems Theory[1]

It may, therefore, be better to arrive than to 'crack on', for then the saga of our travels can be shared in "comradeship and serious joy". In time, travelling has to stop: there comes a destination, unless, of course we pursue a nomadic path as passing spectators. Economic and technological 'growth' metaphors should not be allowed to hide from our eyes that intrinsic and life-strengthening joy to be found in intimacy of mind with others. Old age is dull indeed without it. He who has but one grandiose story to share will be poor company. He lives only in the macrocosm: the microcosm – those small, deep, momentous events of our lives, is

---

1   both cited in 'Growth Isn't Possible' NEF 2010

unperceived. I`d rather spend an evening with Einstein than Marx.
G.K.Chesterton[1] comments as follows on Dickens` `Pickwick Papers`:

> "…comradeship and serious joy are not intervals in
> our travel; but rather our travels are interludes in our
> comradeship and joy. The Inn does not point to the road:
> the road points to the Inn."

Even when we have the conservation of life as our serious concern, we may yet continue to travel along the destructive path. To rely solely on the hope of new technology to reduce our carbon emissions, for example, is to allow that no drive to change our destructive practices is necessary. So we can go on as we do, manufacturing what people want as well as need, without actually destroying the natural environment. New technology will surely solve the problem of pollution[2]. That is at present a forlorn hope. Much new technology has inevitably generated new unsustainability. The time has come to stop relying solely on technology at the expense of focusing upon our life practices, our planting and growing, our travelling, our purchasing and selling, our breeding, our eating and so on, to make sustainable and richer our personal and communal lives. Then we may value those technologies that can help save the world. At the present time as we are commissioning them, so we are ignoring our own destructive practices.

---

1   Cited in Aidan Nichols `G.K.Chesterton as Theologian` (2009) p.241
2   as do Clive Hamilton`s "Prometheans" - those relying on technology`s advance to cut carbon emissions using devices, many of which are yet to be invented. "Soterians", by contrast, see the need to improve our behaviour and policies now: technological advance is invariably a source for new problems. See his `Earthmasters` (2013)

CHAPTER 4: ON GROWING INWARDLY

"Most excellent man, are you who are a citizen of Athens, the greatest of cities and the most famous for wisdom and power, not ashamed to care for the acquisition of wealth and for reputation and honour, when you neither care nor take thought for wisdom and truth and for perfection of your soul?"
- Socrates, in Plato`s `Apology`

`There is a time when a man distinguishes
the idea of felicity from the idea of wealth;
it is the beginning of wisdom.`
- R.W.Emerson   Journals (1830)

Who Needs a Master Narrative?

Probably the most essential `particular` for humanity, at least in times past, has been what Don Cupitt has called a `master story`.[1] The master story has, from early times, formed an ultimate map for living. The religious traditions form such a narrative. In the secular world of modern society, such maps are losing their power. Why, then, does an understanding of the sacred narratives of world civilizations still matter in the educational curriculum of the secular school? Perhaps the most obvious argument is that poor understanding of these things inevitably promotes prejudice and the harmful caricature of cultures other than one`s own. But there is much more to be said than this. The task of religious education in the secular school is to enable learners to not only learn the surface meanings of narratives held to be sacred, but to grasp their deeper meanings for how people live, and to see that, in nominally Christian lands, they remain as bases of culture, whatever we have to say about our own beliefs.

---

1   See his `What is a Story?` (1991)

The tradition of faith defines a community, and that not simply in the local sense, but internationally. Once we understand practices and ideas from the Christian tradition, we begin to see its distinctive contribution to history, how it has decayed, and how it has transformed life. Likewise the same applies to other faiths. Even in the secularized, liberal and individualistic world we live in, it is the lasting heritage of Christianity that gives us our humanistic values. The loss of awareness of the values and concepts brought to us through Christian life makes us faceless amongst the peoples of the world, but if we hold to the things we have learned from our master story, we can maintain our distinctive contribution to the quality of human life. Such concepts include: life as a gift with which we are entrusted and which carries responsibility, temptation and falling, penitence, forgiveness and reconciliation, reverence for the natural world, humility, caring love and sacrifice.

Perhaps this last is the most distinctive and far-reaching of all as it involves the letting go for the well-being of others of some benefits to which we might be considered entitled. Such is the expression of love. Love does not dwell on its own entitlements.[1] Religious and ethical ideas are `commissive` in nature: they challenge our manner of life. Unless they are reflected in the manner of life of whoever claims them as their own, the claim is empty.

The master story enabled individuals to know who they are, what they stand for, what binds them to their fellows in loyalty, what are the great goals to pursue in life, and the path to follow to realize them. The message in such sagas is not simply about one`s own path in life, but on the common path, to which one`s own is conjoined.[2]

---

1   In `Kisses on a Postcard`, young Kenny complains that the blackberries should not be shared out because he picked nearly all of them. Rose rebukes him – `and who was it worked for the food on your plate, my boy?`

2   Almost needless to say, the Muslim master story, as much as the Jewish, has its inhumane side in, for example, the teaching regarding `Harb al Muqadis` the holy war, the treatment of women as in, for example, the promise that seventy-two virgins will be created for even the meanest male believer who dies, and the permission for captured women to be kept as wives. (Sura 33.50)

The Torah (Five Books of Moses) is for the Jewish nation its supreme guide. It tells of their origins, their special calling, their marks of identity, their role in the world, their future hope, and of the will of God who has chosen and guides them. It locates their home in a special land, and provides them with specific physical locations which celebrate the events in their story. It enables the people to account for their own tragedies in their history and to preserve their identity and dignity whatever others may do to them. The prophetic and poetic books of the Jewish Bible confirm and enrich this history, spelling out for them the paths of folly and the path to follow, and conditional promises for the future. The celebrations their story commands are timeless reminders of the nation's role in the world, and have been celebrated for thousands of years. The Bible also reminds the Jewish people why it is that they are settled in many places across the world, and explains their exile in terms of failure to obey their God. It not only gives this people its pride, but also its humility. The story is both chart and compass. It warns against the dominance, if not the acquisition, of external goods and teaches love of neighbour and the world.

Islam has its own master story in the holy Koran. This sacred book tells its own origins, locates its inspiration as dictated *verbatim* by the angel Gabriel, and prescribes the Five Pillars of Islam as the sole requirement for believers. Holy sites are located through the momentous events that took place there, and pilgrimage to them is enjoined. Islam is simple in essence. It is the way of peace through consciousness of, and submission to, the Will of the Eternal. By their behaviour, dress, and observances, Muslims confirm submission to Allah. The Islamic saga tells a people who they are and how they are to live. It extols virtue and condemns vice. Within it is to be found teaching pivotal to its destiny in the history of mankind. Temperance, modesty, respect for parents, care for the poor and infirm, and hard work, are all to be the daily round and rule of each person in the community. The community is to be of one mind and heart, with a common understanding of the ultimate meaning of life. The Muslim pilgrim to Mecca walks seven times around the holy Kaaba, drinks holy water, climbs holy mountains, stones the devil, vows and shaves his head in token of his submission to the Eternal One. These are living metaphors. To refute or support them with evidence is to misunderstand them. They symbolize devotion, loyalty and single-mindedness.

The master story enables individuals to know who they are, what they stand for, what binds them to their fellows in loyalty, what are the great goals to pursue in life, and the path to follow to realize them. The message in such sagas is not simply about one's own path in life, but on the common path, to which one's own is conjoined.[1]

By contrast, today a sense of shared community is not often clear amongst 'developed' nations. The population at large lives in the shadows not only at the individual level, but also nationally and beyond national boundaries. Have things been like this for long, and have they become worse? Might we do better to learn to revere those old sacred stories as the generators of our languages, our roots, and key ideas, rather than as forms of words we are not allowed to sift and critically appraise?

Alasdair MacIntyre finds the chief source of loss of cultural identity in the Enlightenment, as we have seen. The very structures of theism were undermined. David Hume showed that the Creator is unnecessary to us if we deliver ourselves from the presumption that the universe is designed. For Hume, the anthropomorphism that the universe is the work of a designer-God or gods appears quite without warrant. The analogy with a human designer fails to stand the test of criticism: Why not, asks Hume, liken the universe to a vegetable, which has its principle of order wholly within itself?[2] This is certainly no less acceptable than others, if analogies have to be made at all. As a design, the world is flawed, since violence and destruction abound in its course of development. Thus the exercise of unfettered reason ensures that traditional story, understood as a descriptive and explanatory account, is slowly but surely done to death.

German scholars, like David Frederick Strauss, whose 'Life of Christ Critically Examined' was translated by George Eliot, presented us with accounts of the life of Christ freed from the melodramatic and impossible

---

1   Almost needless to say, the Muslim master story, as much as the Jewish, has its inhumane side in, for example, the teaching regarding 'Harb al Muqadis' the holy war, and the treatment of women as in, for example, the promise that seventy-two virgins will be created for even the meanest male believer who dies, and the permission for captured women to be kept as wives. (Sura 33.50)
2   Dialogues Concerning Natural Religion (1779), part VII

elements in the New Testament accounts of his life and death.[1] Charles Darwin, reluctantly, but in his willingness to let truth lead wherever it would, expressed a theory that not only accorded with Hume's ideas, but gave evidence for them from natural observation. In short, the development of life could be explained without reference to the master story that had been told for centuries, that is, without reference to the Creative Hand. We acquired an account of the evolution of life, especially human life, that was seen as scientific and objective. It offered a considerable degree of closure on the great questions of human origins. It asked nothing of the reader or hearer, and showed no path to salvation. It even carried the implication that survival depends upon strength, ingenuity and the luck of endowment and location.

Nowadays the masses of us have stories that the publisher sells or the film-maker thinks will earn good returns at the box office. These speak with many voices, making no coherent sequence, and having no unified themes and ideals. They rarely inspire people who want to make some sense of life in general and of their own lives, confirming the fearsome presupposition that `my life is for me to live as I fancy and I am answerable to no one but myself`. Clues are scarce that might inspire a life of devotion to truth, virtue and the well-being of the world. Consumerism and popular entertainment serve, on the contrary, to cocoon people from life's ultimate issues, dulling any sensibility they might have to the momentous fact that they appear for a brief while in a world that offers them life abundant and asks of them just a little in return.[2]

So what might save mankind from loss of direction, loss of communal identity and sense of pointlessness? We have experienced the charisma of Christian evangelists who pleaded for an uncritical return to the master story, such as William Booth and Billy Graham. The influence of such people in filling a spiritual vacuum was far-reaching, and their successors continue such work, which, though intellectually paralysing, can be a moral force for good, lifting people, least for a time, from the pit of loneliness, guilt and despair.

---

1   D.F. Strauss `The Life of Jesus Critically Examined` transl. George Eliot, first publ. in Britain 1846
2   See e.g. Giddens A., `Modernity and Self-identity` ch.5 on such perceptions.

 By contrast, Dietrich Bonhoeffer perceived that God only has a place these modern times on the boundaries of life, in birth, marriage and death ceremonies, and at times of crisis, but is remote from the everyday living of our lives. The technique of the Church, he perceived, had become invariably to `sniff out people`s sins`, to make them feel a need for redemption and reconciliation to God – something Enlightenment thought could not deliver. This Bonhoeffer saw as a last-ditch attempt to win hearts and minds, a preying upon sins of weakness. He called, not upon discredited supernaturalist hopes, but for a life of love, following Christ as `the man for others`.[1] Bonhoeffer planned a totally fresh non-religious understanding of faith and of following Christ in response to total disillusionment with the Church and its religiosity. The key message for him was that "the concern of Jesus for others *is* the experience of transcendence."[2] How could anyone understand the meaning of love without being changed? The truth in the story goes far deeper than a matter of issues about what happened, whether God exists, or whether the Messiah will return. It is truth that cannot be understood without following its path.

For Bonhoeffer:

"The Church is her true self only when she exists for humanity. As a fresh start she should give away all her endowments to the poor and needy… she must take part in the social life of men, not lording it over them, but helping and serving them. It is not abstract argument but concrete example that give her words emphasis and power."[3]

So, like Kierkegaard a century and more earlier, Bonhoeffer`s insight was that the development of the human spirit had little to do with the traditional systems of ideas about heaven, judgment and hell. Man`s old

---

1   Letters and Papers from Prison (1943-5) Bonhoeffer transforms his understanding of Christianity from supernatural beliefs to a manner of life in which the believer gives his life for the causes of love without expecting anything in return. He revives the mythical understanding of faith.

2   Ibid `Outline for a Book` Ch.2 (SCM 1953) p.179 my underlining indicates the emphasis to be placed on `is`.

3   Ibid.pp. 180-1

master stories would now have to be seen in a new, non-literalist light. Why? Because that was always their proper role. They grew through their transformative power for individual and community. They demanded change. The true Cross was something to bear, not to search for under Eastern pavements.

Objective, dispassionate research cannot find the power of the stories – they are, objectively speaking, fictions. With literal belief in the history, cosmology and paradise of the old story, so also has departed the very manner of understanding that the master stories required. But this has to be relearned: objective investigation was never appropriate in the quest to understand them. Their metaphors are the seedbeds of the mind. The master fictions are not what they appear, superficially, to be. Fiction opens up the way and enlightens the spirit.

Therefore, we do well to revere the old master stories. These embody insights and images that we forsake at our peril. The mistake, made since as long ago as Plato, is to fail to penetrate their surface and perceive how they can yet speak to us. (It was Plato who thought myths, seen by the philosopher as untrue stories, were to be taught to the lower classes in order that they might know their place.) How can I revere a story that I know to have cruelty and folly within its pages? One reason to sift it carefully is because we have not noticed that its dark content is negated and superseded by its most powerful and effective insights, truths that we all too often fail to perceive, and when we perceive them, fail to assimilate. Just as much modern art conveys the darkest despair and destructiveness of humanity, so the dark stories of ancient texts give us a vision of our darkness, and without that, we do not seek the light. These dark episodes are, it seems to me, the secret message cutting deeply into our consciousness that also comes as we contemplate the works of Damien Hirst or Francis Bacon, both radical modern artists. Our world has given up the sacred, and with it sanity of spirit.

The Shoe Seller of Marmaris

My friend and I visited a shoe seller in a poor district of Marmaris, Turkey, in the days before tourists were taking over the town. She needed a cheap pair of shoes to wear in the sea. We had a large banknote. The man had no change. He insisted we take the shoes. The next morning we took the right money to him. He refused with a smile and a gesture of friendship. No word was spoken. We had no language but the language of the joy of sharing. It was then that I began to learn the meaning of Islam for common folk. It echoes Bonhoeffer himself when he wrote that "the transcendent is not infinitely remote, but close at hand".[1]

Muslim scholar Fareed Zakaria writes:

> "The historian Paul Johnson has argued that Islam is intrinsically an intolerant and violent religion. Other scholars have disagreed, pointing out that Islam condemns the slaughter of innocents and prohibits suicide. Nothing will be solved by searching for 'true Islam' or quoting the Qur'an. The Qur'an is a vast, vague book, filled with poetry and contradictions (much like the Bible). You can find in it condemnations of war and incitements to struggle, beautiful expressions of tolerance and stern pictures against unbelievers. Quotations from it usually tell us more about the person who selected the passages than about Islam. Every religion is compatible with the best and the worst of humankind. Through its long history, Christianity has supported inquisitions and anti-Semitism, but also human rights and social welfare."[2]

More, however, needs to be said if we are not to close the ancient texts forever. There follow extracts from some of the clearest teaching of the holy books of the Middle Eastern religions. This teaching forms the spiritual climax, I would say, of these master stories. This is not to claim anything about the context of such extracts in historical terms, or in terms of their relationship to other passages from the Koran or Judaeo-Christian Bible. Whatever scholars might have to say on such matters, my purpose in selecting them is to *emphasize the ideas* they express. Ultimately, the requirement of the faithful is to love.

---

1   Ibid. p.175
2   cited in article by Samuele Bacchiocchi in `Endtime` Issue no.85

"The deep human response for which Allah Most Merciful calls us is to the commitment to justice that transforms daily life into continual acts of kindness and generosity toward all persons regarding them as one intimate family" (16;89-90)

"Please encourage those who aspire to Islam to be gentle and selfless, to turn wholeheartedly toward the Source of Being and to call out to Allah Most Merciful every morning and evening longing only to gaze directly into the Face of Love" (18;27-31)

"Those who make a display of piety but have not committed their whole lives to compassionate action are like those who perform daily prayers as habit or as convention without true awe, humility and longing. Since their religion remains mere pretence, the vessel of their being has not been filled with active kindness by the Source of Love." (107;1-7)

And so also the Bible teaches this:

"You have heard that it was said, `You shall love your neighbour and hate your enemy` but I say unto you, Love your enemies and pray for those who persecute you, so that you may be sons of your Father who is in heaven..." (Matthew ch.6 vv43-5)

(A teacher asked Jesus-) "...which is the greatest commandment in the Law?" Jesus answered, " `Love the Lord your God with all your heart, with all your soul and with all your mind` This is the greatest and the most important commandment. The second most important commandment is like it: Love your neighbour as yourself`." (St. Matthew ch.22 vv36-40 This cites the Torah of the Jews in Deuteronomy ch.6.v 5 and Leviticus ch.19 v.18)

"To love is to obey the whole Law" (Romans 13.v.10)
"Beloved, let us love one another; for love is of God, and

he who loves is born of God and knows God; for God is
love" (1 John ch 4 vv7-8)

For Jew and Christian, much of the holy book they share is now
entirely of the past. We do not follow the commands of Leviticus about
uncleanness or sacrifices, neither do we stone people who gather sticks
on the Sabbath. King David learned that true penitence must come from
the heart, and that only with this attitude could sacrifices be offered on
the altar. Centuries later, the prophet Micah advanced further: "What,"
he asks, "does the Lord require of you but to do justice, to love mercy
and to walk humbly with your God?"[1]

For the Christian, Jesus Christ lived out the teaching on love. Fiction
or not, it matters little, his are stories of love. He healed the diseased,
including the low class and foreigners. He healed women and befriended
them. His life and death were the visible enactment of the love of God
for mankind. His dying love showed the world the way of salvation.
Thus, the master story empowered the believer to follow the forever-
present Master and it was seen to be his love and mercy, his rule over the
destiny of the world that would bring history to a glorious end. The Good
Samaritan, for example, is a story and a symbol known to hundreds of
millions of people. It encapsulates the call to love one's neighbour in such
a way that it has the power to shake us out of our racism and bigotry – if
we bother to reflect on it. Neither does it matter whether or not the Good
Samaritan actually existed. (If he did, then he and the other characters
were idiots for travelling alone along that bandit infested road!)

Reflection is as rare on this point as it is paramount. Once anyone devotes
himself to the teaching in the text, it becomes a principle of his thinking
and a precious value. The teaching will enable him to perceive that much
of the ancient text generally held to be 'sacred' is declared unimportant
by its own supreme insights. His reverence for others, his showing
of love to them, a love which is not dependent upon an appreciative
response, and not requiring that he has affection for the recipient, will
change his life. He will try to understand the minds of others, learning
from them. He will teach them by the power of his deed, by his patience
and his desire for no reward. That unconditional love utterly neutralizes

---

1   Micah ch.6 v.8 (8th c. BCE!)

the authority of any content militating against it which may be found in the text of the traditional scripture.[1]

It is a matter of great importance to perceive that caring love overrides such superficial but highly-prized principles as `the right to better oneself`. The latter might well be brought into subservience to caring love, so that billionaires invest their wealth in improving the quality of life for the disadvantaged, after the manner commended by Aristotle as `magnificence`. Unfortunately, in the globalism of today, the charitable activities of the world`s richest people can be counterproductive and dangerous[2]. It is, on the other hand, tragic to find wealthy professing Christians ignoring caring love and invoking divine providence as an excuse for their lifestyles. Many, if not most, of those opposing health care for all in the USA are also professing Christians.

Nothing changes the mind of the world without the power of love. Striving to embrace others within the bounds of one`s tradition and institutions becomes arrogance, disrespect, and abuse of others` minds. Love in action is never an invasion because it only gives and serves. It says nothing but itself. It cannot be sold, advertised, or dressed-up. We should not be mistaken about this – all peoples and nearly all individuals respond to love which is enacted wisely. All recognize goodwill and respect. Enmity is never ended through oppression, whether by the gun or indoctrination. If we listen to the stories terrorists tell, then, perhaps, they might listen to ours.

The Love that Led a Viking Chief to Hell

Here is a parable which I found somewhere many years ago.[3] It is in my own words:

---

1   If we read Philip Pullman`s `Jesus the Good Man: Christ the Scoundrel` we find a shocking new version which serves to explain strong opposition between the ethical power and novelty of the man Jesus, and the quest for fame, power and control which motivated his twin brother (sic), Christ. As Pullman writes on the back of the book, `This is only a story`. It is not, however, a mere provocation.

2   For an accusation of arrogance and ignorance amongst the world`s richest charitable entrepreneurs, see Mazower pp.418-421

3   I have looked hard for my source, but without success as yet!

> `A Catholic missionary priest took his team to the northern settlements of Europe. On his journey he entered a Viking village and brought his message to the chief. "I have come to offer you salvation from sin and deliverance from eternity in Hell. Only repent and be baptized into Holy Mother Church in the name of Christ, and you shall be saved!" The chief discussed the issue with his fellows, and returned. "Tell me, O wise one, are you telling us that our forefathers dwell in the Hell of Torment?" "That is so," replied the missionary. "We, therefore, prefer to dwell in Hell with our forefathers," replied the chief.`

That surely spells the death of the God of the orthodox. I cited at the beginning of this chapter the texts of love from Christianity, Judaism (the Torah) and Islam. These have massive authority, which they keep even if a person no longer subscribes to the belief system of the faith. I may reject belief in God and the atonement as doctrines, but I cannot reject the call to love without denying my humanity and my sense of responsibility for others and the world.

The texts of love themselves serve as warnings about a vast array of other material to be found in the sacred books which is taken by the fundamentalist as binding. To love one`s neighbour, who includes easily-despised immigrants, (as played by the Good Samaritan no less!), is to show respect, to care, to listen to their voice. How can love be reconciled with pressuring the needy into submission to a system of dogma? What transforms a life is the spirit of love. To think of this when also reading the miracles, parables and sayings of the Messiah, is to notice things not said. The story plants a seed that is not words, yet which grows in the being of the hearer. In the story, `blind` Pharisees were not healed, blind beggars were. The magical element is not the point. (If heaven had gatekeepers, they`d not keep you out on the basis of whether or not you believed in magical miracles – if they did, a tyrant would surely be in charge.)

It is clear that modern societies in developed countries have to varying extents become starved of spiritual meanings because their cultural history has presented them with false alternatives. The Medievalism that embedded their lives in symbolic rituals, parables and moral commands lost its voice when the Reformation taught a simpler faith needing no priest and offering direct communication with the divine. Whilst that reform opposed the degeneration of icon to idol, the passing away of sacred plays, objects of veneration and pilgrimage, it also saw the loss of the mythical. These things were the mysteries, and mystery became a mere edge surrounding belief, and lost its role in human wonderment, dread and hope.

The loss of shared faith led to moral loss and to community loss. Morality and community have no necessary dependence on the presence of religious culture, but only religious culture bestowed real power upon moral rules. (As in the belief that God sees us all the time.) One's eternal destiny depended on penitence and obedience. These ultimate meanings were the given truth to be accepted, and formed the bedrock of social life.[1] The consumer society finally ignores bedrock, having no philosophy of life. It thrives on the sands. It is the new 'opiate of the people'. It appears impossible for the majority to establish and share a coherent and progressive life narrative partly because their world offers a multitude of conflicting versions of how life is best lived, none of which speaks with authority. 'How should a person live?' is a question rarely deemed worth the asking. The good life has become, in its moral dimension, equated with little more than having no serial criminal record.

Richard Rorty lamented the loss of social hope:

"Modern, literate, secular societies depend on the existence of reasonably concrete, optimistic and plausible *political* scenarios, as opposed to scenarios about redemption beyond the grave. To retain social hope members of such a society need to be able to tell themselves a story about how things might get better, and to see no insuperable obstacles to this story's coming true… (But…) As Orwell put it, "The democratic vistas seem to end in barbed wire"[2]

---

1   I borrow Wittgenstein's fine analogy of foundational truths ('grammatical' truths) as the bedrock of ages. See 'On Certainty' section 97
2   'Contingency, Irony and Solidarity' p.86

'strong sustainability' will require, 'radical changes in our relation with the non-human natural world, and in our mode of social and political life'[1].

Such principles are to be anchored in our life narratives and our life narratives anchored in a powerful master story if we are to know where we should be travelling in matters great and small and how our lives can change the world. As world citizens, as receivers of news and knowledge from around the world, we share our lives and our common interests far more than in the past. This requires cooperation and common goals which we strive to meet. The world of nations slowly comes to manifest features of a community. Relationships develop; interdependence grows; members learn about each other and visit each other, playing together, exploring each other's worlds. We become united in shared hopes, common problems, mutually advantageous systems and shared visions.

When that story is complete, we still may find ourselves asking the question 'What then?'. The Cave of Myopia may still be with us, even when climate-change deniers have seen the light and put their billions into sustainability. For civilization to survive and grow, more is needed than to fulfil practical targets in the grand narrative about saving the planet. When all our doings are sustainable and we cease to consume without replacing, what do we then do with ourselves? When we have peace and plenty, and having avoided becoming like vermin on the Earth, on what do we focus our efforts? How do we then find our joy?

Yet how can we arrive at this temporal goal, of the sustainable environment in which our contributions have all made a difference and international agreements borne fruit, and still be dominated by calculative reasoning and the pursuit of external goods? Presumably, we, the masses, will have learned a lasting lesson, if only for a while. Perhaps, being human, other foci will rekindle our greed and impatience to possess. The master-story of saving the planet and its creatures cannot be fulfilled unless it is fuelled through progress in the maturing of the world's electorates, and that requires successful mass education of a relevant sort.

---

1   Jacobs and Dobson are cited in 'Growth Isn't Possible' p.19

Saving the World, and Then What?

Without an agreed master story for the current age, a story that defines the global community that we have become, and which is the source of our sense of direction in the world, the wisest and most vital of our formal principles will sit dead in the water.

How might we find our master story, the story in which we are to find vital purpose in our lives that offers us the chance of changing everything for the better?

Is there a clue here?

> Civil servant and environmental economist, Michael Jacobs described six core ideals and themes within sustainable development:
>
> 'The integration of the economy and environment: economic decisions to have regard to their environmental consequences.
>
> Intergenerational obligation: current decisions and practices to take account of their effect on future generations. Social justice: all people to have the equal right to an environment in which they can flourish (or have their basic human needs met).
>
> Environmental protection: conservation of resources and protection of the non-human world.
>
> Quality of life: a wider definition of human prosperity beyond narrowly defined economic prosperity.
>
> Participation: institutions to be restructured to allow all voices to be heard in decision-making (procedural justice).`

According to Andrew Dobson, Professor of Politics at Keele Univers

Eight Precious Stones Not To Be Mistaken For Diamonds

So what are the marks of true human growth? By contrast, let's look briefly at some candidates that are conventionally agreed, but which are quite inadequate. These are certainly prerequisites to the comfortable life – whilst 'man shall not live by bread alone', he certainly cannot live without it. On the other hand, it is possible to enjoy a good and meaningful life in times of considerable deprivation. The main connotations of the good life appear conventionally to be:

Possession of disposable income   **Good health and health care**

Education that leads to work   **Time for leisure**

Attractive physical appearance   **Security from threat**

Freedom of thought and expression   **Gainful employment**

All of these are important and desirable. Some might be considered worth dying for. Most are goals to which a government should aspire for all. Nobody should have to forego them. But they are not sufficient elements in human maturity. Neither are they *absolutely* necessary to our inner growth. They are precious stones, but not diamonds. It is such desirables that can prevent us from perceiving the supreme qualities in the true diamond.

A life of mature fulfilment can be found in their almost total absence. Some of the noblest, most heroic and productive lives are seriously deprived of some of the above features. So what might be the features of the good life that are both essential and much ignored?

"While all excesses are in a way hurtful, the most dangerous is unlimited good fortune" Seneca (1st.century AD)

Without wisdom, the outward appearance of prosperity and stability feeds the cancerous growth of greed and excess. The good life, in any enduring sense, is a life committed to the transformation of oneself and one's world, whether or not one is poor, oppressed, or suffering.

In contemporary life, this deep meaning of goodness is almost lost. For example, low achievers, the poorer among us, those in ill health or old age or the less beautiful in body are hardly to be admired. There is seen to be nothing in them to admire or wish to emulate unless they somehow perform a heroic deed celebrated on the media. The everyday virtue of the lives of the underprivileged is rarely considered. The power to love is fading, not on the big screen of `Red-Nose Day` or disaster appeals, but love for our everyday relatives and neighbours.

Love is primal because it is vital from birth if growth in being is to proceed. With no experience of love, the baby will easily lose its own potential to love. Love feeds our beings towards maturity. Love is imperative because humanity and the world cannot progress without it. Knowing all this and agreeing with it as a glowing idea is not yet to realise the good life. Effective action makes its virtues one`s own.

Love is the decentring of the self away from self-concern to concern for the beloved, whether family member, friend, neighbour, community…

    …and away from this restricted circle to the well-being of world community.

    …and away from an institution itself towards the world it serves and from which it gains its wealth.

To love is to find one`s being as much in the being of others as in oneself.

Love requires for its effectiveness wisdom. This requires a whole array of human qualities. Without courage, determination, persistence, honesty, knowledge, consideration for others` opinions, self-discipline, patience, generosity, and a host of other virtues, love cannot act effectively. Without all these the spirit may be willing, the mind foolish, and the flesh weak.

Caring love demands no particular emotion of the lover. It is rational action irrespective of emotion. It is required of us for our own sake and the sake of the world in which we live. We get on with loving because we listen to our souls and ignore our likes and dislikes.

It is paradoxical that such love can sometimes be more strongly promoted in the absence of some of those ingredients listed above in the common view of the good life. The tragedy of humanity's advance into modern life is its loss of love. Ease tends towards self-satisfaction. Hardship may drive the soul towards deeper meanings. Popular goods, whether external or internal, are of little benefit in the long term unless they are managed with love. Communities tend to develop effectively more out of shared hardships than shared pleasures.

The following important prerequisites of maturity, themselves aspects of love, tend to be ignored:

1. Developing stable and meaningful relationships with each other. The media all too often attend to poor relationships. Schools are made to support economy-related aims at the expense of relationship-related aims. Even sex education tends to be taught biologically, for economic and health reasons, at the expense of the human relationship focus, which is harder, in the current climate, for young people and teachers to understand[1]. Deeper relations with others depend upon like-mindedness. Things to share together that go deeper than just casual exchanges about the present-at-hand are central to proper social belonging. It has been said by many that human relationships *are* the meaning of life. When these are missing or fail, our world seems shattered and we have to dig deep to find the point of our living. More than anything else, our relationships strengthen our will to live through the worst experiences.

2. Having a developing system of life ideals respectful of the human and natural world about us. Without such, a person is ill-equipped to participate in helping to preserve a world for future generations, and will lessen the scope and effectiveness their life chances. Schooling tends to neglect this aspect of development. Recent initiatives in the UK in the areas of personal, moral and social education, citizenship and climate change are attempts to rectify this. They will serve a failing cause if the nation's leaders are known to be corrupt, when family and community members behave selfishly and without respect for others, when what is

---

1   It's so 'uncool' to warn against promiscuity on anything other than medical grounds. James Bond never asks, 'Hold on, what does this mean for us?' Such implicit moralizing would kill the picture because it would threaten the audience with reality.

taught inside school seems almost impractical outside.

Perhaps the greatest difficulty when it comes to forming a programme of learning on the subject of beliefs, values and behaviour comes from the popular understanding of religious texts and rituals as literal descriptions of a supernatural world. Unless we learn the deep meanings of such narratives, that is, those meanings that are for us now, whatever our thoughts on the subject of what exists beyond this world, we will not be transformed by them. Unfortunately, neither the world of education nor that of the `common man`, at least in the USA or UK, is ready for such, so programmes of study in religions and ideologies drift about with no goal of a transformed life beyond the removal of prejudice. Until such times change, most children will not be able to acknowledge the great traditions and, at the same time, to know that the revelatory power of a story does not depend upon its age and origins. It is surprising, perhaps, that an implication of this is that theology matters: we must shrug off the old literalism and relearn the symbolic and commissive meaning of our traditions.

The traditions of faith give people their language, their concepts of value, their stories which serve as parables of life. Living ideals and standards of behaviour are mediated through such stories. From the Greek Epics, Jataka Tales of Hinduism, stories of Buddha and Mohammed, to the tales of Jewish or Christian holy folk , ideas of maturity come to modern minds, being formative of culture through the ages. It is upon such that the whole heritage of fiction and saga has been built. Neither should we think that the earliest stories have quality not to be found in `modern` counterparts, Andersen`s Fairy Tales, Lewis`s `Narnia` stories, Hoban`s `Mouse and His Child`, Hughes` `Iron Man`, Pullman`s `Dark Materials` for example. I dare also to add the Star Wars film and book saga! One should include a host of inspiring novels, histories, dramas and poetry. These can be, as much as the ancient story, powerful stimuli to human development. And, in a more mysterious way, their themes breathe with living power through music, drama and art. They are also freed from the now trivial, once-crucial clutter erected around old master stories, so they can often do a better job.

3. Being able to use leisure creatively. When leisure pursuits focus upon the satisfaction of physical desires or upon intensity of sensations at the expense of `practices` they tend to diminish our lives rather than enhance them. By contrast, in pursuing them we have regard for the enjoyment of them for themselves. Having such a dimension to our lives enhances our self-esteem and makes us more outgoing. It takes the vacant look from our faces. The lack of conversation which led us to withdraw from social interactions is transformed into a desire to meet and share.

> **Creative leisure** - gets us fit physically, mentally or, preferably, both.
>
> - builds our self-esteem by stimulating our minds
>
> - gives us rich conversation by giving us subject matter and ideas to share
>
> - provides problems to be solved and targets to be met, thus enabling progress, and sharpening our ability to focus, or concentrate
>
> - enhances specialized skills

4. Living realistically. Reading the above might easily enrage due to its strongly idealistic nature. However, we cannot live meaningful lives without ideals, and these may not be fully realized. We strive to promote them. Being realistic means being aware of the real need for power, control, competition, and the firm rejection of outmoded ways of thinking and producing. It is common to regard the successful person as one who overcomes the competition without regard for how it is to be done, tough in business, unsentimental in dealings with others, and hungry for further success. However, we must learn both to *compete and cooperate*, the result leading to a new level of achievement.

> **Lutz Long** was a famous athlete who was the German representative in the long jump at the 1936 Berlin Olympic Games, and was, of course, expected to win the gold medal. During the competition, he was leading after Jesse Owens,

 a black American, had made two foul jumps by overstepping the take-off mark. Long noticed that Owens' jumps were so long that he might well win were he to take off further behind the board. Long took Owens aside and advised him that he should do this. Owens did so, and beat Long into first place. After the event they paraded around the arena together, German and Negro, much to the annoyance of the Nazis. Long was unpunished for this, and remained a loyal German, being killed in action at Salerno in 1943. His achievement was not to be determined simply in athletic or military success, for he did not fully succeed in those aims. His inner qualities displayed the depths of his being in ways that winning the gold medal could not. The heights he attained survive even the tragedy of an early death in battle.

Competitive values must come second to valuing the quality result all competitors seek. Gaining the prestige of higher status is vainglorious, and the true winners know that. Their gaze is focused on the desired result. Long was not prepared to take gold knowing that another could probably have jumped further. Underlying successful cooperation in a project is a love of quality in the end result. One never ceases to be amazed and delighted with the Anglo-French Airbus project. Neither Nelson nor Napoleon would ever have imagined such cooperation. To sustain technological success we need people who put the value of competition second to that of shared cooperation for the sake of quality.

`Ecstatic Valuing`, Without Which We Cannot Grow

Walsh's matrix of values illustrates beautifully how our values might be properly prioritized[1]. It shows clearly both the importance and the

---

1   Paddy Walsh, in his award-winning work, `Education and Meaning`, develops a matrix of values, all of which are ubiquitous and potentially healthy. The conceptual structure in his book is masterly, even though, like most works on education, it will now be gathering dust in attics due to its age (1993).

incompleteness of popular versions of maturity. Walsh develops a hierarchy of four value types, the possessive, experiential, ethical and ecstatic. Each is less readily prized than its predecessor simply because higher levels of valuing become progressively fragile. The most common, and perhaps the most tragic, feature of individual life stories is the failure to develop ecstatic values. This hinders our growth to adulthood, as we fall into the trap of losing such values whilst becoming preoccupied with possessive, experiential and even ethical concerns.

A foretaste of the meaning of `ecstatic` as used by Walsh can be seen in the following example. This highest level of valuing is indispensable to the healthy mind. I have this print of a London evening, probably in the 1940`s. Its creator has saved a way of life for us to recall, or discover for the  first time. Whilst such quality of result is not what makes a work worth attempting, what matters most for my purpose is the devotion of the artist. The painter immersed himself in the task. Careful examination reveals not only the mastery of light, colour and design, but the selection of a scene that could hardly have been photographed, neither did he paint on the spot, nor even in that decade! There was a vision here, highly evocative of a time when human goings-on were almost as today, yet crucially different and easily forgotten. The artist, who I am proud to have known, did not work in order to justify his existence to anyone. Yes, through it he supported his family, but his thoughts were not taken over by such. His work like any other, may have had its stressful moments, but was no burden upon his life, being his play, in the sense that the practice was an end in itself, his own fulfilment. It had power and beauty, and brought truth to the viewer.[1]

The most easily understood are those necessary **"possessive"** values. Examples are wealth, status, work, power and freedom. Clearly, all these are important, yet all have their limitations and dangers. We all want them, but are in danger of making them the main focus of our lives, so

---

1 `In Town Tonight` by Don Breckon, courtesy of Meg Breckon.

that good reasons for seeking them tend to be lost. Rightly pursued, as already emphasized, they are not sought for themselves, but for what they lead to. In other words, they are the means to attaining higher values. It is also evident that not everyone can achieve them. For some to do so is for others to fail. They can, therefore, be divisive, and the cause of conflict. They have to be kept in proportion. Such are the `external goods` of Aristotle.

Do we really seek the company of those who have made money-making or social status an end-in-itself? What do they talk about? Even if brief encounters seem beneficial, there is small chance of conversation about mutually-loved activities which are a delight in themselves. The conversation generates competition rather than intimacy or true bonds. What about `work`? As `my job`, it is a conversation stopper when people are present who can find no job. Only when work has an element of play, and life-enhancing play at that, can respect and inspiration develop out of the conversation. For `play` in work is creative activity, and is valued for itself. By then it has become elevated to a higher status, that of `ecstatic`. We return to the important subject of play, for children and adults, later.

A less apparent, deeper layer of valuing is the `**experiential**`. Life is valued for the richness of experience it affords. There is the challenge of the unknown, the unsolved problem, the unexplored height, whether it be physical or theoretical in nature. It might seem to us that the pursuit of such things is what gives life its point, and that this forms the peak of spiritual development, for the self that testifies to the richness of life`s experience is no waster, no slouch, and has the chance of being a joy to know! But, as Walsh points out, such a life is, without deeper layers of valuing, futile, for genuineness of being requires something other than experience as its inner value. We may be reminded of the `done-that-been-there` mentality, in which a person measures his life according to the breadth and duration of his experience. It is the perennial danger of the scholar, the traveller, the pioneer and innovator. Walsh speaks of the "nemesis" of being "into" experience, but not properly "in" experience.

The masses might not climb mountains unless a tourist train lugs them safely to the peak. As long ago as 1864, John Ruskin raged, in gentlemanly manner, of course, about mass tourism, a pursuit too easily mindless of the awesome nature of the Alpine world through which tunnels and cuttings were carved to enable the masses to go there and pass on to the next scene. To pass straight through an honoured place is not to know it. We would do better to linger, look and listen, to stay and learn its life[1]. Touring, with bases of some duration, is one thing, travel another.

There is an ethical fault in the relentless pursuit of new experiences. People, creatures and the world itself, are not treated with respect. This suggests that we must pursue a deeper layer of values than both the *possessive* and the *experiential*. We give authority to `**ethical values**`.

Ethical values regulate our behaviour when we realize that we must avoid cruelty in all its forms and develop rules and principles which promote this goal. Take, for example, the principle of `respect for persons`. This is a vital feature of the good life in a humane society. It ensures that we are on our guard against treating others on the basis of prejudices about their age, status, appearance, gender, race, etc. It helps us listen to them before we make judgments about their views, and it helps us learn from them. Notice that `respect for persons` is not a `rule` to follow because it does not specify precisely what to do and what not to do. Rules do this, but, being rules, they are inflexible and can be used inhumanely. The rule `do not steal`, for example, has to be considered in the light of principles like respect for persons whenever a particular situation arises. (Stealing in a particular situation may be good if it saves potential victims lives, feeds the starving, prevents self-harm, etc.[2])

This is fundamental. There is little hope for a truly global society until we

---

1   John Ruskin`s powerful diatribe against mass tourism is cited in de Botton `The Art of Travel`.p223

2   Lawrence Kohlberg (1981) developed a hierarchy of stages of moral thinking through which he claimed that the developing person ascends to a certain level. This hierarchy emphasizes that moral rules are helpful things for people to follow, but that they are also severely limited in their usefulness when facing certain vital situations. Ultimately, the final, and supreme level of moral thinking employs `moral principles`, such as `consideration of the interests of all involved` to help one arrive at a fair judgment. Such principles are at the heart of rational decision-making, as Habermas also claims. They do provide a structure for our thought: some moral dilemmas remain, however, rationally insoluble.

apply those principles of respect for persons, openness, consideration of interests, equality of opportunity, etc., making them the ultimate arbiter of the morality of actions. This is all of vital importance, *but we have yet to hit upon crowning essentials of the mature, or truly good, life. One could be ethically committed and faultless in conduct yet missing the true springs of a meaningful life.*

Ethical values themselves depend upon a more all-embracing form, which Walsh calls `**ecstatic values**`. In ecstatic valuing, he points out, the focus is in no way upon the self, what it might acquire, what it might achieve, or even how it might conduct itself, but upon the object itself. Whether the object of experience is human, animal, inanimate, past, present or future, engagement with it is motivated by fascination, reverence, and the desire to become immersed in its life. Thus the passions are directed away from mere possessive, experiential, and even ethical concerns, which challenge, trouble and even overthrow the self, towards concerns within which the state of the self is forgotten. It is this forgetting which contributes to its growth. This is the diamond we seek.

We may now perceive why Walsh adopted the term `ecstatic values`. `Ecstasy` comes from the classical Greek, *ek* (outside) and *stasis* (stand). Ecstasy, as employed here, is not an emotional state. The ecstatic person is not focused upon herself, considering how she is judged by others, her image, status, apparent success, etc. *The focus is upon the activity or practice itself.* She is immersed in it, loving it, knowing that this time spent need not be surpassed. It is not pursued for what it might lead to, but because it has its own fascination and reward. Contrast that with the anxious person, who strives to become more `important`, to get rich, to become well known yet who derives no joy, skill or understanding from what they get up to in life. It is the loss of the ecstatic that generates strife and loss of mental health and reduces the possibility of being really worth knowing. Ecstatic valuing is about rising above the necessities of coping in life and being able to enjoy practices for themselves, being unmindful, at least for the duration of one`s engagement in the practice, of how things are going in mundane terms.

But how can someone experience such engagement in a creative activity for its own sake, for the pleasure it brings, when preoccupied

with how the next rent and fuel bill is to be paid? How can people whose possessive needs are not met, possibly attain to the `ecstatic`? How can life become play rather than struggle in the absence of money, food or security? With difficulty, of course, and that`s why the objects of possessive values become ends in themselves. That said, people who already have internal goods to delight in have a refuge in times when external goods are in short supply. They have foci of delight that cost them nothing – from games to the love of nature, reading, sharing ideas or enjoying music and art, and not to forget, climbing mountains. Whatever happens on the possessions front, their faith in the value of life itself is not easily emptied. We can endure poverty, ill health, etc., far more easily if we have self-esteem. The possession of internal goods delivers us from our esteem problems, for we perceive that we have quality of life! We still have cause for joyfulness.

The demise of ecstatic values is an aspect of a wider loss. Ruskin spoke in the time of the Industrial Revolution when mankind became obsessed with technology. Technology served to help deliver the British from revolution, or even worse, starvation. But it was also technology that sharpened the focus upon calculative thinking: what is thought about is an object to incorporate into our instrumental world. Where language is dominated by calculative thinking distinctive sensibilities become atrophied and people can see themselves only in terms of the subject-object distinction. Calculative thinking is earning the status of an ugly sister, whilst meditative thought remains a perpetual Cinderella, whose importance is unperceived.

Meditative thinking, by contrast, does not take as an *object* what we think about, but rather recognizes what is thought about as another *subject*. People, for example, in the circle of our lives, no longer serve as a mere appreciation society for us, but become true presences, themselves to be enjoyed and valued as much as we value ourselves. Meditative thinking is hardly likely to be nourished as we speed through the scenery or gallop round a historic town without indwelling it in some way, not necessarily physically, but mentally. Knowledge of a place is a vital prerequisite – meditation and fresh insight are not possible on an empty mind. Reverence is an integral aspect of meditative thinking, and is at the heart of what `ecstatic` means. It cannot be rushed. As a general rule, by the way, we'll surely have the chance of a better holiday if we stay in the one place, providing we choose it well and learn its cultural ways. It might change us forever.

The Birth and Salvation of Learning

We should not see ecstatic valuing as the distant attainment of an elite. Children possess this. It is vital to their development. J------- is eight years old and well known to me. At three he adored vehicles, and could repeat at a glance the make of every car he saw. He watched TV and saw advertisements for cars such as Subaru. He saw the large 'S' and heard the vowel sounds. He was learning to read without a teacher. The motivation derived from ecstatic valuing is perhaps the greatest key to learning to read, for it gives a child the courage to guess, and lucky guessing accelerates ability. His parents have not forced this upon him, but showed clear enjoyment of his passion. He has loved what he has seen, and his parents have reinforced that love. Clearly such ecstatic experience may widen to other or deeper loves. The child has found the world to be magical. He loves to learn. He knows his interest is valued. The growth of the mind has accelerated, and he is now widening his subjects of fascination.

I have a close friend, H---------, much of whose time was spent with her big sister as a small child. Whilst parents were busy, they made their own joy together. Miniature roads were constructed through plants and bushes, toy cars and trucks busily travelling to and fro. Father's very large packing case became a sailing boat, in which 'swallows and amazons' type adventures were created. I myself, at about six years old, laid out on the kitchen floor a large sheet of brown paper, took my colours, and drew a map of the world, with my mother calling out names of countries whilst doing her washing at the sink. The map lived for some years, having all the appearance of a failed attempt at Mappa Mundi. None of this activity was designed to formally teach us anything, but we all learned much, and above all, grew to love our world. The sisters became scientists, I became a geography teacher. The birth of ecstatic valuing is found in the play of childhood.

Sadly, this playing is in stark contrast with the play of a child who is inspired by scenes of fighting, driving crashes on the road, and the killing of monsters: what joyful activities could thence arise, and how could they engender social growth and sharing? A perverse joy in hurting and destroying readily results. Parents are the key to success or failure here. We may leave children to play together, as well as playing with them, but whatever we do, we need to equip them with stories and toys that deliver them from fascination with the darker aspects of humanity. In childhood it can only harm them unless, in their story making, the forces of evil are overcome by the good and true, and are not the focal theme.

Notice the generation of creativity and its transformation as we mature. There appear to be at least **three levels**, each of which can be applied to a wide variety of activities:

1. **Idiosyncrasy** Infants will be allowed to make something of their own and on their own. It is precious because it is richly meaningful to them, not because it meets conventional criteria of quality. (I recall my own oldest daughter's hovercraft made at nursery school. It looked nothing like one to the careless eye, a cornflakes' box with cut and paste work. What a joy it was to her, partly owing to the delight shown by her parents at her own abilities, of course. It made her work valued by adults.) To make something of one's own is one of the first steps towards confidence in learning. If that dies, higher levels will never be reached. Parental or teacher interference can be fatal at this stage.
2. **Conformity** As children mature, to this form of creative skill will be added creative work according to criteria of quality. Beyond infancy, from about six to eight years old, conventional standards will be employed in the finding of solutions to problems, whether they be concrete or abstract. A teacher is, therefore, important from here on, not simply as a guide, but as an instructor. Rules must be taught and skills acquired. The infantile idiosyncrasy in making or painting is superseded by submission to the conventions of measurement, drawing, writing and making things. This applies from junior schooling to undergraduate levels. Learners should

be ever mindful of the conventional if they are to master or transcend it.

3. **Autonomy** The highest form of creative work involves the breaking of new ground in a subject, novelty that grows out of established knowledge and skills, but which transcends them. At best this may provide a radical new idea of the criteria for excellence in the matter at hand. Not many will reach this stage of creativity, but there can be no harm whatsoever in trying. Even the notorious urinal of Duchamp (1917) would make no sense without an understanding of conventions in fine art, against which it stood in stark protest.

Also, to fail at this highest level is no shame: many have trodden that path. It also follows that the task and goal must be sought `ecstatically`, not primarily as means to other ends. **Reginald Mitchell** created a disastrous failure in 1925, his beautiful S4 seaplane. This was to be the first cantilever high-speed monoplane in the world. With no external bracing needed, it looked and went superbly. Aesthetically unparalleled, it was, however, ten years ahead of its time in terms of the science of structures and forces, and, as a result, it crashed. External bracing had to return until the appearance of more sophisticated materials, as were supremely employed in Mitchell`s thinner-winged Spitfire 11 years later.

What seems to be of paramount importance from early childhood is the signalling of enthusiasm. The child discovers whatever it is that pleases the parent, be it a smile or gesture, and repeats it at will. New, life-enhancing experiences and abilities are soon discovered. This comes from the primal energy of spirit that indicates that all is well. There is, probably in all babies, grief of separation, when the mother figure who constitutes their world, disappears for periods of time. This is a time of threat during which creative powers come into being. The blanket or the teddy bear stand in for the parent figure. The imagination comes into life and play can begin.[1]

Parenting requires not only intimate stimulation and informal education which stimulates the child's mind. It also, paradoxically perhaps, requires that space and time be given for the child to 'do its own thing'. Thus there needs to be time when the child relieves its own lack of stimulation by 'making its own joy', finding its own source of inspiration, and strengthening confidence and hope in life.[2] Such freedom may, of course, be abused by children, since, for most perhaps, the 'temptation in the garden' experience must be gone through.

The starving child, the child whose body has been wracked with pain, who has received the constant grief of neglect, and sensory starvation (seeing forever the same ceiling or cot bars) is the child whose spirit is in danger. Indifference and despair can possess its being. We can hardly imagine how a loving mother, starving and sick, with no medical care, nothing to warm or stimulate her child, feels when she looks into its face.

Small children who have a stable caring environment from birth, parent figures only absent for short periods, with their own bed and special toys, have stability and the warmth of love. These stimulate confidence and expectation in later life.

 It is not simply maternal love that matters: paternal love is as vital, and even in the time of maternal loss, the love of a father can save a child from despair.[3] Pandita Ramabai

---

1   The importance of the 'transitional object', the thing that is precious and is not 'me' yet not 'mother', is emphasized by D.W.Winnicott in his 'Playing and Reality' (1971, Penguin). It is the bridge between the inner and outer worlds and the prototype of all symbols, located in 'the space between'. Kim Simpson's chapter in House (2011) on 'The Unfolding Self' says much that every adult should know about young children.
2   'Ned and the Joybaloo' by Oram, I. (Andersen Press) addresses this subject in a children's picture and text book.
3   As was the case with my mother, whose mother died when she was four, and who had wonderful memories of her father's love for people, gardening, animals and the countryside.

was one who lost her mother when very young, but her father was forbidden, as a Hindu, to educate her. He defied this rule and taught her Sanskrit, his own sphere of special expertise, and in her growing years, she amazed the masculine academic world. She then spent her life striving for the rights of Indian women to become educated.[1]

It is also wondrous how some children maintain their love of life despite the complete loss of parent figures. **Joey Deacon**, who we met earlier, maintained his passion for life and his love of people despite not having had any education all his life, and having been placed in a hospital for the severest categories of mentally handicapped people when his mother died. She had always believed in his intelligence. His father devotedly visited him as often as he could until he also died, in 1939. Joey was unlucky enough to have been born a generation too soon, his mental powers being hidden behind speechless spasticity. He had learned to love people and was apparently not mindful of the awful injustice committed upon him. He lived for other things. Joey had no sense of possessive valuing, and little time for calculative thinking; the experiences he might enjoy were extremely limited. (Once, he writes, a really pretty girl visited the ward, a peak experience for Joey. `She wouldn`t fancy me`, he wrote.) However, some mysterious life force kept the lights on in Joey`s life. The autobiography got written. Joey`s mind had developed through means unknown, but he needed to develop language and ideas, none of which he was physically capable of expressing until reaching old age. Possessive valuing might well have destroyed him.

As already emphasized, ecstatic valuing is a vital ingredient in all education, not just for the top stream, yet it is the most vulnerable ingredient, being largely qualitative rather than quantitative. Love of the activities in which children are best engaged is the most vital manifestation

1   In 1889 Ramabai established the Mukti Mission in Pune, India`s first organization for girl education and women`s equal rights with men, which still thrives. Mukti means `liberation`.

of a good educator simply because it is itself an expression of valuing the foci of study for themselves. And the propagation of such love is the supreme mark of successful education at any level, from severe learning difficulties to adult learning.

Love of the world in this sense is possessed or lost by anyone. We need to be forever be on our guard lest the pressures of hardship, of competitiveness, of sexual desire, of wealth-acquisition-and-possession, of self-advancement in whatever form it takes, distract us away from respecting and enjoying practices, people, creatures, the environment – all *for themselves as opposed to whatever they might lead as gain for us.* It is a long, hard road for us to travel if we are to recover from the domination of instrumental values to the freedom and peace of the ecstatic, but to do so is to enrich and probably lengthen our lives. This author has travelled the route himself and stumbled into many a hole on the way.

The current pressure to 'move children on', to accelerate their formal learning to count, read, use computers, can seriously inhibit their ability to play. Playing is spontaneous, social and self-guided. The imposition of formal learning targets and programmes upon children, even up to teenage, tends, for the majority, to reduce their enjoyment of life, their hope for their own futures and their love of other people. Life becomes an obstacle course. Take, for example, one target amongst the plethora required by the UK government for preschool learning:

> (From 40 months children should…) "Complete a simple programme on a computer; use ICT to perform simple functions such as selecting a channel on the TV remote control; use a mouse and keyboard to interact with age-appropriate computer software."[1]

That is outrageous. If children can do those things, fine, if properly supervised, but to require such skills in a formal learning assessment for measuring quality and progress shows complete ignorance of human development and makes carers, teachers and parents anxious and

---

1   Early Years Foundation Stage of National Curriculum, 2008

competitive.[1]

We have, in order to discover or rediscover ecstatic valuing, to take stock regularly, to look at the extent to which we pursue as ends things that should be no more than life's necessary means – promotion, money, getting noticed, measured performance etc. – and to learn enjoyment in life for its own sake. We may take time to share leisure and conversation with the ones we love. We may read on a subject that has lurked in the background for too long. We may take that demanding country walk we once fancied doing. We may join a sports club again, or at least get the bike out. We may plant seeds. Above all, we may play more with our children. These sorts of things, and a million other possibilities, are the activities that exemplify ecstatic valuing. They are food for the spirit, and can deliver us from our slavery to work. There is something also mysterious about them. The questions they raise, the solutions they offer, the further questions… the ideas, the language, the images, the problems, all have brought us to being again, out of mere existence.

To be, as a fully-functioning human being, is to have one's mind nourished by a thousand delights that have no point beyond themselves, and to learn that there is no closure. We die before the mysteries of objects of contemplation are resolved. I have just enjoyed reading Steve Jones' `Darwin's Island`[2]. He writes about `The Thinking Plant`, and amazes me with information about the sensory powers of vines that perceive light and change their strategy for reaching it, sending new shoots up nearby taller trees than the one they had originally chosen for support. Darwin's experiments in his own garden, with his own son as assistant, led to new discoveries about plant behaviour that led eventually to today's understanding of the processes involved when such achievements are reached. It has opened my mind to a dimension about which I knew almost nothing. I have entered a world of wonderment and mystery. Nature is highly sophisticated, even in plant life, to the extent that every new discovery continues to bring more problems to be resolved. Science involves ecstatic valuing and meditative thinking.

---

1   Government ministers and civil servant teams in the UK largely come from public schools and universities. These people ignore the expertise of specialists in child development in policymaking.

2   `Darwin's Island: The Galapagos in the Garden of England` (2009 Abacus London)

It is clear that all four forms of valuing, possessive, experiential, ethical and ecstatic, are valid and vital. We need to possess the normal necessities of life, but may not transform our level of existence beyond having possessive values. We also need to have the stimulation of a range of meaningful experiences in order to delight in our world and become true participants in its well-being. We need to be able to regulate our valuing of possessions and experiences through ethical principles which guard against exploiting people and places for our own ends. Most easily omitted are these spiritual values which it is not an easy matter to define, yet which are as vital as other levels of valuing.

It is the forgetting of these that has led to widespread malaise in modern life.

> "Many of the `teaching to test`, assessment-driven characteristics of the primary school are now invading our nurseries and other early years settings. Ed Balls, (the then) Minister for Children, School and Families, wants (and believes it to be appropriate that) our children to `hit the ground running`. The language of industry is rapidly colonizing the art of education."[1]

In times when life was hard, people had to value possessively in order to have food, money for rental payment, and to keep a job. We might think that, in such times, ethical and ecstatic valuing would have been put aside, but that was rarely so. It may also surprise us to learn that, in wealthier days, possessive and experiential valuing still predominate, and do not take less dominant a place in our lives. This is because human beings have usually found reflection, meditation, and creative work less attractive than the pursuit of activities which can easily be envisaged to yield results.

How easy it is to miss out on that intercourse of minds which furnishes deeper joys in life together. The human being is equipped to become a creature of meaning. The meanings in his life are not genetically coded in, as with bees and herring. He perceives it. He must learn it, make it, share it, enrich it. He is also a creature of his time, and uses the narratives of the time, fact and fiction, to furnish himself with knowledge, understanding

---

1   Edginton et.al in `Too much, Too Soon` (2012) p.40

and wisdom. More than this, he sifts and questions these, tests them in his life, shares his thought with others, and becomes a desired friend amongst those who value living conversation rather than idle talk.

It is in the shared life of infant and parent where all that must begin, to be developed in the play of infants and the more programmed learning of later childhood.

CHAPTER 5: ATTAINING LOVE OF THE WORLD

> `The core and ultimate value of life can lie only in such states as exist for their own sake and carry their satisfaction in themselves...
> There really are such...we call them play.`
> - Moritz Schlick Philosophical Papers 1927

> `For true love is inexhaustible; the more you give, the more you have. And if you go to draw at the true fountainhead, the more water you draw, the more abundant is its flow.` - Antoine de Saint-Exupery

Let`s pause for a moment. What is this contemplation that we must employ if we are to progress unhindered in our search for inner maturity? Nobody can reflect without some outside influence or they`ll end up back in that faceless, presupposition-less, nonsensical `reason`, which MacIntyre warned us about. All thinking starts from accepted presuppositions, or first principles, known in ancient times as *archē*, especially when claiming that such-and-such are good for us! We are all `somewhere` culturally speaking. We all have presuppositions without which we have no starting points from which to travel in reflection on life. "Don`t let`s deceive ourselves into thinking our reflections are any less `culturally determined` than others", we might say. This can, surprisingly, be a mistake.

Open reflection has a vital place. It seeks to expose and question our presuppositions wherever possible and wherever it is important to do so. It can take us back to beginnings – to our *archē*. It erects no barrier to enquiry and criticism. It may, of course, lead us to new commitments in our thinking, and new presuppositions, but it does enable us to progress as we do so. On the other hand, no open reflection can happen in a vacuum. It functions on the basis of what has been learned hitherto. I read Steve Jones` `Darwin`s Island` and my thinking was influenced by what I learned, and I found myself to be inspired – here are wonders indeed! I now have answers and also many new questions. By contrast the religious dogmatists whose mental life rests upon divinely revealed truth have enclosures to their imagination that are firmly fixed: `Either this is the Word of God or we are lost`. But all boundaries to our imagination are questionable. To transgress them is to dogmatists, (whether in religion, politics, economics, music, etc.) apostasy, and to break them down, damnation. For such folk, to shake free from the grip of the system will be harder than emigrating to Siberia. Thankfully, the best religious positions are not these days dogmatic and exclusive, but expressive of attitudes of love, reverence, and openness to mystery.

Liberal humanists, who may or may not be also devoutly religious persons, will make their stand only on certain presuppositions without which there can be little peace for society or the world, and without which there can be no interchange of ideas. `No interchange of ideas` implies `no meaningful conversation`. These presuppositions on which they stand include the importance of freedom of enquiry and expression, impartial respect for persons, and truth telling. (Hardly dubious presuppositions!) This liberal position is not held in opposition to religious outlooks as such. As humanists, they believe, ethically, that "cruelty is the worst thing we do" (Rorty), and that love, as care and respect, undergirds enlightened ethical practice. To love is also to listen, not simply to verbal statements, but to the practices and metaphors belonging to ways of life of which we have yet to find understanding. To be devout does not imply dogmatic rejection of open reflection – faith can proceed as a way of life expressed and enhanced by ritual and symbolism. The expressions of faith may be what Ian Barbour called "ontologically shy", that is to say, not ready to hammer out convictions in a rigid system of propositions, yet ready to show a sense of the sacred in manner of life[1]. Their symbols reveal and hide at the same time.

---

1   In `Myths, Models and Paradigms` (1974)

Love of the World

Love of the world promotes -	Love of the world counteracts -
Enjoyment of activities, people, places, creatures for their own sake	The desire for self-aggrandizement in the eyes of others through wealth, status, power
Insight and deep understanding, patient deliberation	The pursuit of immediate, impulsive pleasure-seeking
Love of oneself	Self-loss, abuse and destruction
Valuing, and desiring the well-being of, individuals	Pursuing actions which diminish others
Intimacy with others and one`s world	Cold indifference to others` interests
Contentment with what cannot be changed in one`s life	Disgruntlement with one`s lot
Strength and assurance during difficult times	Weakness and confusion
Personal attractiveness irrespective of one`s age and appearance	Over-concern with one`s physical attractiveness
Motivation and energy	Resignation when the game appears to be up
Openness to the unknown and acceptance of the brevity of our existence	The closed mind: seeking distraction from the unpalatable
Thankfulness	Indifference to the fact of being alive
Optimism and hope for the future	Scepticism and despair of the world

`Love of the world` is, in the Christian tradition, a seductive vice. The Christian is taught not to love "the things of the world, the lust of the flesh, the lust of the eyes, and the pride of life"[1], for here `the world` refers to fallen, corrupt lifestyles that fail to see beyond pleasures and possessions to the eternal kingdom of love. But love of the world as understood in this work has a different emphasis, focussing upon reverence for human beings, for creatures and the natural world. It is not altogether in opposition to the ancient meaning, for this love also resists egocentric hedonism and lust for power and wealth, but it is not in any sense `other-worldly`. It does not look beyond the created cosmos to a perfect world beyond the grave, for it sees our lives as having their being here in this finite and fragile cosmos. Thus it is the gift that enables us to age and die in peace.

This `love of the world` is not exactly the same as the *agapē* (Gk. `caring kindness`) of Christianity. Central to its development are wonder, reverence and, perhaps above all, intimacy, whereas *agapē* is rooted in action motivated by the caring will. The agapeistic love required in order to love one`s neighbour (taking `neighbour` in the sense of anyone with whom we have dealings) is required irrespective of one`s feelings about them. It is impartial kindness which can be dispensed to the most unattractive people. It has a rational basis, rather than an emotive one. Hence it can be commanded, as indeed, it is written that Christ commanded it. We cannot instruct people to be reverent: reverence comes from within. All we can do is to encourage them to show respect.

As human beings we thrive on intimacy. It is to delight in the object of affection, not seeking to mould it to its own vision of what it should be, but at the same time seeking to promote mutual good. It is the sharing and enhancement of quality and can be likened to *union* with the object of love. Such union with the world is a manifestation of true human growth.

Learning to Dance

Reverence and intimacy of mind between humans is most powerfully symbolized through metaphors of dance and courtship.[2] The metaphorical

---

1 1 John ch.2 vv15-17
2 I am indebted to Padraig Hogan`s `The Custody and Courtship of Experience` (1995) `Courtship` might have unwelcome undertones to the unversed. `Dance` might do the job of `courtship`, but it lacks the force of the latter metaphor.

use applies to the wider sphere of what used once to be called 'intercourse'. This is the encounter between people who share experiences and ideas without attempting to dominate each other. As dance, intimacy is mutual. When dancing with another, both parties consent and each must respect and complement the movement of the other. The dance symbolizes a desire for closeness-with-freedom. It conforms to the social expectations and patterns traditionally laid down. The dance may enable each partner to explore the other's response and perhaps allow the possibility of relating more closely. Unspoken messages may be passed during the dance. When it ends, one or both may go their own way. The cultivation of love proceeds through an initial encounter with the beloved through which one learns their being, is attracted, and maintains respect. One does not abduct, exploit or diminish them in any way. The encounter may end then and there or proceed, perhaps, to new depths.

Developing love for a being, whether human, fauna or flora, cannot be promoted through dominance and exploitation. If a forest is seen merely as $1,000,000 of wood pulp, its being cannot be explored and it cannot be listened to. If a woman is seen by a man as a potential sexual conquest, her being cannot be understood and revered. (Men can also be victims here, but it all too rarely displeases them.) Intimacy may, however, be conceived as we observe the rules of the dance.

As courtship, intimacy is gradual and gentle. Courtship is a means by which two beings may explore each other's potential as a mate, the pain and damage of rejection being less than it would were instant union attempted. Courtship allows time for each to learn from the other and for each to change in order to relate with mutual respect, whilst allowing differences to remain. Courtship enables confidence and trust to develop, as well as hope for future intimacy. It takes time and devotion, and is not likely to be achieved on a Saturday night encounter at the Paradise Nightclub.

Children learn to love the world through a teacher who loves the world. The best teachers do not thrust a syllabus at them, enforcing learning in order to get good test results. Neither do teachers simply provide good learning resources and leave students to get on with it. Their role is to stimulate youthful sensibilities, not towards themselves as teachers, but towards the focus of study. They inspire the child with their own love of the subject, and stimulate a similar love in the child. They may become loved by the pupil, not simply for their personality, but for what they have given.[1]

Teachers need not work to be respected and loved, and should not do so. Doing so may win them the adulation of the immature, but in maturing life, the child will look back and spot the game for what it was. Good teachers work because they love what they teach and that children learn it. Such learning cannot always be appraised by the necessary measures required for administrative purposes. It can always be perceived, if not measured, by the transformation of the mind of the child.

What might be the criteria for spotting a transformed mind? Transformation of mind preserves and develops the natural wonder we bring to the world as children. It raises a person from indifference and boredom towards lively interest and involvement in exploring and enjoying the world. That is the first and overriding quality sought by the parent or teacher. Once this foundational attitude is laid, the interest needed in order to retain images and concepts, thus creating a web of valued meanings, can develop.

Love of the world is a gift of childhood. It may be regained as a result of experience and reflection later in life, but is essentially innate and delicate. It is something instinctive and primal in the young, not an accomplishment of the educated élite. Many people who have had no formal education have developed a profound love of the world. This may be limited in the range of its foci, but is nevertheless deeply authentic. By contrast, many who have passed through an education system have had their instinctive sense of wonderment and curiosity deadened, and lost the will to love. Home life can do this just as effectively.

---

1   Of the mountaineer, George Mallory, Robert Graves wrote: "He was wasted (as a teacher) at Charterhouse. He tried to treat his class in a friendly way, which puzzled and offended them."(Goodbye To All That`, 1929)

Recovering Primal Love as Reverence, Presence and Play

Now we look at three important figures whose perceptions may help clarify the way we may understand and deepen our love of the world, Martin Buber, Moritz Schlick and John Berger. Buber's contrast between the exploitative and the reverential, Schlick's understanding of play as a mark of deliverance, and Berger's insights into 'presence', are each vitally illuminating for us. They indicate aspects of a state of spiritual health, the absence of any of which reveals the self in trouble. To lose, or fail to develop in any of these, reverence, presence and play (Yes, play!) is to regress from essential features of maturity.

Rediscovering Reverence

Buber was a massively influential Jewish philosopher who wrote 'I and Thou'[1]. The central theme of this most difficult little book is the distinction between two sorts of relationship – 'I-Thou' and 'I-It'. Buber's distinction has become seminal in our understanding of how we may relate to the world. In an 'I-It' relationship, we view the focus of our attentions as a resource, of use for some purpose. We may see a tree as potential timber or as  an aid to drainage or shade. We may see a friend simply as one who will help and protect us. We may keep sheep simply for the purpose of wool and meat. Clearly, 'I-It' relationships have to occur if the human race is to survive. It is part of the requirement that we control the world as much as is in our best interest. However, this urge to manage and use resources for our survival can, and often does, take over, thus preventing us from understanding the being of that over which we have control.

By contrast, in an 'I-Thou' relationship, the possession of power over the

---

1   1923, translated into English in 1937. This is a difficult work, made more obscure by the author's self-confessed acknowledgement that clarity of expression weakens the mystique appropriate to a great work. My understanding has been largely gained through introductory works such as John MacQuarrie's 'Existentialism' (Penguin 1973)

other party is not a concern. The concern is to hear, see and learn from the other. It is stimulated by fascination and wonder. It perceives the other as a being independent of one's own, and profound and precious. It is drawn to that other through its own primal instinct to love. Thus any object, person or creature can become a 'Thou' to oneself. This is not an option for us humans. It is a root of meaning in life. In an 'I-Thou' relationship, key aspects include 'encounter', 'meeting', 'listening', 'mutuality', and 'exchange'.

For example, the forest becomes to me a place evoking my awareness of its beauty, its relative timelessness by comparison with myself, and its fragility. Yet these are not the only things the forest has to say. If I listen I will learn more. I may learn more, not just from being there, but also from the art of others, who deepen my sensibilities as I stand in the wood. I pass through the primitive agelessness of the ferns in a wood, I love to arrive at an old tree, living symbol of the brevity of my life and survivor through all the troubles of humanity around it. If the wood has so much to say, how much more can it be so of our 'I-Thou' relationships with creatures and with people?

In an 'I-Thou' relationship we become intimate with our beloved yet it is not our possession (even if we have the freehold on it). Indeed we yearn to share our relationship with others and the insights it affords. That is the birth of conversation and art, origins of culture itself. The love on which an 'I-Thou' is founded is strictly non-possessive. The lover wants the beloved to be loved by all. An 'I-Thou' relationship costs nothing and excludes nobody.

There is also in the work of Buber something more than 'respect'. To respect is to avoid abusing, misusing, oppressing, destroying, the focus of attention. It is to avoid racism and other prejudicial biases, and to give fair opportunity to others. We *revere* the 'Thou'. To revere the beloved, the world of persons, creatures and nature is quite another matter than merely respecting them. To respect is to behave in certain ways towards others. To revere is to have a certain attitude towards others. We revere when we are gripped by a sense of the profound in the focus of our experience – the object itself. To revere is to sense the marvellous, an element of transcendence of our understanding. We feel so much for which we have no words.

Buber perceived the loss of 'I-Thou' dialogic relationships in the modern world. The emphasis is increasingly on physical resources, on controlling and making things for practical use and on competition. This focus detracts from our capacity to listen to others and the natural world. To listen is to enjoy the subject of attention for its own sake, to gradually perceive its deep quality and to honour its being. Buber saw the attainment of 'I-Thou' relationships as rare, even between humans.

One message to us is that others are as important as ourselves, that they have the same quality of being as us and must be listened to, remembering that voices and words are not necessary for people and creatures to address us. This is a sensibility that is at the heart of being human. The less we possess this, the less human we are. Buber would also say, as a Hasidic Jew, that, whilst we cannot find and speak intelligibly about God, God finds us as we live in the 'I-Thou'.

Rediscovering Presence

What does John Berger have to say that gives yet more substance to all this? Berger has won top awards for his books on history and art and gained the Booker Prize for his novel, 'G'. He describes 'The Shape of a Pocket' as his most important work. In it he examines various works of art, including photographs. He hardly does more than meditate on the artist and his work. But in this way he is telling us what art is, and doing so, not in a list of propositions and arguments, but in engagement with the particular. One cannot easily generalize about art. Art is particular. One does well not to slavishly bring theory to a work of art. It says itself to the beholder in the here and now.

Berger takes us to the particular, to the chosen subject and to its context in the narrative of history and a life. He then ventures, near the end of his book, to say something very explicit, something that requires little comment but which must be allowed to speak for itself. It condenses the whole book into a rich capsule of meaning that can only be felt as we allow the book to speak in its particulars. The quotation is not just something to remember but something to live:

`When all the members have been separated and all the parts sold, what is left? Something more to sell. A whole is more than the sum of its parts, so we sell the personality. A personality is a media product and easy to sell. A presence is the same thing as a personality, no?

Presence is not for sale.

If that`s true, it`s the only thing on the earth that isn`t.
A presence has to be given, not bought.

Three hundred girls from Thailand.

I`ll take them. Ask Melbourne if he`s interested.`[1]

The most profound things cannot be put into propositional form without loss. Art, the art of poetry, music, painting, drama, must be called upon in order that there might be some chance of vision. For it is out of the depths of emotions raised through our encounter with the particular that images and concepts are born. And with these we can start to think.

That persons are not objects to be owned or rented for our pleasure, to be destroyed at the whim of the mighty, is one of the unlearned lessons of the ages. The lesson was taught even in the old religions and also unlearned in them! Millennia have passed and the lesson is not truly learned. Nowadays we believe the violator must not suffer the fate of his victim because it would be a primitive cruelty to kill him, or even to humiliate him. But in the old stories, the violator sacrificed his life because he violated the life of another, and such punishment showed collective abhorrence of the crime and reverence for the victim. Paradoxically, it can be the very loss of reverence for life that steers us in the direction of not executing people who wilfully kill others.[2]

---

1   The Shape of a Pocket. p.248
2   My thought, not Berger`s.

These are thoughts arising from the imagery of Berger's poetic lines. Powerful imagery, born out of the particular, generates and fuels concepts – concepts having connotations, implications, logics of their own, all of which enable us to reflect, discuss and act with understanding. It is, however, a strange and vital truth that even clear, logical language, the language of debate, of science, of the law, of daily talk, can become ossified and soulless. It is the language of functioning, of getting things said and done according, no doubt, to schedule.

By contrast, it is that language of imagery, of symbolism, of the arts, that returns the hearer to those seminal experiences of life which enable a revaluation, a new perspective, a tearing down of the old inadequacies and oppressive conventions, and which revive life again. These enable a seeing beyond the surface, a sense of authentic encounter with the being of the world. My understanding of Berger leads me to consider that art is not – now to generalize – an escape from the real or an improvement on the real. It is a 'coming home' to the real.[1] The quality of a work of art is something to do with its ability to arouse the beholder. This brings him or her to a reality that arrests their attention and enables them to 'notice' in a new way. It enriches and sharpens the senses. The artist perceives the real in the subject and conveys it powerfully to the viewer – if the viewer has eyes to see. This is so for poetry, drama, music, novel, etc. These things are no *divertissements* from life's realities. They *disclose* the realities with power and directness that literal words cannot. (You cannot say what feminine beauty is, for example.)

Take such subjects as the medieval ladies painted by the Flemish artist Rogier van der Weyden in the 15th century[2]. Such paintings portray both the beauty and the dignity of woman. They portray human presence with great power. The first is a young woman, painted in 1435, as she almost faces the painter and looks directly towards him, and is therefore, probably the artist's wife. The second, painted about 1460, is, by contrast,

---

1   I am indebted to Richard Palmer's work for this term. See bibliog.
2   Both can be found on the Internet. The earlier painting is in the Berlin Staatliche Museum, the latter in the Andrew Mellon Collection, National Gallery of Art, Washington.

clearly a beauty of higher rank but also young. She exemplifies the enhancement of feminity, grace, deportment, and fashion. Her gaze is downwards. Here is propriety, yet without submission. Her status requires the maintaining of distance. The former picture also portrays the care in personal presentation that is essential to convey a sense of self-worth and place within the community whose standards she respects. Such art conveys to me a  sense of the stability of customs which are integral to, and symbols of, traditionality. They make for social stability and sense of both purpose and role.

Without such we hardly know who we are, being but largely anonymous figures in a crowd of individuals, grasping feebly at belonging to some form of communality by means of hairstyle, clothing or bodily markings, yet hardly knowing the meaning of what we are about, and so simply wanting to impress. Does one have the impression that, over the centuries, something may have been lost? We realize that we come to a work of art from where we stand in time and place. For these pictures also tell us that modern dress has a completely different expressive power. It says something else about our estimate of life, about conformity, about community. Is individuality without communality all that remains?

> "The cultural revolution of the latest twentieth century can
> (thus) best be understood as the triumph of the individual
> over society, or rather, the breaking of the threads which
> in the past had woven human beings into social textures"[1]

Are we infected to the core of our being with the assumption that we are but evolutionary accidents, that dignity is a sham, that mankind is but a predator? Is that why it is the fashion in the Western world for younger generations to go about in torn jeans with saggy bottoms and chunky trainers, and carry meaningless, even shocking, logos on their `T-shirts`? (And do older generations do the same under the spell of an assumption that maturity is reached and gradually lost once you`re no longer young,

---

1   `Age of Extremes` (2002edn.) p.334

as Hobsbawn suggests[1]?) Might all this explain why an estimated one in five British citizens have tattooed or pierced their bodies, a last attempt to dissociate themselves from the conventional?[2] Can people who do these things possibly revere themselves, let alone the world? Perhaps they can, and show their deep alienation from so-called 'civilized values' through a return to the primitive.

Rediscovering Play

Moritz Schlick saw play as the meaning of life by contrast with the 20th century emphasis on work. His use of the term is sophisticated: he does not mean we should be flippant or lazy. A deeper meaning is sought. In his 'Philosophical Papers'[3], he addressed the problem of the burdensome nature of life for the average worker. He spoke of the 'curse of purposes', which is that workers tend to strive for goals which are not integral to the work itself. Furthermore, these purposes are justified because they serve to maintain life by putting bread on the table, etc. This leaves us with a stark sense of pointlessness – 'the content of existence consists in the work that is needed in order to exist'. By contrast:

> 'The core and ultimate value of life can lie only in such states as exist for their own sake and carry their satisfaction in themselves.'[4]

Writing in the early 20th century, Schlick was prophetically aware that mere economic success leading to affluence would be no solution to this problem. Now that workers have complex rights and safe working conditions, as well as limited working hours, the problem is exacerbated

---

1   Ibid pp.325-
2   "What can be sufficient inducement to suffer so much pain is difficult to say: not one Indian (I have asked hundreds) would ever give me the least reason for it." (Joseph Banks 1769) The British of today give a hardly more enlightened response: they just like it.
3   1927,1979 His essay 'On the Meaning of Life' is reprinted in Hanfling O. (ed) 1987,
4   Ibid. p.62

rather than reduced. Unless people's work becomes integral to the values they choose, it diminishes their fulfilment. Work becomes a state of oppression irrespective of the safe and secure conditions they might have.

Whilst there will always be forms of work that carry little or no intrinsic reward or pleasure, it seems that either a person needs to do work that is also pleasurable and rewarding in some way, or that, in the absence of such, they need to be given time for, and assistance with, leisure pursuits that they can choose and enjoy for what they are. Therefore, the activities that are dear to us in life are akin to play, for play

`is the name for free, purposeless action, that is, action which carries its purpose within itself`[1].

Schlick cites Schiller's famous passage:

`Man plays only when he is in the full sense of the word a man, and *he is only wholly a Man when he is playing.*`[2]

Schiller continues by showing how both aesthetics and science are expressions of play. This could become confusing: if a man works as a cleaner and enjoys it, taking a pride in the results, can it be called "purposeless"? Of course, that is not so. By using this word, Schlick is showing that the cleaning is enjoyed for its own sake: the employee loves his work and the quality in its product, which also enhances his quality of life.

It is of more than passing interest to note an alleged remark of Wittgenstein, a friend of Schlick: "I don't know why we are here, but I'm pretty sure that it is not in order to enjoy ourselves."[3] Both men's perceptions are important facets of life's meaning for us. I think we can live with both of them. Play is, for Schlick, activity pursued, being attractive in itself to the participants: playing is a facet of the *telos* of humankind. It accords, of course, with MacIntyre's `practices` and our `LEAs`. He is concerned

---

1   Ibid. p.63
2   Schiller's `Letters On the Aesthetic Education of Man`, tr.R.Snell 1954 p.54, all cited in Hanfling, loc.cit.
3   cited in Hershey, P. `The Beginning of the End` (2004) p. 109

with the demeaning nature of activities imposed upon people that are unattractive to them but which have to be undertaken in order to survive. For both Wittgenstein and Schlick, our lives need meanings that we can truly own. We may not always enjoy our play, for doing the things we love to do can be painful at the time of doing them. For both Schlick and Wittgenstein, our lives must be meaningful to us, not just to others, such as our bosses. Both oppose lives of empty pleasure and slavery.

This need for play is pertinent for learning how to love the world. We cannot do so when our lives are dominated by the pressure to meet goals that we do not hold dear in themselves, or that are clearly not really worth the effort. Prestige, fame, wealth, supremacy over others, admiration, etc., are all perilous because they deepen the condition of focusing one's life upon oneself – a foolish and hopeless task. The focus has to be upon that which transcends the pressures exerted upon ourselves when we fail to rise above empty rivalry, and passionate promotion seeking. In play, our energies are wholly devoted to the 'game' itself. Work of all sorts and degrees of skill needs to become our play if possible. It is here that virtue is born and enhanced. Self-control and discipline, forethought, precision in craft, honesty, self-criticism, balanced judgment, listening to advice, all are examples. They are marks of growth.

On the subject of 'dirty' work, what about refuse collectors, sewage workers, bank clerks, social workers, call-centre workers, prison officers, etc.? And what about those jobs that require little skill at all, like inspecting confectionary as it passes along the conveyor? Much of their time and effort is stressful, and some is sheer drudgery. However, it is also possible to make the most ghastly work become one's play, although most cannot be expected to achieve this. Picture a Hindu man of low caste, emerging from a Mumbai sewer through a manhole into the midst of seemingly crazy traffic. I saw one man on TV, covered in filth, naked to the waist, wreathed in smiles as he pointed to the sewer and shared a joke with his friend. Perhaps he knew that his work was a gift, that he was privileged to be one of few who had the strength to do it? Some people are gifted with the ability to find humour in the most unlikely places, thus lightening the load of life, even finding their true calling in darkness and danger. Given a mindful perspective, the sewage worker overcomes the smell and the rats: he is needed; he is one of few who can do this; he finds meaning in the task. Ultimately, darkness and light come from within. Such people deserve the highest honour. Knighthoods in the UK should go far less to civil servants, footballers or light entertainers, but to sewage workers, social workers, teachers and carers!

This might not, however, make those unskilled and repetitious jobs pleasurable. So long as these persist, pleasure at work has to be created for the worker as a stimulus, such as music whilst working and social pleasures. White, ever the realist, speaks of the need to acknowledge such "heteronomous" work as deserving of a reduction in hours, allowing greater leisure or more enjoyable paid part-time work.[1] If most jobs were limited to a 20-25 hour working week, with the lower paid suffering no wage cuts, and higher paid ones accepting reasonable cuts in salary, opportunity for more spiritually-enhancing activities could be made available. The rationale for such a policy would include the need to reverse the assumption that a person's life consists in the abundance of goods they possess, and to include the consideration that, with physical needs met, we need to be able to participate in a variety of practices that offer both pleasure and competence.[2] Such a radical development would surely reduce crime and serious illness.

To play is to love the activity beyond one's own participation. A fan can thrive on football long after he (or she!) has ceased playing. Pursuing means of expression, invention, investigation, the exploration of life – these are all life-sustaining independently of one's own wealth and circumstances. Play is also a focus through which mutual enjoyment can grow. The mind has something to share with others; thus it can survive the deprivations of poverty, injury and age. A person who has such loves becomes interesting and more desirable to know! Contrast this with those who live entirely for purposes relating to external goods – they tend to become tiresome and boorish.

1   White J. pp117-8, where he contrasts this with "autonomous work".
2   See `21 Hours` NEF (2010)

To birds and mammals, as I observe things, life has its greatest point in the here and now. It is to be enjoyed, and the striving is all to achieve that end, not to struggle just to survive, but to enjoy as many moments as possible. None of the higher species lives just to meet the need to dominate, to eat, to reproduce. I think I first learned this when watching a film of wild baboons taking turns at sledging down a hill using an old steel sheet. We can learn from a dog, who may sense things we may have long forgotten.

Holly was my golden retriever, coming into my life at a time of loss that threatened my health. I am unhesitant about lining her up here in the same work as Socrates! She was to be my distraction from the grievous problem, and that she was! I learned from her the unreserved joy of her passion for life. There was – believe me – the climbing of trees, and that not just to chase squirrels, but to entertain. And how she loved the sea! The more daunting the waves, the more she would charge into them, being thrown up, over and back, as I watched in terror. Her energy was boundless, and she loved an audience.

In Cornwall on a very wet and windy day, as I looked out of the window I saw the rooks flying around and above their rookery. They engaged in the most perilous aerobatics, swooping round and up and down at high speed, defying the gale. As I asked myself what they were up to, it occurred to me that they were just enjoying themselves. The task of life's struggle suspended, they were living out their truest being. I contrast this with the troubled soul, despairing of discovering 'what it is all about', imprisoned in cynicism, overworked and overanxious. To truly live is to enjoy each moment, exercising our best powers. This is the ultimate aim of all our lives. It is an attainable paradise.

There's nothing new under the Sun, especially in education (II)

It is worth reflecting on the damage done to children's development if play takes a back seat in their growth from infancy through childhood. **Robert Owen** (1771-1858) established a school for the young in New Lanark, the mill complex purchased by his philanthropist backers,

> including Jeremy Bentham. Rather than impose reading, writing and arithmetic upon four year olds, such things were not introduced until the age of seven, as play, dance, music and shared games were seen to be more important. They served to inculcate good habits and qualities of cooperation and friendship. The manners of the children brought up under his system were `beautifully graceful, genial and unconstrained; health, plenty, and contentment prevailed.`

To speak of play as the meaning of life is not to avoid hard terms like responsibility or work. Mother Theresa`s `play` was to love the poor and dying. She sought nothing beyond it. She never tired of it because she found her `*eudaimonia*`, her blessedness, in it. To enable a beggar to sleep in peace or a dying man to feel valued, that *was* the point. For us lesser mortals, there is also pain in play – we try to achieve a result and it has to be improved, which requires discipline, brings failure, demands persistence, and so on. But the pain is never the whole thing because we love the object of desire whatever the quality of our own efforts to attain and enjoy it ourselves.

It is easy to get carried away with romantic ideals about contemplation, treating creatures as beings in their own right, honouring individuals as they deserve, and turning the life of pressure and drudgery around. In practical terms, how might people be provided with an environment that positively enables them to find more in life than is offered in the high pressure environment of the workplace and in the circumstance of having no work place at all? In the former they may become simply resources fulfilling tasks they neither set nor understand, and in the latter they may easily succumb to the notion that their lives have no point anymore.

A much shorter working week could help tackle overwork, unemployment, overconsumption, high carbon emissions, compromised well-being, entrenched inequalities, and the lack of time to live sustainably, thus enabling us to care for each other, and simply to enjoy life. It would enable many more people to join the workforce and allow for measures to reduce damaging levels of inequality.

In themselves, of course, such practical moves are not sufficient, and they may well be wasted. The quality of our lives depends not simply upon our leisure opportunity, but on our attitudes and understanding of our own needs. Unless our education enables us to find LEAs for ourselves, we are not likely to grow inwardly by working less.

> We need to refocus upon so much that often passes unnoticed and undervalued in our lives...
>
> and to be unshaken by unattained ambitions, though we would have liked to attain them...
>
> ...to be delivered from the domination of strivings to look prettier, to perform more effectively, to impress others, to belittle others, to be the subject of pleasant conversation, to be wealthier, to climb higher up the social ladder, to be a great lover, to lose weight...
>
> ...and it is to be able to leave preoccupation with all these things aside, and to see and love a person, a creature, a place, a situation, reading, viewing films, for itself.

There is joy for anyone who can do this: we are on the road to maturity. We may still wish to look prettier, have more influence, be liked, etc., but these things no longer cloud out the fundamental delight in living that is the source of our greatest strength, and so they never really bother us.

Personal maturity is energized by that primal love that began in infancy and matures as we grow, progressing despite all the setbacks and shocks it suffers along the way. The eyes that look upon material goods, a potential relationship, a work of art, a distant exploration, as things to possess that might be added to the enhancement of one`s standing and worth, have been dimmed. Seduction has occurred. Reflective thought has failed to guard the self, and those dark forces that define much of society have invaded our being. It is this return to the obvious that is so difficult and yet so necessary.

"The aspects of things that are most important for us are

hidden because of their simplicity and familiarity. (One is unable to notice something because it is always before one's eyes.) The real foundations of his enquiry do not strike a man at all... we fail to be struck by what, once seen, is most striking and most powerful."[1]

We can be quite sure that our financiers and politicians are well endowed with talent and intelligence. They were once well educated, for the most part, yet subtle forces have too often darkened their vision. Greed for money and power dulls the mind, distorts perspective, and holds them, and their voting public, in delusion. Have we really outgrown that little story of Jesus, about the man who grew rich and stored his wealth in ever-bigger barns, sat back in his armchair, no doubt the one in the oriel window overlooking his estate, and gloated over his great gains? That evening, probably in that very armchair, he died of a heart attack. Of course it seems to many a very silly story.[2]

Imagine telling the mother whose baby is dying in her arms through malnutrition because her breasts are dry that one key aspect of the meaning of life is `play`! The playing society that furtively imprisons without trial, that condemns boatloads of refugees to the open sea, that consumes fuel for pleasure, that ignores the hunger and pain of the innocent, is obscene, and an obstacle to the growth of its citizens. It has failed the challenge to love.

Personal Fulfilment, Some Paradoxes

Can any sense be made of the following memorable words from St. Paul in this day and age? On the face of it, the paradoxical descriptions of human blessedness are fanciful nonsense. We need to look more carefully if we are to find their deeper meanings. If we cannot perceive these we remain victims of the masquerade permeating so-called `developed` societies.

"As sorrowful,yet always rejoicing; as poor, yet making many rich;

---

1   Wittgenstein `Philosophical Investigations` 1.129
2   St. Luke ch.12 vv13-21

and having nothing, and yet possessing all things."[1]

For Abraham Maslow, the celebrated father of humanistic psychology, the supreme and crowning fulfilment for individual development is `self-actualization`. For him, there is a pyramid-like hierarchy of needs that must be met before a person can attain to this peak.[2] Self-actualization, self-fulfilment and well-being are all attempted expressions of the *telos* of personal development. However, there are differences between them. In particular, the difference between Maslow's `self-actualization` and the concept of `maturity` is important. `Maturity` and `blessedness` are better expressions of the *eudaimonia* that has its roots in the Bible, Aristotle and other classical philosophers such as Seneca. `Self-actualization` is not appropriate to this, because it is dependent upon our having met lower order needs such as sexual love and good health. For Maslow, we can only grow into a fulfilled life once these are met.[3]

Maslow's Hierarchy of Human Needs

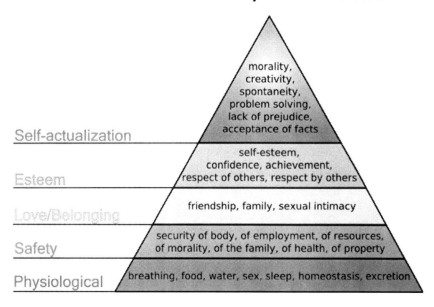

---

1   2 Corinthians ch.6.v.10
2   Maslow, A.H. `Motivation and Personality` Harper & Row 1970 (2nd. ed.)
3   Aristotle, who to a slight extent would agree with Maslow, saw the possession of some external goods as important to the realization of *eudaimonia*. He also acknowledged that being friendless, weak, ugly or childless would reduce opportunities for virtuous activity by comparison with the more fortunate. Nicomachean Ethics 1153b17-19

Nevertheless, even if the peak experiences at the tip of Maslow`s pyramid bear some similarities with the idea of maturity in this work, there are differences. Such differences might even undermine the validity of conceiving human maturity through the pyramid analogy at all. The luck of life may have some influence on the spiritual growth of many, but it is a strange and wondrous fact that disadvantage often spurs growth in ways that an easier life does not. By contrast, Aristotle, Maslow, and more recently White and the Skidelskys, place emphasis on the dependence of well-being upon material wealth and good fortune in life. **Once we come to understand growth in terms of virtue and love this emphasis is flawed. These writers, like Maslow, have little interest in the human capacity for self-transcendence in adversity or prosperity. Such self-transcendence is a vital aspect of growth towards maturity. It is the spiritual life within us. As active agents that choose our own attitudes and activity, our growth can be enhanced by hardship if we have the inner resources.** To say this is not to wish hardship on people, but to draw attention to a deeper, more durable and inspiring awareness of human potential. Indeed, it is partly through a transforming education that the inner strength of character needed to overcome and persevere in the face of pain and failure become practical. Upbringing and education, from the earliest to latest years of our lives, must have its tough activities if real progress is to be made in mind and spirit.

However, maturity can be attained in the absence of the meeting of many lower needs, and it is even possible to claim that, in many cases, it would not so wonderfully have been attained in the absence of deprivation. Our spiritual needs arise at Maslow`s third level and upwards. It is hard to imagine anyone mature in their development if they lack self-esteem, self-confidence, or a sense of achievement in any sense. What is this sense? What must have been achieved?

Seneca (A.D.1 – A.D. 65) makes the point clear for us:

"Fortune can only snatch away what she has given; but she does not give virtue, and therefore she cannot take it away. Virtue is free, inviolable, unmoved, unshaken, so steeled against the blows of chance that she cannot be bent, much less broken. Facing the instruments of torture she holds her gaze unflinching, her expression changes not at all, whether a hard or happy lot is shown to her. Therefore the wise man will lose nothing that he will regard as loss; for the only possession he has is virtue, and of this he can never be robbed. Of everything else he has only the use on sufferance."[1]

How is it that a person can lack sight, sound and language, forego sexual needs even though having a healthy body and strong mind, and yet reach a state of maturity? We are always being taught that sexual experience is one of life's most vital ingredients. Is fulfilment possible without it? How is it that a person can experience sexual failure or social ostracism and yet transform society? Surely success is not possible unless one has found acceptance by those in authority? Many men and women have foregone, or been unable to fulfil, such basic needs in order to attain higher goals.

Perhaps a supreme example is that of Helen Keller (1880-1968), surely one of the highest overachievers of all time! Born blind, deaf and dumb, the miracle of her growth inspired millions. It always pays to listen to her: "If I regarded my life from the point of view of the pessimist, I should be undone. I should seek in vain for the light that does not visit my eyes and the music that does not ring in my ears. I should beg night and day and never be satisfied. I should sit apart in awful solitude, a prey to fear and despair. But since I consider it a duty to myself and to others to be happy, I escape a misery worse than any physical deprivation."[2]

"Most people measure their happiness in terms of physical pleasure and material possession. Could they win some visible goal which they have set on the horizon, how happy they could be! Lacking this gift or that circumstance, they would be miserable. If happiness is to be so measured, I

1   Cited in Grayling A.C.(2004) p.57 From Seneca's `De Constantia Sapientis`
2   `The World I Live In & Optimism` (1903), 2009 p.102

who cannot hear or see have every reason to sit in a corner with folded hands and weep. If I am happy in spite of my deprivations, if my happiness is so deep that it is a faith, so thoughtful that it becomes a philosophy of life, — if, in short, I am an optimist, my testimony to the creed of optimism is worth hearing."[1]

Such people defy Maslow's pyramid. They reach the top by virtue of their qualities of courage, single-mindedness, love of life and love of others. Their own failure to achieve wealth, physical pleasures, a conventional education, job and a secure home life is transcended by the power of their inner resources.

A further exceptional, example of a person deprived of fundamental needs was George Loveless, leader of the Tolpuddle Trade Union of 1833. Despite being subject to injustices perpetrated by the local and national Establishment, he never lost his dignity, humility, and courage to stand up for the starving labourers and their families. Transported to Australia for the crime of swearing secret oaths, he and his colleagues endured four years of slavery and separation from their homeland and loved ones. George's steadfastness through all disaster was to make him and his friends the catalyst for sweeping changes in workers' rights.

"I would call upon every working man in England, and especially the agricultural labourers, who appear to be the lowest, degraded, and the least active, to shake off that supineness and indifference to their interests, which leaves them in the situation of slaves. Let every working man come forward, from east to west, from north to south; unite firmly but peaceably together as the heart of one man; let them be determined to have a voice in, and form part of, the British nation; then no longer would the interests of

---

1   Ibid.p.87

> the millions be sacrificed for the gain of a few, but the blessings resulting from such a change would be felt by us, our prosperity, even to generations yet unborn."[1]

To give one's life in a deliberate act of self-sacrifice for the survival of others serves as a supreme example of maturity. Such an act cannot simply be motivated by belief in life beyond the grave. There resides within those who achieve this the strong hope that love begets love, and the assurance that to act in love is to complete one's humanity.

 The paradox of the greatest sacrifice appears powerfully in a tragic but celebrated incident. In the USA four heroes are remembered every year in February throughout the land, on Four Chaplains' Day[2]. It celebrates a story of self-sacrifice and bravery by four army chaplains from different branches of the faiths and exemplifies a shared commitment to humanity.
After midnight Feb. 2nd/3rd 1943, their ship, the USS 'Dorchester', was torpedoed by a German submarine in freezing waters. On board were 904 soldiers and sailors, including many wounded. As the vessel quickly sank, taking only 24 minutes to do so, the four chaplains calmed the men, helped the wounded into the lifeboats, few of which got away, and helped them on with their lifejackets. However, some men had no lifejackets, so each chaplain gave his own away. The last anyone saw of them, they were standing on the deck, arms linked and praying together. There is more to life than staying alive.

But they will not likely have this in mind when the challenge to action

---

1   G.Loveless 'The Victims of Whiggery' 1837 cited in Norman, A. (2008)
2   They are: A Methodist, Reverend George L. Fox; a Jewish Rabbi, Alexander D. Goode; a Roman Catholic Priest, John P. Washington; and, of the Reformed Church in America, Rev. Clark V. Poling. Four Chaplains' Day is celebrated on the Sunday nearest Feb.3rd each year.

comes – they will be solely occupied with the thought of saving others. The supreme goal of the human spirit has been attained and put to work. We cannot call such lives 'wasted'. They were tragically lost, but their last actions won them something, an immortality they certainly did not seek. It is a sort of immortality perceived and bestowed by human beings in the here and now. It teaches us the power of love to conquer death. This is what 'conquering death' means. Such a death is the climax of a life and leaves seeds of love.

It is of more than passing interest to reflect on those who, in deep despair of oppression and injustice in society, made martyrs of themselves. Jan Palach burnt himself to death in Prague and became, as he hoped, a symbol of the desperation of the Czech people for freedom from the Soviet oppressor. His was the ultimate form of statement that his people were not to be enslaved. The imitators who followed his example are largely forgotten by comparison. The religious call such martyrs 'blessed': in common thought they are disastrously impetuous. The attainment of one's personal *telos*, can come, if rarely, in death.

Of course, martyrdom is the destiny of an exceptionally rare few. Growth to maturity, even with martyrdom, is surely the best climax of our short lives. But those who have never hit headlines and never had to sacrifice themselves have attained this without ever being honoured for their success. It matters less if we die forgotten than if we die remembered for not having loved the world.

 Florence Newby can exemplify millions of people: she is hardly remembered by anyone living apart from myself, being her nephew, and a roomful of others. Florrie had prominent teeth and a raucous laugh. She never married, worked at Vauxhall Motors and the Shaftesbury Society, retired to produce the church magazine, visit the sick, and to loan her house to others in need. My Aunt Florrie was always a model of good cheer and humour,

and loved the simple things of life, hearing good music, planting flowers, and taking unpretentious holidays. She had no degree, little wealth, and few conventional talents. But she gave her time, effort, and devotion to everything and everyone she loved, and changed her world for the better. She had moments of deep joy, as when she listened to classical music! She had nursed her mother during a long and painful terminal disease. Finally, Florence suffered the same thyroid cancer as her mother, and lingered, voiceless and in pain, in hospital. I visited her many times. I treasure her notebook.[1] There are countless anonymous high achievers like her.

---

1 I keep her written messages to me, scrawled on a thick pad, as a memento of her courage and indomitable cheerfulness. One night her personal TV was removed, probably since she was thought to be past viewing it. She wrote to her nurses "I'm not dead yet you know. Give it back!"

CHAPTER 6: THE ROLES OF STORY IN HUMAN DEVELOPMENT

> *"The story form is a cultural universal; everyone everywhere enjoys stories. The story, then, is not just some casual entertainment; it reflects a basic and powerful form in which we make sense of the world and experience. Whatever the case, it is clear that children are readily and powerfully engaged by stories."* - Kieron Egan

> *"I could a tale unfold whose lightest word*
> *Would harrow up thy soul, freeze thy young blood,*
> *Make thy two eyes, like stars, start from their spheres,*
> *Thy knotted and combined locks to part*
> *And each particular hair to stand on end,*
> *Like quills upon the fretful porpentine."*
> - William Shakespeare, *Hamlet* (1600-02), Act I, scene 5

The secular master story, that of our role in the salvation of the planet, gives a perspective on reality, awakens the imagination, and offers vital roles in life for us all. Without such, there can be no life narrative that also reflects world awareness and a perspective on the future of mankind. It is an unfinished story that ultimately unites us by giving us shared goals that must be reached.

Story is central to human development, and always has been, and through it we grow into a sense of the world and our place in it from babyhood to adulthood. Through story we develop a sense of narrative progression. Our lives have beginnings, middles and ends, and the desired climax is fulfilment and final contentment – true `peace at the last`.

Keiron Egan expresses such through a number of works. He has been one of the most productive writers proposing unorthodox approaches to teaching in recent times. His output is considerable and his thinking original. His view is that any teaching using story to convey a lesson, almost anywhere on the curriculum we choose to look, is more likely to enable the child to grasp and retain ideas than teaching that is didactic. Didactic teaching imparts information through direct instruction in which the teacher alone is active and children are expected to listen, record, or to follow instructions. Few of us learn best like that. We *remember* narrative sequence. We are more likely to absorb ideas that are part of a narrative whole, a coherent stream of events and ideas that leads to a climactic end. If we can be brought into the narrative, so much the better.

Egan shows how our minds develop through narrative. He sees human development through story as following four sequential layers, or stages, **the mythic, the romantic, the philosophic and the ironic.** Whether or not exceptions occur, here is an important sequence of story development, both in the growing mind and, perhaps, in the evolving of cultures through history.[1] Egan calls each of the four layers "sense-making capacities", each being quite distinct. However, we move upwards to the next without losing the lasting benefit of previous layers. "In its evolution, consciousness does not slough off its earlier stages, but incorporates them in transmuted form in its later stages."[2]

Story as Myth

In infancy and early childhood, children are not typically concerned with the external workings of things or with the objective world, but with becoming a pleasure to those who love them by being good (or provoking them by being bad, especially when frustrated in their desires!). They seek, essentially, to be good, rather than evil, and to be safe from the dark forces they sense around them. Their many frustrations can, of course, lead not only to difficult behaviour, but, more seriously, to self-hatred and despair. Through such things as fairy stories the binary concepts of good and evil, honesty and deceit, trust and suspicion, etc., are grasped

---

1   Egan saw his sequence of four stages as a form of `recapitulatory` theory. Individual development reflects cultural history. See his `Romantic Understanding` ch.8
2   Egan p.188 , citing Ong W., `Interfaces of the Word` (1977)

and applied. Children learn what trickery and trustworthiness are, what it is to be brave rather than cowardly, and how the dark things of life can be faced and overcome. The task is predominantly to find acceptance in a world of beings and powers that might be a threat. This belongs to the **Mythic** stage of story development.

Bruno Bettelheim, in his seminal work[1], saw the imagery of fairy stories as enabling children to confront life's terrors, bringing unconscious dreads gently into thought, and to see that, for all their power, they can be overcome. Whilst such stories are not, strictly speaking, myths, they can have a mythic role. The cannibalistic witch can be tricked into her own oven to sizzle away in the place of her victims. The fear of mother's darker side can be unconsciously displaced to the witch and thus located in the world of nasty dreams. Such stories have many variants crossing many cultural divides. Bettelheim saw `Beauty and the Beast`, for example, as a variant of the story of Cupid and Psyche, with its Greco-Roman origins, sharing the common theme of the wondrous yet threatening power of love. Thus stories serve to promote emotional growth. The very fact that such story has a beginning, an uncertain middle, and a happy end, provides a template for all life's hopes and struggles.

A central feature of myth is melodrama. The story may have cosmic and lasting significance for human life and the fate of the cosmos. Demonic forces invade the world and only the chosen one can know the way of salvation and lead people to it through mighty acts. Myths may serve to endow natural phenomena with profound significance. A myth may live on through many ages, conveying the master story for Christian, Hindu, Buddhist and Muslim. It will generate ritual, feast and rite of passage, and have great didactic power.

It is important for us throughout our lives to visit the mythic dimension. Some may still commit, in serious hope, to the drama as truly historic and replete with life-protecting and guiding power. Thus it is for those who believe Christ's crucifixion not only happened, but negates the weight of our sins, and for those, like Gandhi, whose last prayer was to the deliverer, Rama. We may, alternatively, sense that such stories are not literally true, but that they alone can convey insights stimulating a sense of life's

---

1   Bettelheim B. (1976)

significance *sub specie aeternitatis*. For example, there arises from some of the greatest master stories of the world the thought that personhood is the key to `what it`s all about`, so that ultimately reality is personal, however vast and chaotic the phenomenal cosmos might appear to be. We so often seem to forget as adults that myths can bear truth for us at any age. That is why such tales are more than entertainment: they convey and enrich a sense of the awesome mystery of life, the forces underlying it, and the critical struggle within us of forces over which we must gain control if we are to avoid bondage and destruction. They rekindle in us a sense of grandeur and the destiny which is, at least potentially, in our own hands.

> The classical myths can furnish far-reaching metaphors for human self-understanding. Take the myth of **Cassandra**, for example. Given the gift of prophecy by Apollo to celebrate her beauty, she failed to return his love. Frustrated, Apollo placed a curse upon her which ensured that no one would listen to her prophecy. Cassandra has become a symbol of those who speak the truth and are never heeded. The story has versatile application as a metaphor of the human condition. It can certainly serve, however, to illustrate how it is that those in power easily fail to respect the voices of their opponents, whose love they have failed to win. The results can change history: dictators in some Arab states may be learning this as I write. The versatility of myths gives the possibility of deepening understanding in any age. Warren Buffett repeatedly warned that the 1990s stock market surge was a bubble, attracting to him the title of 'Wall Street Cassandra'. Laurie Layton Schapira is an analytical psychologist who perceives the `Cassandra Complex` to be highly significant in our understanding of destructive personality clashes between the sexes, the male being Apollo-like, and the female being Cassandra-like.

Myths and sagas employ key concepts that transcend cultural boundaries, such as temptation and falling, the struggle between forces of life and forces of death, dangers that trap the unwary, the path to overcoming the seemingly invincible foe[1], sacrifice and the cost of victory, the road to deliverance peace and salvation, and finding true wisdom. These stories enhanced the sense that people had in past ages of life as a struggle, of paths that must be followed, leading to a goal that is our true destiny. Is it not one role of music to stimulate our sense of this struggle? We notice how epic music expresses mythic themes. Such diverse works as themes from the films `Lord of the Rings` and `The Empire Strikes Back`, Handel's `Messiah`, Haydn's `Creation`, Mozart's Requiems, Beethoven's Ninth Symphony etc. provide examples.

It was certainly during the Renaissance and later Rationalist and Enlightenment periods of West European thought that mythic understandings were eroded. For medieval people, myth was everywhere, in the village with its central focus of the church, and the building itself, with paintings of the paths to heaven and hell leading to the spiritual centre at the altar and sacred host, the very body and blood of the Saviour. Shared reverence, dread, fear and hope and joy abounded. The loss of such denied common folk meaning for their sufferings, and hope for eternity. Perhaps above all this, the bonds of local and wider communal life were loosened, slowly giving way to the aimless individualism of today's secular world.

In the West, the European Reformation arose from a growing awareness of oppression and corruption by the Church itself. The discarded `bathwater` indeed carried away the dirt of superstition and greed, but `babies` were thrown out with it. The living, present, force of images and of saints had been guides and encouragements to a gentle and honest manner of life for ordinary folk, even when surrounded by poverty, pain and death. Suddenly, with the aid of monarchs, a way of life had become outrageous, superstitious and corrupted. By contrast, the relatively slow development of naturalistic explanation and discovery of distant places on Earth took the scholar and explorer into new forms of thinking, and towards the loss of the mythic. Dragons became crocodiles. Scepticism spread abroad and downwards to the common folk.

---

1   Like Perseus' mirror shield, used to kill Medusa without suffering the fate of all who looked into her face – thinking `outside the box` as some would say. It may remind one of the phantom armies and sounds of armies created by the Allies in WWII.

There can be little doubt that the loss of the mythic accelerated the loss of reverence, awe, humility and consciousness of life's brevity. With it went the loss of enchantment, so that a world of real tragedy, emptiness and lack of meaning dawned upon increasingly cynical minds. By contrast, the Oriental world, at least in India, has experienced less momentous secularization of thought, especially amongst the poor. The common folk still live amongst the gods, and know their power.[1] In the secular world, the loss for us is great in terms of the psychic force of the mythic beings and powers around us. These conveyed an all-embracing sense of destiny, an awareness of the all-seeing, with the conviction that all our doings are known. Thus the common folk could sense that ultimately, all, rich and poor, old and young, live under the power of the divine, in whose eyes earthly status and power count for nothing.

We eventually outgrow preoccupation with the struggle of our mythic fears and hopes, dread of dark forces and belief in magical powers, although vestiges may remain with us all our lives. Such concerns move from centre stage, except in times of high anxiety and trial, and give way to the romantic outlook, in which our passions focus upon the world of the 'daytime'. Losing the mythic is tragic. It is all fiction of course, but it is fiction that conveys a profound sense what it is to *be*.

Story as Romance

During childhood the mythic stage is accompanied, usually from about eight years of age, by the **Romantic** stage. Here children develop an interest in the realities of the external world. Factual stories about the past, present and potential future excite them. Historically, the romantic age in Europe is that of the explorers such as Marco Polo, Vasco da Gama, Columbus, Magellan and Cook. The later expeditions of exploration and achievement stimulated the romantic view, later to be further nurtured in the minds of the young by such as Mungo Park, Matthew Webb, the Wright Brothers, Scott, Amundsen and Shackleton. Our romantic outlook

---

1 For example, at the Shri Swaminarayan Temple in Neasden, London, massive queues of devotees offered milk to the statue of Ganesh, who consumed it. (Sept.1995). The gods are also offered food and drink for each night: guides tell of its disappearance by the morning.

is one in which we love to know the real extremes of things, of speeds, of distances, of size, of human achievement, of endurance, of love, cruelty and pain. Life becomes for us a drama in which the achievements of mankind, wonders of nature and the life of animals, become gripping. Through such, engagement with the life of the world in things great and small is nurtured. From this time, scientific explanation is becoming important as we seek to understand the workings of things, the nature of plant and animal behaviour, and why people act as they do. However, it is the incorporation of such issues into narrative that brings them to life and makes key concepts precious. It is through focusing on other human lives that we can come to understand ourselves and endeavour to emulate the deeds of hero figures.[1]

This form of story making is employed by the best writers in popular science and teachers of science in schools. Steve Jones` best-selling works, to which I have already referred to, are about `biological science`, or `the behaviour of plants and animals`, and might be said to contain information for passing exams. But if they are seen as Jones sees them, as intriguing stories, the opening up of secrets and of the almost unbelievable capabilities of plants and animals, we begin to see that learning becomes `surprise`, the discovery of processes which intrigue us, without resolving all the problems of understanding. It would be wrong to limit ourselves here to books. Stories involve us, partly because we love narrative, partly because we can absorb knowledge through them without having to consciously memorize, and partly because they furnish us with images, the powerful seedbeds of ideas.

Surely this romantic stage in our development best teaches us that we can overcome obstacles, conquer our fears and surprise everyone, best of all ourselves. It may not be best to teach heroic story in the formal atmosphere of the classroom, except, perhaps, in serial form for a short time at the end of the day. Great stories of human achievement are best read in the child`s own time, and where parental encouragement can stimulate enthusiasm. They then become truly their own, stored in the

---

1   It is important to avoid gender prejudice during the romantic stage. I still possess a copy of `The Boys Book of Heroes`, no women included, from the early 1940s! One is the more impressed by those eighteenth century `Bluestockings` on to Seacole, Lottie Dodd, Amy Johnson, Fanny Blankers-Koehn, Nancy Wake, and so on, who all broke the mould!

archives of the mind for future use. The more iconoclastic the story the better!

Abu Raihan al-Biruni, born in 973 in present-day Uzbekistan, was a brilliant polymath who calculated latitude and longitude for many locations, believed the Earth to be spherical, and constructed a16ft high globe to show the known and imagined features of the planet. He spoke and read many languages from East and West. He also studied rocks and minerals and created the idea of specific gravity. This was important for arriving at his later conclusions. His most inspiring thoughts relate to what some historians call his `discovery of America`. Whilst he did not travel there, he hypothesised that, as the land masses of the known world only crossed about 11/25th of its circumference, it would be very odd were there to be 14000 or more miles of ocean from Europe to Japan. Furthermore, water being lighter than most rocks, would not the Earth become imbalanced? Why should the forces that gave rise to dry land on 2/5ths of the Earth, not also do so in the `World Ocean`? He was also a Muslim. Here are some of his words:

"...in an absolute sense, science is good in itself, apart from its (content of) *knowledge: its lure is everlasting and unbroken...*(the servant of science) *should praise the assiduous* (ones) *whenever their efforts* (arise from) *delight* (in science itself) *rather than from (the hope of achieving) victory in argument."[1]*

Fantasy and science fiction are sophisticated versions of the romantic brought close to the real world by often having their starting points at general locations and in known places. They then take the reader into an

---

1   Item from an article by S.F.Starr `So,Who Did Discover America?` History Today Dec.2013 pp.40-45

envisaged world, one that opens up possibilities for the future of mankind, such as space travel and ecospheres, to mention two of the less terrifying. Such excites the growing child, and need not nor should ever be left behind. It enables us to imagine possible worlds, parallel universes, as those now considered by physicists. We also love these parallel worlds of writers such as Tolkien and Pullman at later times in our lives. They enable our minds to play, but they also kindle in us powerful emotions of awe, terror and joy. Through them we learn superlatives, those of the natural world and of human achievement, and the open nature of the future.[1] They give our spirits food for imagination, perhaps enabling us to be more prepared for the great things that may come out of our world of small things.

Story as Philosophy of Life

During adolescence and young adulthood, we develop new interests in the story form. We now attain a **philosophic** stage, in which the symbolic power of mythic stories and the realism of romantic stories are accompanied, and in a sense surpassed, by the search for an ultimate story, a story which unites experience and explains life in terms of wide-ranging general truths. At the philosophic stage we want to see the world through a commanding web of concepts. The story of humanity might be understood as the quest for power and control. On the other hand, the acquisition of wealth, of territory, of sexual experience, might each be felt to explain the human world, and we are likely not to settle at this stage for a combination of such, but for one of them as `the key` to understand humanity. Grand perspectives may themselves not be life enhancing, however. The life narrative of child-becoming-adult may be crippled into cynicism, as when all people are seen to be at heart self-seeking and corrupt or sexually motivated. This underlines the significance of open discussion with young people at home and in school. Informal versions of fascism still walk our streets. The philosophic story will have its climax in a vision of the future – `what might come to pass?` `Can

---

1   It is interesting to note that such stories are far less interesting and inspiring if they contain only good qualities. They take on greater fascination when human weakness, wickedness, tragedy and pain are a threatening ingredient: "In heaven all the interesting people are missing" (Nietzsche)

tragedy be as likely as triumph?' `How safe are we?' `What is the human role in the world?' Clearly the whole curriculum of arts and sciences is a key catalyst of philosophic ideas, so long as it is taught as suited to the learners' developmental stage, to address the problems they and the teacher mutually set! For example, the theme `What is Human Life For?' calls upon views from religions as well as recent literary and philosophical writers (like Schlick, discussed above, or William Golding.) The advances to be gained for the learners are far more likely to remain with them than hierarchies of abstract concepts, and will enable them to express their own imaginative response. Imaginative abilities are an essential requirement for asking profound questions, seeing new connections, and thus using knowledge in exciting, and sometimes frightening, ways. The philosophic capacities are employed to develop a vision of hope, for it is through these that we form the widest perspectives of all, our ultimate cognitive structures for understanding life. Truly meaningful philosophy includes the investigation of the significance of learning for our view of life, its past, present and future and our role as creatures. It is, however, only through liberal education that a balanced view of human nature can be developed: we are neither uncritical optimists nor hopeless sceptics.

"What is the use of studying philosophy, if it does not improve your thinking about the important questions of everyday life?"[1]

Wittgenstein also used a picturesque analogy, seeing our thinking as trapped, like flies in fly-bottles, not knowing the way out. Philosophy can enable us to find that way out and become liberated, with better chance of avoiding the next trap set for us. Modern philosophy is widely seen as an academic backwater, dealing with obscure and unnecessary problems relating to the nature of meaning. That should not be so. It is also about the big picture in which we live our lives, coming to understand our prejudices and confusions. Our philosophizing leads to the arrival at a grand perspective, changing everything for us.

---

1   -Wittgenstein, in letter to Norman Malcolm

Now is the Time we Need a Grand Perspective More Than Ever

"This is the first century in the world's history when the biggest threat is from humanity... It's a question of scale. We're in a more inter-connected world, more travel, news and rumours spread at the speed of light. Therefore the consequences of some error or terror are greater than in the past." [1]

"We're at the level of infants in moral responsibility, but with the technological capability of adults,"......... "There is a bottleneck in human history. The human condition is going to change. It could be that we end in a catastrophe or that we are transformed by taking much greater control over our biology." [2]

There is a way out of the chaos arising from the current individualism, for which the narrative of so many lives is but a wandering indulgence. We live within a story that could and should unite the world community in singleness of identity and purpose. What might legitimately distinguish good from evil in the current world, and doom from salvation? What might clothe us with an identity which cannot be gainsaid and which we might be proud to share with all people? What might the story be that shows us how everything we do makes a difference one way or the other?

And what might the story be that depends not on supernatural religious beliefs, but finds its power through language and concepts originating deep within the stories of the past, of the Fall, of Babel, of the Flood, of the Passion of Christ, of the Enlightenment of Buddha, Vanity Fair, Nicholas Nickleby and the multitude of modern novels, as well as in all our modern knowledge? In short, what is the prophetic narrative for our time which shows us the destructive forces spreading through society, state and world, and how they can be combatted?

This story, of the reversible decay of the human spirit, the loss of creatures and fouling of sky, land and sea, is, we are discovering, unfolding in the

1   Lord Rees, Astronomer Royal BBC Business News 24/4/13 'How are humans going to become extinct?'
2   Nick Bostrom (Oxford Univ. Future of Life Institute)

world! It is irresistible to the reflective person and worthy enough to become a key focus of world education. It calls for a revival of values being grounded in and powered by the love of the world, humanity and other creatures. All past master stories were, we now see, powerful and truth bearing, but now they are becoming truth-bearing fictions. These have given us perennial symbols forming image frameworks for our lives. We search for enlightenment, for regeneration, for faith, for single-mindedness, a shared paradise. The story for us as world citizens today is one in which we find ourselves taking part; it is not for us simply a matter of initiation into a particular tradition and institution, enriching though that may be for us. It is the story of our own destruction or salvation in an ever-suffering world. It defines our `now`, our `soon` and our envisaged future. We have no reasonable choice but to be true to its message.

Perhaps it is that the all-embracing perspective fails to do its job. It embraces, but only in a limited manner, with limited language, and devoid of inner awareness. Somewhere along the line of our philosophizing, we have become overconfident. Systems of thought are tools, not the last word. They help but also hinder. They are never the final word. They may not even motivate us to pick up litter or recycle our waste.

Story as Irony, and the Problem of Relativism in Master Stories

And so we arrive at the **ironic** form, one in which the massive general perceptions and rigid viewpoints of earlier philosophic perspectives are rendered more sophisticated, qualified and tentative. Thus caveats become rife, and particular situational experience becomes of greater interest than the achievement of an overall view of life, though the grand view remains as a communal map – something to pore over and refine together. Life is ironic insofar as so much of our knowledge appears to contradict itself, and things are not at all what they may, on conventional thinking, seem. Perhaps in frustration, we return in later life to the love of the particular, the here and now in all its glory.

`Ironic` persons will be interested in particular insights and the complexities that render simple and clear understanding extremely difficult, downplaying, but without forsaking, the general perceptions gained through the urge to find universal truths. One will recognize that clear, universally-applicable insights are usually over simple, that rules tend to have exceptions, and that the understanding previously assumed is so readily shaken by later experiences. Closure – the discovery of answers that are conclusive and final, is seen not to be possible, even though it is forever sought, and may have been necessary in the past if traditional authorities were to be consolidated. Now it is seen that, out of the systems of thought that were once taken to be final, come new questions and new paradigms that transpose past learning into a new key. The ironic stage may be largely a creation of the last century, during which anthropology and the study of cultures led many to the conclusion that a shared philosophy of life is impossible. The focus for understanding the human situation now becomes particularistic. Insightfulness comes from an imaginative indwelling of our own and others lives and cultures, not from a grand overview that interprets and evaluates them.

If that is so, what chance of a universal master story now?

Richard Rorty (1931-2007) was perhaps, after Kierkegaard, the ironist philosopher *par excellence:*

"I shall define an "ironist" as someone who fulfils three conditions:

1. She(sic) has radical and continuing doubts about the final vocabulary she currently uses, because she has been impressed by other vocabularies, vocabularies taken as final by people or books she has encountered;
2. She realizes that argument phrased in her present vocabulary can neither underwrite nor dissolve these doubts;
3. Insofar as she philosophizes about her situation, she does not think that her vocabulary is closer to reality than others, that it is in touch with a power not herself."[1]

---

1   Richard Rorty, Contingency, Irony, and Solidarity., p.73

Educational development in terms of story experience reaches its maturity here, claims Egan. True or not, this need not diminish the importance of earlier phases, any of which, it seems to me, a person can voluntarily revisit, and in all of which deep insights can be found and visions rekindled. The ironies of life are only perceived by one who has had much experience and has endeavoured 'to make sense of it all'. Whilst some general insights remain profound and forever valuable, they will inevitably be qualified and even surpassed, for we never reach the end of the journey to understanding. The real world has a variety of voices, each with truth to share. Nothing, not even a great synthesis of ideas, is the final version.

> Does this imply that, once we reach mental maturity, we know that no agreed master story is possible? This depressing situation might be confirmed as we read the work of philosopher and film-maker **Hilary Lawson**. He deepens the gloom felt amongst many. A short extract paints the scene: "…we are lost. Lost in a world that has no map, not because it has been mislaid or forgotten, but because we can no longer imagine how such a map could be constructed. In our post-modern relativistic age we find ourselves adrift in a sea of stories that cannot be fathomed nor anchor found. For we find ourselves in a world without certainties; without a fixed framework of belief; without truth, without decidable meaning. We have no unique history but a multitude of competing histories. We have no right or moral action, but a series of explanations for behaviour. We have no body of knowledge, but a range of alternative cultural descriptions."[1]

Once we write, as I do, of non-fictional story, of a story that relies upon the truths of science, and whose challenge to us depends on the rational moral principles that apply to all mankind without which human verbal communication would be effectively unachievable, we are bound to face up to a central claim of post-modernism. This is that all knowledge and reasoning is perspectival – relative to the knower's first principles, which, presumably, are theirs through the cultural accident of living in a

---

1   'Closure: a Story of Everything' (2001) Preface p.ix

certain time and place, and being educated in a certain direction. Thus all thinking is socially derived and therefore has no objective validity.

Lawson develops a thorough account of this phenomenon that pervades our philosophizing – philosophizing in the most all-embracing sense, embracing arts, sciences, ethics and religions. The master story depends, he would claim, upon the viewpoint of people who, by the nature of things, live within *a perspective on life,* perspectives being endless, and for which no criteria for choosing rationally between them exist. We all have different stories to tell, from Australian Aborigine to Orthodox Christian, to Maoist and quantum physicist. And many make syntheses of such stories, becoming Marxist Christians,etc. I have yet to meet a Marxist Christian Australian Aborigine, but some could be living quietly in Kiev or the Kakadu. There are said to be no criteria for choosing one particular way of life: foundations cannot be appraised, and understanding is only possible if one lives within the perspective.[1]

Whilst I am perhaps guilty of a rash dismissal of this cultural relativism and its consequences, I, nevertheless, do not for one moment accept that its significance destroys the idea of a global narrative for humanity today. Why not?

First, we are one species in one world, a world that has few isolated pockets of ancient tribal life or forbidden cities. We speak languages all of which have enough overlap of ideas to possess a strong element of translatability: few, if any, concepts are esoteric to the tradition. By immersing himself in such a culture, the anthropologist seeks to learn the true meaning of its practices, and to express them in terms that the outsider can understand. The idea that cultural relativism somehow immunizes each against criticism from without is plain nonsense. Once people come to understand a perspective that is not their own, they may see the world differently, even to a radical extent. The new perspective might be seen to have simpler, less cumbersome and more all-embracing

---

1   Upon this foundation arises a further problem, that of `self-reference` (Lawson Ibid. Prologue pp.xxi-xxvi) Once we accept the dogma that `all perspectives and theories are relative to the system of presuppositions and concepts within which the protagonist lives`, we find ourselves making a claim of universal truth. See also Appignanesi & Garratt on `Theories of Everything` (2000) pp.108-9

explanations of things than does their own. It may authenticate itself in its ability to offer solutions to practical problems like cures for illness and effective farming.

We may call this ability to understand another culture `insight`[1], which constitutes a new dawn for the mind. It is now possible to see things otherwise. It is now possible to revere what was strange and nonsensical, even if one may not come to adopt it oneself. One need not do so, for the practices that enhance reverence may function well in one`s own tradition. But, at the very least, one`s own view of life will become more sophisticated and more conciliatory through learning the power of other traditions. Cultures interact on the basis of mutual translation, not simply of languages, but of concepts and values. European-Americans can understand the view of the world held by native tribes of North America. We can learn from them, for example, that the idea of `owning the land` is foolish nonsense. Likewise, rainforest tribes can learn from the modern world and assimilate the benefits of modern science, and we can learn from them. That is because there is always a basis in common interests and moral values, even when many radically-opposed views are present. (That these are radically opposed can only be perceived through concepts applicable to both!)

Second, shared threats to survival and prosperity promote shared debate and compromise, and may create unity of purpose against a common threat. This is one way in which a synthesis of cultural traditions develops. We take the best of each other`s stories and synthesize them into a more adequate and widely-applicable version. As this sharing of perspectives grows, so those which promise greatest benefits for mankind have the tendency to prosper and supplant native cultures. Supplanting tends to occur as, for example, when Roman Catholic countries tend to become increasingly secular. But is this entirely a good thing? The humane and reverential insights of a tradition need not be lost but live on in integrated harmony with the wider perspective. The difficulty lies in the theology of the institution: it has to march on.

---

1   I first came across this account of `insight` in Stuart C. Brown `Do Religious Claims Make Sense?` London SCM 1969 However, Brown claimed that understanding and belief are simultaneous, whereas I think insight gives understanding and imaginative respect, of not necessarily belief.

The post-modernist attitude to cultures is a cul-de-sac of attraction only to intellectuals from a largely sociological background who falsely imagine they have put the notion of global society and a common humanity to rest once and for all. Their pursuit of this position has led to obscure and unintelligible writing, itself devoid of truly philosophical story[1].

The maturing person no doubt finds weaknesses of mind and will; the grand story will have to admit of, and submit to, exceptions and ongoing problematical phenomena; every arrival at clarity and certainty will gradually move on to the perception of jarring insights which humble the Grand Eureka. It is, therefore, never wise to dogmatise, or to refuse all opposition. In a democracy, the would-be dictator must be allowed to speak, but not to prevent others from doing so, and it would be wise for him, and his audience, to listen. We may, horrific though it be, discover one day that the established foundations of democracy are shaken to the core simply because democracy cannot save itself, and only an authoritarian system can forge a way though otherwise insoluble divisions. The story may yet have twists in what might appear to be its tail.

We are also mindful as ironists that every solution brings a new problem, that all answers bring new questions, that every truth has a context outside of which it is unintelligible, but outside of which whole realms of invention and discovery await us. That is why we should always listen even when we think we know.

And even Rorty rediscovered the vision despite, on his own admission, having read too much Heidegger! As Habermas puts it in his obituary to a revered opponent and friend: "Nothing is sacred to Rorty the ironist. Asked at the end of his life about the 'holy', the strict atheist answered with words reminiscent of the young Hegel: 'My sense of the holy is bound up with the hope that some day my remote descendants will live in a global civilization in which love is pretty much the only law."[2]

---

1   For a readable and succinct account of the post-modernist view see pp.464-479 of David E. Cooper's `World Philosophies: an Historical Introduction` (1996)
2   In `Sign and Sight` 12th June 2007.

Story as Journey and Story as Destination

We tend not any longer to call upon the holy books and ancient institutions for this saga, even if their accounts of our place within it, of our own tendency to love of the darkness, and need for love of others and the world, are as valid as ever. They remain the treasure houses of vital language for a narrative that enables humankind to see itself accurately as the most developed of creatures and at the same time the most damaging to the prospects for our world. The master story always was a shared narrative pointing the way to a transforming future.

Modern education and the ghastly experiences of modern warfare have tended to unite the liberal democratic world against paths prescribed in the ancient master stories of the world. We have become emphatic about the rights of individuals, of the sick, of children, workers, and immigrants. We abhor the oppression of women, the slaughter of animals by bleeding them to death, and the taking up of arms against those deemed to be damned. No one can really claim this liberal world lacks moral awareness. The much-maligned press pounces upon political hypocrisy, scandal and abuse of the helpless. All this is clear evidence that the world is developing a clear sense of humane moral ideals, even if some societies appear to flout them. Pariah states may still exist, but there are few that survive long by oppressing the mass of the people to fulfil their leaders` ends.

The tradition of values, goals and ideals residing in a narrative giving a vision for all will have to be global and all-embracing. What MacIntyre disparagingly calls "the language of everywhere and nowhere" will, at least to some degree, become the language of everyone and everywhere. Communication technology is driving us there. "**Globish**" has come to stay. Globish is the name given to the worldwide English of the Internet. English, or at least some abbreviated and ungrammatical offspring of it, has become the medium for communication across frontiers.[1] But before dismissing the need for `small communities`, we need to imagine a synthesis of the global and the local, for those old traditions remain as our treasure houses. Without them, we would hardly understand what

---

1   See McCrum, R.(2010) `Globish: How the English Language became the World`s Language` Viking

forgiveness, penitence, sacrifice or spiritual rebirth might mean, let alone understand their power to deliver. For this reason, it need not be imagined that each culture forsakes its past outlook and values.

Martin Jacques, an authority in Chinese affairs, has pointed out that as China develops, it is not likely to lose its Confucian attitudes. As nations become more prosperous, they become more confident of their traditions and attitudes, the single party and elite leadership standing in opposition to the multiparty democracy preached by the West.[1]

I recall Chesterton's remarks, cited earlier[2], about the inn as the goal, rather than the journey as the goal. In a small community one finds intimacy, meaningful conversation, shared fun, celebration, sorrow and loyalties. It is the home of "serious joy". We find true personal growth at the local inn as well as on the journeys towards global community. We are indeed members of at least two communities which themselves challenge and refine our own path in life.. At the 'village inn' we may call upon mythic imagery and romantic icon to enrich our thought and conversation. On the big journey we are philosophic – holding before us the grand perspective, a master story that guides our love of the world towards a sustainable future – but also remaining ironists – ready to acknowledge the imperfection of our knowledge, what it might mean about how we should live, including the extent of our freedom to 'do our own thing'. Yes, we can also commune at the Inn on such big matters!

As individuals, we are contributors to the well-being of the community. Our work includes political activity, supporting movements that promote radical economic and social change.

> "Today's economic system must be transformed into a 21st-century economy "as if people and the Earth matter". Many people see this transformation as one aspect of a larger historical change—the end of the modern age and the transition to a post-modern age, marked by a new awareness of our common humanity and our kinship with the rest of creation." (James Robertson)

---

1   Jacques M (2012) p.12-
2   Ch 3.

There is something incomplete about my emphasis on the new `master-story-that-is-not-fiction`. It is dangerously instrumental, and belongs to "the instrumental society"[1] insofar as its ultimate goal appears to be the salvation of the world from ecological disaster and the human race from self-destruction. It thus might occlude deeper meanings less obvious than the presumption of consumerism. The unfolding narrative being revealed through modern science lacks inspirational power; it delays the question `what for?` Were we to achieve a state of planetary equilibrium, what then? The factual story says nothing about the meaning of my life or human life as a whole. I cannot be here just to avoid harming the world. Chesterton`s inn gives us a clue.

Fiction is the medium that enters our souls. It lives within throughout our lives and steers our life narratives. Science may not give us final facts, but it gives us the nearest thing to them, and we ignore the `non-fiction` at our peril, of course. The differences between the master story for today and fictional works (such as fantasies, myths and novels) on the same issues are many. Not only is fiction likely to reach a wider public, but also its penetrative power is far greater. This book has claimed to present a factual story, in a direct manner. It has dwelt on such things as the atrophy of our humanity through the pursuit of Life Diminishing Activities at the expense of Life Enhancing Activities, on the nature of these and what they offer us, on the distinction between external and internal goods and the current dominance of the latter, and on the pre-eminence of love in a mature life. This has been worth the effort, for it grapples with the problem of getting a perspective on our lives. Even if this `factual story` does help some readers organize their thoughts, and develop a richer framework of understanding, *it is not likely to inspire, thus instilling vision and energy to attain well-being for ourselves.* Inspiration is the task of the `fictionalist`:- the film-maker, the novelist, the poet, the dramatist, the artist, the musician.

Fiction enables us to turn from objective knowledge about the outside world and its workings towards our inner life. It challenges our values, our integrity of being and all our plans. Of such we really must visit a great pioneer.

---

1   Charles Taylor`s term in `Sources of the Self` p.500-

The Danish philosopher Soren Kierkegaard (1813-55) was incensed by the inert philosophical systems of European thinkers. Even if they might have attained to some objective truths about what is real and good, and those processes determining the workings of the world, such objective truths remained detached from how people were to live their lives. Truth must, he saw, be lived in, passionately, if it is to have

any relevance to life. For him, "an objective uncertainty held fast in passionate inwardness, is the truth".[1] If a book is merely interesting and its ideas accepted, it may not yet have become living truth.

For Kierkegaard, objective truth, which he called 'philosophical' truth, was not the same thing as 'subjective' truth. The former makes no difference of itself to our manner of living. It is impersonal, public, a tool for humanity to contemplate or use for good or ill. Subjective truth alone is the power in one's life. It is what is believed and sought with "infinite passion and concern". Kierkegaard understood this deep inner commitment as true faith. All our knowledge is wasted unless it changes us. He was opposed to the dead orthodoxy of a religion that emphasized belief in the creed rather than living the attitudes and values implicit in it.[2]

Living truth was, for Kierkegaard, awareness of guilt, of penitence and forgiveness, of learning love, of salvation from an inhuman life. He brings to all subsequent times the understanding of human spirituality in a way that demotes interest in systems. How one lives is the thing, and it is the priority for which stories, myths, sagas, parables, novels, etc. serve as media. Personal transformation comes not from learning objective

---

1   Concluding Unscientific Postscript. p.182 Bob Zunjic's article in Wikipedia on Kierkegaard's 'Concluding Unscientific Postscript' (1846) is an excellent introduction to 'inwardness' as the truth. (www.uri.edu/personal/szunjic/philos/conclud.htm)

2   Kierkegaard was deeply Christian, but rejected the focus on doctrinal accuracy prevalent at the time. In his view "Pilate asked 'What is Truth?' and then crucified it". I am also reminded of Richard Peters' dictum: "Truth is not a destination at which we arrive, but an aegis under which we travel."

truth (or that which is accepted as such). It is born out of `epiphanic` or `eureka` moments, in which the learner is not told or instructed anything, in which nothing is systematically learned, but which come from within the listener and within the story itself. They come with unforgettable power because they penetrate deep within and change us, to a greater or lesser extent, forever. They are visionary.

Consider the difference between a text box of bullet points and an allegory of life, such as `Pilgrim`s Progress`[1]. With an image, the author does for us what no structured psychological analysis could possibly achieve. Reading Bunyan`s description of `Vanity Fair`, we find external goods, instant pleasures, and the best variety of entertainments. ("...he that will go to the (Celestial) city, and yet not go through this town, must needs go out of the world.") There is the `Hill of Error`, up which they walked with ease, but which was "very steep on the farthest side"... the `Enchanted Ground`, "where the air naturally tended to make one drowsy"... in which was to be found `The `Slothful`s Friend`, an arbour "finely wrought above-head, beautified with greens, furnished with benches and settles".

No longer need we call upon any literal understanding of magic, miracles, divine intervention, or paradise beyond death. These may have been indeed, the `opiate of the people`, but they were vital when the impoverished and downtrodden needed `opiates` to keep them from madness and despair. Now a growing proportion of mankind has outgrown the need for such things. Slothfulness is nurtured by new opiates, for which there is no excuse.

Martin Heidegger was a strong critic of lifestyles in the 20th century western world. He drew particular attention to the "scribbling" in newspapers and throw-away novels, the dominance of Hollywood, and the national worship of boxers and dictators. Such things he saw as reflecting a society that has "fallen from being". The masses accept mass-produced, stereotypical styles of life. Such is `fallenness` – they have lost themselves like patrons of a rowdy drunken public house whose talk is

---
1   John Bunyan, 1678

hardly intelligible, and in which labels, clichés and slurs predominate. So much for `serious joy`!

What Heidegger sought was a new `language-event`, that is deliverance from the empty language of the crowd. The key question for the individual to ask is "Am I free for my world or taken over by it?"[1] The solution is not, of course, an arrogant, superior egoism, but membership of communities of living minds, minds that grow, not by following every fashion of the moment, but by listening to voices of art, music, literature and the sciences, finding fresh gems yielding new perceptions and deeper insights – to behold what may have been already there but which was passed over in ignorance and haste. A good film or play may also serve!

Our fictions are a multitude of powerful and imaginative creations of writers past and present. The `throw-away` stuff merely diverts us from learning to grow up. Quality literature, drama, film, music, accords with the pursuit of inner well-being. It enables us to understand humanity, to feel its pain, to know heroism, to express delights and shun the fanciful. It does not take us into sexual violence and murder in order to excite our instincts but to awaken us to human depravity. Quality literature enables insight, delivers us from false ideas and destructive valuing, promotes a sense of proportion, and enriches our lives. This is not instrumental, but it is a facet of the true life of the human spirit. All this feeds our minds, strengthens our conversation, and deepens our relationships. It is not the diversity of narratives that is a problem, but an all-too-common paucity of meaning. Rich meanings not only accord with the way humans are, but generate insight into what they might become.

The Old Testament prophets offered a vision of the people`s future which was *conditional*: to follow the commandments of the Almighty would lead to prosperity: to follow the way of idolatry would lead to national destruction. What is more, a point of no return would be reached when time to repent and change their ways would run out. Exile, slavery and dispersal amongst the nations would be irreversible, even if, one day, a

---

1   Being and Time p.68

remnant should return. The message for today has every similarity in form, if not in *dramatis personae*. Our penitence must involve all races if we are to preserve a promising tomorrow for our descendants, some of whom we have brought into this world.

 "Where the mind is without fear and the head is held high; Where knowledge is free: Where the world has not been broken up into fragments by domestic walls; Where the clear stream of reason has not lost its way into the dreary desert sand of dead habit; Where the mind is led forward by Thee into ever-widening thought and action; Into that heaven of freedom, my Father, let my country awake.

- Rabindranath Tagore (d.1941)

CHAPTER 7: EDUCATION AND LEARNING TO COMMUNICATE

"Most people do not listen with the intent to understand: they listen with the intent to reply" – Stephen Covey (1989)

"You're short on ears and long on mouth" – John Wayne (Big Jake 1971)

One vital mark of education for human maturity is learning to communicate effectively with each other. This entails mutual respect, willingness to listen and learn, and to express one's views clearly and critically. The principles of mature communication have been clarified by Habermas and contrasted with the corrupting influence in contemporary life of institutions dominating our lives. Should there be doubt about the human inability to communicate effectively, some frightening examples from the supposedly highest intellectual levels may clarify matters.

Negotiations took place at the **2009 Copenhagen Climate Change Conference** in which the representatives of 192 nations were present. These did not lead to legally binding agreements, simply to statements of intent, which are, in themselves, worth little. They are not even promises. The world waited in vain and protesters protested in vain. How might suspicion, wrangling and uncompromising self-interest amongst national representatives be transformed into openness in communication and an overriding desire to save the world? The problems here are, at least in part, those of the individual `writ large`. That is because leaders are at the heart of deliberations about such major issues, and these leaders will need to acquire certain attitudes, goals and skills if they are to be anything other than a spanner in the works. In short, `How can these important people learn to grow up?`.

The problem of turning debate into action is further highlighted as **UNEP**[1] tells us that we now have `treaty congestion`. World leaders have signed

---

1   United Nations Environment Programme 2012 (Guardian Weekly 15.06.12)

up to 500 internationally recognized agreements in the past 50 years of which only 40 led to "some progress" out of 90 carefully examined, and "little or no progress" was detected in 24, including climate change, fish stocks, desertification and drought. "Further deterioration" was posted for eight goals. Prof. John Knox has shown how the USA has failed to enact 10 or more international agreements, including the Basle convention on waste and the UN convention on the law of the sea. It is relatively easy to sign up to programmes, but far harder to implement them. Perhaps the greatest obstacle lies in a clash of interests with big business, which is important for jobs and wealth creation. But can we eat our cake and keep it? The problem is an example of the failure of real rational communication, which involves honesty, single-mindedness, foresight and sacrifice.

Further confirmation of the chaos into which supposedly humanistic organizations readily fall can be seen within the European Union, whose very constitution has been undemocratic from the outset[1]. Mazower sees its initial idealism and vision to have been taken over by bureaucracy and committee rule, controlled neither by politicians nor electorates, the latter having largely given up voting. His argument goes far beyond Euro-scepticism and points to the European project's role in atomizing and alienating society[2].

Habermas is perhaps the foremost European writer to defend and advance the importance of rational principles in effective dialogue, countering the post-modern stress on devious usages and hidden agendas said by sceptics to infest all communication.

Learning to Communicate: Reflections on Habermas

The contemporary philosopher Jurgen Habermas (1929-) has made a mighty contribution to the study of, and prescriptions about, human rational communication. The principles of communication devised in his work are a fundamental requirement for all representatives engaging in

---

1   See Marta Andreasen: *Brussels Laid Bare*, Devon, St Edwards Press, 2009 for an analysis and first-hand account of EU oligarchy in action.
2   Adam Zamoyski, in Literary Review Oct.2012 would concur with this.

dialogue and negotiation with a view to reaching agreed and binding settlements. Needless to say, it is a requirement widely ignored, even amongst people we imagine to be educated.

Habermas exemplifies Socrates dictum that `the unexamined life is not worth living`, in the sense, of course that he represents its converse! Habermas sees reason as a tool of communication, not as a sufficient tool for disclosing the nature of the cosmos, by contrast with rationalistic philosophers of past centuries, such as Leibnitz. For him the evolution of human reasoning skills must be advanced in order to balance and restrict the "**strategic**" and "**instrumental**" uses of reason which have become a tool for social control. For the sake of reaching mutual understanding between parties, strategic and instrumental uses of reason tend to deny "**communicative**" uses of reason, even if they have important functions.

Habermas shows little concern for MacIntyre`s love of small communities, each loyal to established traditional ways of life. For Habermas, not only is there no turning back to such, but the "project of modernity" is not yet complete. To achieve this, communicative reason must be accorded its proper place in community life once again. What does he mean by all this?

The human being has a unique capacity for reasoned communication which has evolved into the democratic institutions of the present. These have the capacity to display human rational powers at work, although even so-called democracies have a long way to go before the rational possibilities inherent in them are fully authoritative. What are these values intrinsic to rationality? Whilst a more expanded account follows, for the moment it might be said, for example, that anyone who values reasoned communication will, to be consistent, be impartial between speakers. (The fact that a view is expressed by a particular person thought to be poorly educated must not reduce willingness to appraise that view on grounds independent of whom the speaker might be.) This will be further clarified when we consider what has become known as the `Ideal Speech Situation`, below.

Habermas perceives that contemporary society has had its inherent possibilities of 'communicative competence' inhibited and suppressed by the over-powerful domains of *market forces, state domination*, and *the power of institutions*. These all determine the course of our lives far beyond any duty we might have in promoting them. They have become our oppressors through the dominance of their place in current political and economic policy. *They have presented assumed first principles of living for our unconscious assimilation, thus colonizing our minds.* (We accept, we follow, we conform… we imagine no other course.) Only an education leading to self and social understanding, especially focusing upon forces competing for our ideas of success and failure and the goals we choose, can enable us to find ways out of this straitjacket.

Habermas regards this 'strategic and instrumental rationality' as supplanting genuine rationality.[1] Citizens are not involved in any genuine debate about policy that matters to them. Any thinking about the things that matter to a community is done for them by those appointed by them to do it. That would be fine, except that the highly questionable values of the state are not opened to question, which erodes democracy and, with it, any sense of shared community. People's freedom is given away and their choice of what to do with their lives is eroded.

Strategic and instrumental rationality has supplanted the rationality of the 'lifeworld'. Habermas is claiming, quite rightly, that reflection on quantifiable things, especially money and power (expressed in votes) dominates political action. The reasoning that belongs to what Habermas calls the 'lifeworld' is perverted and ignored.[2] The 'lifeworld' consists in the informal and everyday concerns of life, of the family, of non-party politics, of culture. This informal world of shared interactions provides a basis for mutual understanding and social cohesion. It expresses the values and virtues that mark out qualities in people, and the contrasting marks of corruption. Habermas' key emphasis is that the lifeworld has

---

1   For examples of how these forms of practical thought have come to dominate our lives see Appendix 3 of my 'Eudaimonia' (2011)
2   In the UK, deep financial cuts made by local authorities as a result of government reduction in funding has led to the closing of libraries, the suspension of children's nursery education, and the demise of Local Education Authorities. Schools have had vast administrative responsibilities thrust upon them in order to save money. Citizens are thereby deprived of dynamic sources for their personal development.

been "colonized" by the values and ideals of the market, of institutions and the state.

Change should only originate through the 'lifeworlds' of communities – as citizens challenge and review the systems that dominate their lives. We tend to forget that real democracy gives people their voice, and this can only be rightly expressed through communicative uses of reason. What might these communicative uses of reason be?

Famously, Habermas posited the '**Ideal Speech Situation**' (ISS) as exemplifying the requirements for reasoned communication between parties. Participants in deliberation, for example, about a desirable state of affairs which they all agree upon, as at the 2009 Copenhagen Conference on climate change, needed to adhere to certain rules.

These rules are:

> 1. Every subject with the competence to speak and act is allowed to take part in a discourse.
>
> 2a. Everyone is allowed to question any assertion whatever.
>
> 2b. Everyone is allowed to introduce any assertion whatever into the discourse.
>
> 2c. Everyone is allowed to express his attitudes, desires and needs.
>
> 3. No speaker may be prevented, by internal or external coercion, from exercising his rights, as laid down in (1) and (2).[1]

Whilst this gives us no solution to specific cases of dispute, it does begin to suggest a counter to the negative attitudes and behaviour we may display. Discussion has little point if we stand by such negatives because we are simply not prepared to listen to other points of view and weigh them up rationally. Habermas later wrote in 'Discourse Ethics' that the

---

1   Habermas 'Discourse Ethics' p.86

requirements of such as the ISS are logically presumed even by anyone who tries to argue that they are invalid. For example, anyone arguing against the features of the ISS is already committed to those features. Were this not so, he would not be engaged in reasoned discussion: he would do better to throw a shoe.

Why is all this important? It is foundational to democracy and to parliamentary debate. Also, it is all too scarce! The goal of genuine debate is surely not to maintain a position out of loyalty to one`s friends or because one must not be seen to make a `U-turn`. It is not to demean one`s opponent with *ad hominem* accusations. It is not even to allow loyalty to party policy to determine one`s actions. Open debate requires willingness to change in the light of convincing evidence and argument, even if changing is tantamount to an admission of lack of forethought. The inflexibility of the `Iron Lady` is only a virtue if that lady has listened with respect, weighed up the evidence, considered the arguments of disputants, confirmed her own rational basis for her position, and stood by it. Inflexibility is the death of international conferences in which sacrifices must be made, responsibilities acknowledged, and compromises accepted. So it is quite clear that national and other representatives at negotiations would do well to confront the discourse ethics to which they are beholden before the outset of a conference. No representative should sit tied to a specific viewpoint or brief from his seniors back home, and if he does have a strongly-held position, that must not only be expressed but justified and debated by all parties. That will enhance, if not guarantee, hope of progress towards world-changing decisions.

But we have a long road to travel before such rationality can be realized. There is an intimate connection between maturity at the personal level and the furtherance of communal well-being. Lifeworlds, promoting as they do discussion and reflection, tend to also be fertile ground for the development of personal autonomy – being able to think and decide for oneself on rational and informed grounds rather than simply through submission to a prevalent view.

Autonomous, or "principled" moral thinking, as expressed in **Lawrence Kohlberg`s** `Post-Conventional Morality`, calls upon rational moral principles held to be the supreme

> criteria for appraising customs, rules, and even claims to human rights. These include the principles of:
>
> non-restriction of freedoms which are compatible with the freedom of others;
>
> openness and truthfulness, only to be restricted when the welfare of others would otherwise be threatened;
>
> equality of consideration for the interests of all; equality of opportunity;
>
> the pursuit of retributive and distributive justice.

These principles form ultimate criteria in rational decision-making. To ignore any of them is to be driven by predispositions harmful to oneself and others. In the absence of such criteria, progress in communication is unlikely. Commitment to them is a mark of the autonomous person, which is itself a mark of maturity.

Cross-cultural Communication

It has long been clear to Habermas that, in his description of the expression of the concerns and values of communities known as the `lifeworld`, "something has been missing"[1] in the principles required for contemporary communication to advance. That `something` is religion, which cannot be excluded from any attempt to enhance human communal understanding and conciliation. Since the rise of Islam as a political force, awareness has grown of the social wisdom of granting that a great section of the world`s peoples give pride of place to religious practices and beliefs in determining their lives. Habermas now sees that, not only must religious communicators subscribe to the principles of communicative action, but that the concept of reason must not preclude a religious outlook on life, even in a secular society.[2] Therefore, the attitude that religious ideas are

---

1   Hence the title of Habermas` essay, which is the focus of his 2007 collaborative work See bibliog..
2   Ibid. p.16

disproved by science, and that any adherent to them fails to qualify as an active communicator, is to be open to challenge. It may be the case that proof and disproof reflect failure to understand religious meaning, as I have argued. If religions are said to describe anything, that is merely on their surface: in their depth, they are essentially about inwardness and reverence, and some consciousness of a dimension transcending the mundane to which we may be answerable.

To these international matters and debates, individuals and groups bring their own spiritual qualities. The climate change conferences are a mirror of the calibre of their participants. Without the vision that our common goal is not self-aggrandizement or national gain but the salvation of the world for future generations, no progress can be made.

The power of traditions to address the current local and global trends in living is expressed powerfully by **Jonathan Sacks**[1]. Sacks takes key concepts from his own Jewish tradition to address current issues. Such concepts have their origins in that tradition but also have relevance to the lives of all. Without such, we are the poorer. He draws attention, for example, to the importance of business in the Jewish tradition, which stands in contrast to long-standing emphases in Christianity about the dangers of material wealth-acquisition. The need to trade, because none are sufficient in themselves, is as old as civilization, and a stimulus to human communication, agreement and respect, so business is essentially a good thing. Clearly, this has stimulated Jewish enterprise through the ages and enabled the wealthy to promote further growth without stifling the conscience. The largely Christian counter to that is to focus upon the depravity of human nature and our tendency to greed, thus erasing any clear vision of the sanctity of commerce. The greatest entrepreneurs, from Carnegie to Buffett have been uninhibited about making billions but equally uninhibited about using it to the good of the world. One cannot help but be reminded of the

---

1   In his `The Dignity of Difference` (2002)., subtitled `how to avoid the clash of civilizations` See, Introduction (above)

little-known ending of the story of Joseph. He gained all the wealth in Egypt by his organizational and business prowess, developed as he steered society through a seven-year famine, but at the climax of his work, presented all the proceeds to Pharaoh. Stories from the traditions conveyed values which defined the heart of a culture. Quite clearly, both Jewish and Christian traditions convey vital truth about humanity that is readily obscured in modern life.

We are all aware of the apparently intractable differences between Islamic life and cultures based on personal freedoms. Such have led, tragically, to horrific crimes against humanity, both cultures having their share of responsibility. The only way forward lies in dialogue and mediation, which must surely begin with those with moderate views conversing with the extremists in their society, focusing upon the foundational sources sanctioning their actions. Scholarship is vital here. Muslims must address extremism: Jews and Christians must address the extreme right in their cultures. That stage must be successful before any intercultural conversation can be fruitful.

We have to learn, not only from Islam, but from the **Confucianism** implicit in Chinese politics, that government by the people may not be what is best for the people. That may lead us to perceive the aimlessness and individualism of the Western secular tradition, so that we place greater value upon educatedness in history and politics, and to enjoy, through worldwide media, the conversations of mankind. In the West, paternalism is abjured, the state's roles kept to a minimum, and any behaviour that appears to harm none is allowed. For a society having its roots in Chinese traditions, the state is the parent of society whose wisdom is to be obeyed and who guides its people towards honourable progress. Society is one collective being, to which the individual is subservient. Personal freedoms are limited by the state in the interests of the people. Stability is paramount.

The quest for autonomy, free expression and democratic powers, as evidenced in the 1989 Tiananmen protests, flew in the face of Chinese tradition. The impossibility of dialogue between cultural groups within China had been obvious for centuries, and suited Maoism. At the present time, the protests appear to have had an indirect and lasting influence: they have gathered international support for opening up China to tourism, business and international trade. This has led to private initiative, wealth creation and ownership. China came to know that its progress internationally and stability internally depended on manufacture and trade. It now knows that its further growth depends on enhancing the lives of its rural poor. By contrast, there is no sign of any easing of China's draconian censorship laws. Even in the light of this knowledge, we, like themselves, can learn much from China's ancient traditions.

> "If you lead the people with political force and restrict them with law and punishment, they can just avoid law violation, but will have no sense of honour and shame. If you lead them with morality and guide them with *li**, they will develop a sense of honour and shame, and will do good of their own accord."
>
> (*a moral, well mannered, example, according to the moral code)
>
> "When the personal life is cultivated, the family will be regulated; when the family is regulated, the state will be in order, and when the state is in order, there will be peace throughout the world. From the Son of Heaven down to the common people, all must regard cultivation of the personal life as the root or foundation"
>
> Confucius c.500.B.C.E[1]

What, however, of Christianity's role in communicating its values to this world which finds itself forever in danger of growing down in spirit rather than up. What can it have to say to an impoverished world? As `dogmatics` is put on hold, so its spiritual power has a chance to change our world. In recent times, the Roman Catholic church has, for example, diverted from its focus on theological fine-tuning, to an awareness of

---

1 For more on *li* and related ideas *ren* and *yi*, see McGreal I.P. (ed.) p.3-

its mission to a suffering world. Recent Popes have themselves become evangelical in the sense that they rejected secularism with its shallow consumerist values, and placed emphasis on the cultivation of spiritual values through the meditative life, as well as caring for the poor.[1] Also the focus upon life's sacredness has found expression in resistance to abortion and euthanasia. All this is, however, in need of expressive force. Were the new Pope to actually become a new St. Francis, with his own pet creatures around him, perhaps a parrot on the shoulder during Mass, and a personal campaign against gluttony, poaching of protected species, and cruelty to children, he would carry great authority beyond the confines of the church.

Of course, it is also important that the churches listen to the world: their intellectual inadequacy and internal corruption must change if the passage of time is not to see them fading to nothing. The Bible may condemn homosexuality, but does not the call to compassionate love provoke a reassessment? The global Internet itself constitutes a challenge to all traditions to engage in the conversations of the world. Clearly education has a key role in enabling learners to honour world traditions despite their differences, without being afraid to question them for their tendency to cling on to divisive and cruel teaching.

Communication Skills as Tools for Life

Once we see the importance of learning to communicate without prejudice, allowing that we may be incorrect in our views, and seeking to learn from others, we have a promising chance of success. More is, however, necessary. Our hearts may be in the right place, but our skills may be lacking.

Probably the most fundamental prerequisite we must attain is self-awareness. To know our own committed views on matters is vital if we are to prevent these from filling our vision and clouding out possible insights that might have made us think on. They must be temporarily put on hold or 'bracketed out' if we are to learn from others who may differ

---

1   See Weigel, G.,(2012) 'Evangelical Catholicism: Deep reform in the 21st century church' N Y Basic Books

radically from us. It is easy to lose our ability to listen, and to question whether we truly understand. Without such, our preconceptions may remain a hindrance. It takes careful practice if we are to show respect to a speaker by listening rather than focusing our minds, even as he is speaking, on forming a powerful reply. In effective communication the other parties must be presumed to be at least as wise as ourselves. They may be sources of important learning for us.

It is tempting but fatal to assume preconceived ideas about other parties to the conversation, thus judging and dismissing their contribution without even digesting it. Bad teachers do this, as do all who consider themselves to be wiser and more expert than others. Mutual concern to solve the problem, hoping to benefit from each other's wisdom, as well as their quest for expert solutions, marks out the mature conversation. The teacher as participant is open to correction, without being non-committal, and focused upon the issue itself, not seeking personal prowess and the humiliation of those who differ. Humility makes for inner calm.

Therefore, teaching and learning require a wide range of communication skills as well as competence in the field to be taught and learned. It is not simply in the classroom, but throughout our lives, that we must remain alert to these issues.

It is likely that the best communicators have inner qualities that lead them to instinctively give credit to other parties in conversation because they have outgrown the assumption of superiority over whoever they converse with. They understand the meaning of Buber's 'Thou' and Berger's 'presence'. The possession of long experience, high academic qualifications or high office must never be allowed to prevent the holder from openness to wisdom coming from unlikely sources.

Teachers learn from the learners. The good political leader listens and learns, as does the best medical practitioner. If medical practices no longer offer personal doctors assigned to particular patients, what chance is there of understanding patients? The patient becomes no more than on-screen data compiled by a range of people. Individuals are no longer known – knowing a patient as an individual enables relevant dialogue and understanding. Such also applies if we are to progress in multicultural dialogue. The new neighbour who belongs to a different faith will have understandings and perceptions that may reveal things more challenging than can be gathered from the encyclopedia.

CHAPTER 8: EDUCATION TOWARDS MATURITY

"Upon the education of the people of this country the fate of this country depends" -Disraeli[1]

"The transforming quality of education is what makes the contrast between education and life ridiculous; for it is by education that mere living is transformed into a quality of life. For how a man lives depends on what he sees and understands...an educated person is one whose whole range of actions and activities is gradually transformed by the deepening and widening of his understanding and sensitivity... " -Richard S. Peters[2]

Good education generates the realist and the idealist in each of us. The life of the realist is useful, but can be devoid of deep meaning. The life of the idealist can be as profound as it is useless, but ideals can enable us to appraise the roles thrust upon us in society. Nothing big can ever happen without ideals. It is our degree of realism that enables us to play an effective role in the maintenance of society as we help meet functional needs, and it is our degree of idealism that enables us to transcend the roles and status given us by society. Without vision, deep change may never occur.

> **"With no vision, the people perish"[3]**
>
> A good children's library will include what we might call `mythic fiction`, taking the form of the arrival of the powers of darkness upon a blissful scene, the struggle with them, and the final victory of love and justice. From ancient parables and fables to contemporary works with their

---

1   House of Commons 15th June 1874
2   1973 pp19-20
3   Proverbs ch.29 v.18

more subtle lessons, ideals may form. Complementing such are the modern works of such as **Jacqueline Wilson**, who takes the reader into harsh, everyday reality, enabling realism, sympathy and action. However…

…it is important to note that this genre of realism may harmfully bypass the **Romantic stage** (see ch.6) in which heroic virtues and grand achievements transcend the grim realism of Wilson's plots. Children need to become inspired by greatness. The dark things of life, like divorce, mental illness and racism require to be balanced and transcended through a vision of life's possibilities for those who overcome.

It is the ideal, life at its most fulfilling, that should be experienced from the very beginning of our lives, in infancy and early childhood. That means fun, play and love of internal goods – being definitive of worthwhile activities – for their own sake. There is little purely instrumental about this learning: its point lies within itself. In early infancy, this is not best achieved through a systematic interventive programme of teaching, but through the oft-subconscious influence of good parenting on the child[1]. Learning comes through interaction between child and parent, whatever that may include. It begins with the first smiles, kind looks and warm touches of the parent, as well as the comforting breast. For the young child in the nursery group, learning comes from a sense of being wanted, from play, from watching others' behaviour and imitating it. Perhaps above all, the child learns to trust in and relax with the first adult figures they meet outside their home. Learning does not come from a systematic programme of instruction and acceleration up hierarchical ladders of attainment.[2] The role of the nursery teacher is to provide activities from which the child may have some choice, to tell stories to those able and ready to listen, to enable the exercise of whatever skills the child wants to employ, whether to build, draw, enact by dressing up, etc. The teacher

---

1   See 'Too Much Too Soon' (2012) ch1 by Penelope Leach
2   Hence the strong opposition to the 'The Early Years Foundation Stage', part of the British government's Childcare Act 2006 which has (in 2011) 17 attainment targets for 3 to 4 year-olds. Its 2008 publication seems to have had at least 9 points of attainment in each of six areas of development!

is a skilled facilitator at this stage, not a systematic instructor. She (for women make the most appropriate nursery teachers) will, of course, record salient data about a child's progress and difficulties in language, motivation, happiness, and social initiative, for sharing with parents. She is not just a mother substitute but also an expert in her crucial role.

Meaningful all-round pre-16 education must likewise focus predominantly upon the *telos* of maturity rather than upon the pragmatic needs of learners-soon-to-be-adults. It should aim to broaden and deepen the possibilities for learners without presupposing what they will do for employment. Thus it focuses on promoting the all-round development of human beings, thus enriching their lives. The most crucial processes of mental development lie in early childhood experience and affect all later progress in life.

By contrast, in recent times, political initiatives concentrated largely upon bringing the skills of the workplace into the mainstream educational curriculum, thus making education more appropriate to the needs of employers. This began, in most UK secondary schools, with the **Technical and Vocational Education Initiative** in the 1980s[1]. The upshot was, at best, that young people could more easily see how schooling is important for their future. They learned industrial processes, how to use computers, how to create websites and software programmes, design and marketing, how to invent and sell products, thus forming realistic career ambitions. *Thus ran the subtle tragedy of modern state education.* Not only would such skills become speedily outmoded as employment needs changed, but this would relegate enduring knowledge, concepts, skills and attitudes to a lower rank. The pupil might be better equipped as an employee in the near future, but hindered in their development as an autonomous being.

Traditional disciplines matter because they furnish the mind with profound ideas, foundational knowledge and transferable skills in arts

---

1   Technical and Vocational Education Initiative.

and sciences. Such form the universally-required platforms for human thought and inner growth. In their absence, interpersonal communication can be but functional and eminently forgettable. They form the basis on which true transformation of life quality can arise. It is, for example, in the acquisition of such things as historical knowledge that the development of a sense of direction in society and personal life is formed. If we know the human past, we also learn the present and future that we wish to promote for mankind.

At the same time, it is also true that learning is an unwelcome chore at any age in the absence of intrinsically-valued pursuits, freely chosen. These are forms of creative activity that are precious, stimulating, and enriching in a person's life. Without them comes self-loss, itself a form of slavery into whatever slot one might be given in society. The student who learns to be driven solely by obedience, ambition or fear of unemployment has lessened chances of acquiring intrinsically-valued activities. Sound education saves the employed and unemployed from an empty life by engrossing them in practices that stimulate their minds towards maturity. This also gives the learner a chance of making her play also her work, as considered in chapter five. These are the true ends which school-based instrumental activities serve to promote.

This suggests that we should build upon the interests that children develop through the play of their early and subsequent lives, and balance such with learning themes selected by the experienced teacher and parent. More than this, however, the form of presentation matters just as much as the motivation of the child. Jerome Bruner was one leading psychologist of learning who saw the importance of modes of presentation in teaching.

Bruner is renowned for claiming that the key to learning progress lies in the appropriate mode of representation of ideas. His threefold distinction outlined here is in opposition to the theory of Jean Piaget that children develop through set stages, and that the teacher must adapt the content of learning to these stages. (E.g. Don't try teaching 'seeing another's point of view' to 3 year olds). In fact, anything, claims Bruner, can be taught to a person at any age provided it is presented in an appropriate mode.

He commends a hierarchical sequence of learning modes, starting at the **enactive**, by for example, interactive storytelling, making objects, ordering them, role playing in situations that yield problems and solutions, scientific experiments, e.g. planning a helicopter rescue mission using a map. (Concepts to be used – start, distance, route, destination, range, speed, compass directions etc.)

This progresses to the use of imaging (called the **iconic** form) in which objects/phenomena/processes/principles are represented in diagrams, maps, or timelines, being aids to understanding ideas and relations by picturing them, e.g. representing circles and their parts by a diagram on the wall.

The development of the **symbolic**, the most versatile and accurate medium, which is the use of abstract ideas in language and number, and which offers great breadth of application for problem-solving and expression. E.g. learning and using `pi`, calculating the area of a circle using `pi multiplied by radius squared`.

This sequence is of value to us at any age, enabling us to gain understanding of difficult ideas to whatever degree we can master. Diagrams and cutaway drawings, hypothetical situations, and three-dimensional models all enable the adult to find some understanding of otherwise mystifying concepts, like black holes.[1]

Thus the curriculum to be pursued is not to be a formal journey through a hierarchy of material organized solely according to its degree of difficulty and the logic of its ideas. This is but one facet which must be balanced with respect for the capacities and interests of the learner. Thus:

The pre-16 curriculum should reflect a balance of many factors:

---

1   See e.g. his `Process of Education` (1960)

The **known achievements** of the learner until the present, enabling the teacher to match tasks to pupils' needs in a progressive way, taking them the next step.

The **known interests and attitudes** of learners as exemplifying their ecstatic valuing (see ch.4), that is, whatever they find fascinating and rewarding. This will promote self-confidence and the desire to learn more.

A **strategy for enhancing the self-belief** of learners regarding their ability to cope and succeed.

Progression in the **representational mode** in which knowledge is to be presented (as above).[1]

The **relevance** of the content to be learned for future life. 'Relevance' may be understood as whatever is felt to be important by the learner as well as the teacher: it arises from an agreement between them. The subjects to be incorporated into the investigations and projects must be shown to be of long-term value to the learner, being transferable to future needs in school and beyond.

The **coherence and progression** of ideas and skills in the chosen themes. The disciplines and fields of study have their own logical sequence of progression in ideas and skills. Progressive sequences of knowledge, concept and skill belonging to each subject have to be reflected in scheme and theme planning.

The need for learners to employ a **broad range of** mathematical, linguistic, historical, geographical, scientific, etc. **knowledge and concepts** through their chosen themes of study.

---

1   John P.de Cecco (1974) `The Psychology of Learning and Instruction ` gave a broad, much neglected, perspective.

Successful schooling leads to motivation, learning in depth, and a degree of breadth, although this last matters rather less than the first two. Overemphasis on the breadth of subjects learned presents the school and child with the need to cover vast tracts of material within a limited time, which tends to detract seriously from the quality of the learning experience. The primary goal for learners is the development of active and able minds able to pursue their own interests in the future. Once students are beyond the age of sixteen, they can then take the benefits to further and higher education, training or paid employment. More than that, they acquire dimensions of thought and skill that enrich their whole adult life, even in old age.

> **Well-educated 16+ school-leavers** are of far greater value to an employer than those who have suffered in a poor school. Their exam results may or may not be good, but...
>
> They have developed confidence.
> They make friends readily.
> They can identify problems and ask questions.
> They recognize error and injustice.
> They tend to adapt quickly.
> They are self-disciplined, being loyal and committed to creative progress.
> They have learned to obey instructions.
> They can express themselves accurately and clearly.

Such employer requirements are regularly changing, especially with the pace of technological and market change, and fresh employees tend to find pre-16 work-related learning to be inappropriate to working life.

This rather conservative stand need not imply that the range of foundational knowledge never changes. Citizenship, political theory and economics, for example, have grown in importance in teenage education in recent years. But such change takes place rarely and evolves slowly. What is certain is that occupations like agriculture, building, banking, marketing, even child-rearing, should not usurp the general education appropriate to compulsory schooling – even if these things are demanded by pre-16s who otherwise will not cooperate. Great skill is required to teach knowledge and understanding in such things as literature, mathematics and religious thought to senior pupils whose dominant concerns are about future employment. It is not the place of educators to satisfy the preferences of the young, or of parents or employers, but to guide them. It is vital that the teacher has enough understanding of the rationale for including initially unpopular subjects on the curriculum to be able to present a convincing case to learners.

That said, agriculture, for example, may deservedly feature in school outside the curriculum as suitable for pupils who learn through it as a medium, and who may not be amenable to any other approach. In Kent, I taught in a school with its own livestock unit, managed by pupils who failed at formal learning, but could learn to read, to understand biological needs, to quantify, record and to take responsibility through tasks they loved. The aim was not primarily to train them to farm but to teach them effectively through their own interests. Such work was undertaken before the school day, during breaks and after school, such was the enthusiasm of pupils.

Education for Human Development

Education, as opposed to training for a specific task, has wisdom as its ultimate aim. Wisdom includes knowledge, understanding and love. In the UK, the state domination of educational institutions tends to obscure this. With their gaze fixed on improving measurable performance, politicians focus upon those goals which voters can understand with little effort. Calculative thinking dominates the public mind, for enabling children to grow up loving learning and having the capacity for intimacy in the senses developed in this work, is not always simple and measurable. Pedagogy[1] is an art, and its neglect as such is a common cause of poor long-term transformation of the learner.

Children may do well on assessments of their knowledge and understanding using measures derived from the national syllabus. Schools are becoming expert at getting measurable results pleasing to ambitious parents. Tragically, all this reeks of superficiality. The question

---

1   Pedagogy is defined as `the art and science of teaching` in Britannica. `Pedagogue` has different meanings between European states.

of what education is properly trying to achieve is largely ignored. If it's self-fulfilment we're after, what do we mean by it? Is getting a job, being secure, being skilled, enough? Is there nothing more important to be sought if children are to get the best out of schooling? At its best schooling generates the dynamic for development towards maturity of being. Anything less is inadequate education.

The emphasis being made in the UK at present is on *cognitive* learning for all preschool children. This includes literacy, numeracy, problem-solving and reasoning, and has become a statutory requirement even for all professional carers of preschool infants. Goals are set by the government for each stage of the child's growth. The picture assumed is that teaching is meant to lead the child up a progressive staircase of achievements in literacy, problem-solving, reasoning and numeracy, these all being no less important than physical, social and emotional development, *even at the preschool stage*.[1] Whilst the goals certainly reflect vital achievements, it is dangerous to make them the systematic focus of preschool development. This tends to occur when teachers want to make sure their children can perform very specific tasks by a certain time in their schooling. Pressure is put upon children to reach goals required of the teacher, who becomes anxious about her career and distracted away from the informal and situationally-related skills so vital at this stage. Thus the whole joy of learning can so easily be taken away, and inspiration lost. Elements of spontaneity and play are of its essence.

> From the beginning of the child's entry to the nursery, learning requires skills and sensitivities of parent and carer that tend to be unperceived by compilers of analytical ability charts. **Tim Brighouse** writes "Caring for babies and toddlers is deeply personal, involving immeasurable qualities such as attunement and responsiveness. A one-size-fits-all framework that needs copious record-keeping risks substituting bureaucracy for care."[2]

To assess and measure through constant record-keeping is to undermine the expert adult's chance of acting as one who aids through play and

---

1   Beverley Hughes, Early Years Minister, UK cited 'Too Much Too Soon' p.37
2   'Review of early years law' Tim Brighouse et.al. TES 31/11/2007

intuitive action. They easily find themselves becoming administrators waiting on bureaucratic appraisal, and their pedagogical art becomes devalued. Educational bureaucracy is capable, in such ways as this, of indirectly destroying the primal sense of curiosity and wonder in children just as can poor parenting. It certainly depresses the parents, who are then made to feel that they cannot usurp the place of the `expert`. As for professional carers, they are also made to feel that play and unprogrammed activities have no serious place in the nursery.[1]

Once the child reaches school age the pressure to reach set attainment targets can destroy the most powerful processes in the teacher-learner relationship. Children can come to hate the pressure of learning, to shy away from engagement in any activity associated with teachers and school that might have inspired and captivated their attention. The majority can learn that they are viewed as poor, lazy and inattentive learners, when the fact is that they have been deprived of the joy of encounter with the world through the classroom. (School stinks!) These then appear in stark contrast with those who achieve good levels, and who, through positive reinforcement, take to all this assessment and grading like ducks in water. Thus the failure of the majority becomes inevitable.

Powerful teaching captures the attention through vibrant media such as storytelling and enacting, enriched through art, music and the sciences, and, in later years, narrative sequencing of themes in the disciplines. Computers and such modern devices as interactive white- and wipe-boards are to be used only as *occasional aids* by expert teachers who understand both subject and pupil, otherwise they can themselves become substitutes for genuine instruction, the acid test for which is that it enables the learner to grasp those concepts needed to integrate knowledge. It thus forms a meaningful and powerful whole, a *body* of learning that contributes to personhood, rather than a mere catalogue of items to be learned and recalled at a future date.

And, by the way, the well chosen subject of study, such as metamorphosis in insects, birth, time, journeys, volcanoes, earthquakes, fossils, inventors and inventing, fashions,

---

1   See e.g. `The impact of the EYFS (Early Years Foundation Stage) on Childminders` in House R., Ch.4.

> voyages of discovery, structures, arrest the attention of the child who has moved from that mythic stage of story to the romantic (as in ch.6). Once aroused, the mind is hungry for ideas that belong **to networks of meaning**, and that lead to pressing questions and areas for further discovery. The dawning of fascination with a topic is likely to become a means to number skills, a sense of chronology, and of place. For example, the ages of rocks and fossils can incidentally enable children to get to grips with huge numbers, and with a sequence of ages and periods, a skill otherwise beyond their years.

Whatever other tests might be applied to mark out teachers of quality, supreme is their love of their subjects and their desire to learn how to communicate with and motivate children to become lovers of such things. There is no better path to learning intimacy with the world than enjoyment of the sound educational curriculum. This focuses upon

learning that is foundational and far-reaching in its significance, being...

...highly applicable to understanding a vast variety of situations in life,

its content appropriate to the stage of personal development to be reached by the particular learner,

presented in an appetizing form, matching and broadening learners` interests,

and forming a ladder of progression in content, ideas and skills.

Lest the picture might become one of simply transmitting ideas into children`s minds, it is equally important that they be encouraged in their own creative and imaginative work. To devise, make or think something free of step-by-step instruction is vital at all stages, from infancy to doctoral thesis! It is clear that the precise choice of activity depends not simply on the official curriculum, but also on the known and likely interests of the child: the work becomes the result of a planned balance between the two.

Once we surrender to the desire to `get the material across`, this vital element of pedagogy is lost.[1] The most lasting knowledge we gain is knowledge found through our own quest. Rushing through an exam syllabus or teaching to get children high Standard Assessment Task results utterly destroys this possibility. The best teachers do not simply travel through a programme of instruction, or teach with an eye to success at audit time. They welcome the pause required to `make something` that requires the ideas and skills to be learned, to allow puzzlement to develop on the road to solutions, and to pursue in depth whatever is found to be fascinating. Education is about the powers of the mind as much as filling it with content.

Such issues as the following should be paramount across the programmes of learning, students being encouraged to think about their current and future life narratives. It is vital that genuine contemplation of one`s life, seen as the development of a personal story, with goals, problems to overcome and hopes for achievements, has its place in the learning programme. This comes from students, and promotes a positive perspective for meaningful futures. It is an aspect of spiritual development in a post-religious culture.

> **Issues stimulating self-awareness, self-appraisal and new directions**
>
> **Life Goals** – life goals for those growing up in e.g. Christianity or Hinduism. What can I best gain from my education? What do I want to achieve in adult life? Why do I consider this ambition to be a good thing? What will I be doing for others?
>
> **Perception of Threats to Fulfilment** – What might be the forces that lead to a destructive lifestyle? How can I resist these? How might I enhance my effectiveness?

---

1   Jerome Bruner `Towards a Theory of Instruction` Harvard 1966 p.53

Projection and Retrojection – When my school career is complete, what do I hope to have gained by it? Looking back on my life in old age, what will please me most about my past? What might I warn the young to avoid?

Use of Time – What am I doing when I consider my time to be well used? What are the most attractive ways of wasting my time? Why are they so beguiling? How can I break free from their hold on me?

Ordering of Values – consideration of the range of personal values that matter to me, and how I rank them in order of importance. What am I doing in my spare time? How is that changing me? What do I gain?

Social Acceptance – In which ways do I want to be like others? In which different? How can I best demonstrate these if I wish to gain respect?

Strategies for Change – How might I cope with improving my use of time and do the things I really should prefer to do?

Perspective on Life – How do I feel about being alive? How lucky or unlucky have I been? Does my life matter at all, to whom and how? If I could change the world, what would I do? What are the greatest evils today? What are the most powerful forces for good?

Location and Migration – Moving to new life or staying at home? A consideration of gains and losses in external and internal goods, and of the personal qualities required for a wise decision. How might living in the Third World be a great idea?

It is an inevitable consequence of *depth* in learning that pupils will not do so well on all the myriad points of assessment with which government policymakers are so often obsessed. Therefore, the important emphasis to be made in all-round education on *breadth* of learning must regularly be sacrificed. (For example, a good teacher will sometimes say, "No, the syllabus could not all be covered because such a long and profitable time was spent by that group on forest management; precious things were learned and questions raised that mattered to my pupils.") The richest lives tend to be focused most on a field of special interest, although, that said, the enlivened mind also broadens its appetite for wider fields of activity. And many have a great love of learning across such a wide field that they never become specialist experts at anything. That's not a bad thing either!

Empowering and Transforming the Profession

Good teachers are one key to lifelong effective learning.

Where might they be found? Top graduates need to be recruited to teaching by means of giving them a vision of its key role. In realistic terms, trainees need at least a two-year course, all of which should be paid and in schools. The student teacher needs a thorough sociological, philosophical and psychological understanding of the paths of human development. This will deepen their perception of what needs to be taught and how it is to be presented.

Teachers must have control of the profession returned to them. The best teachers are not simply skilled communicators: they are also skilled academics and experts. There is a breadth to their knowledge and skill that goes far beyond 'knowing a subject', like history or maths. They understand the developmental stages of children, social influences upon them, class and cultural differences, and so on. They know the way forward for their pupils. Teaching is a multifaceted set of skills, all converging in wisdom deserving high recognition. By contrast, the politicians and civil servants who actually control education lord it over the profession, creating 'new' initiatives, all unaware that these are invariably returns to past policy. In the UK, Her Majesty's Inspectorate, drawn from both academic and practitioner expertise, should be restored to its erstwhile status as key advisory body. Clearly, `Ofsted`[1] should be replaced by her Majesty's Inspectorate, to which a body of more regional advisers would be answerable. This system is, of course, exactly that discarded by the 1985 Education Reform Act of England and Wales. Before then, national experts advised government, and local experts administered and appraised schools and teachers, with an intimate knowledge of social catchment areas, etc. They also created networks of professional development. It worked well, but was not cheap, which partly explains its demise. Successive governments paired it down in the name of innovation, efficiency and, believe it or not, democracy.

Professional status equal to that of medical practitioners is required, healthy bodies being of little use to the development of mature human beings without the development of educated minds. A minimal increase in pay at the starting end of a career in teaching is a discouragement to those who enter the profession for money, but salary scales should at least rise twice as high at the top end as at present. Quality of teaching thus can become properly acknowledged as professionals develop in expertise. The best teachers might be awarded professorship status in education, enabling them to mentor the less experienced, leading to levels of award.

Such requirements will never be fulfilled so long as those in power see nursery and school teaching as easy money for the less than academically brilliant. The early growth of children is known to require profound knowledge and skill of the specialist and to be of lifelong significance.

---

1   `Office for Standards in Education`, a quango in charge of specific school inspections and made up of a mixed body of teachers and members from other professions. Members are part-time and may have no background in education. They inspect according to rigid formulae and timetables, and frequently have never formally studied education.

School education is surely as important as the health of citizens! Not only are teachers as vital as medics, the skills required to become an expert are as complex, and they cover a wider, more dynamic field.

Implementing a Vision

It would be very odd for anyone to claim that their aim in life is to become mature! Just as we may only achieve happiness by not seeking it in any direct manner, so maturity comes indirectly, as a result of seeking specific goals. Such pursuits produce personal integrity, qualities of character, enduring commitment to activities that have merit in themselves, active sensitivity to the needs of others and a positive contribution to making the world a better place. Thus a person's growth advances through their projects in life.

Nobody is excluded from the possibility of developing a life of merit. There are those whose bodily condition cripples them, but who have a powerful effect on other people for their courage and active caring. There are those who try and try, yet hardly ever succeed at projects to which they are devoted – the mountains they have sought to climb always defeat them – yet nobody can deny their virtue. There are those who never measure themselves against the rich and famous, who live in a small corner, yet who transform it.

None of these people *seek* to become mature; they mature through the choices and tasks engaging them. Yet it behoves the philosopher in us to bring the subject to light as a matter of urgency, simply because so many of us are becoming stunted through the false exaltation of external goods at the expense of internal goods – MacIntyre's 'goods of excellence'. We lose sight of our true being as we exalt goals and values that have no right to become life's main focus, except in desperate extremes of starvation and oppression. Basic needs met, we need to turn our focus away from them towards activities that enable us to develop the virtuous life. Good nurture and education inspire this.

There is nothing inexorable about processes of inner growth. Natural selection does not choose the altruistic and thoughtful or educated. Human wickedness can destroy these features in its own species, and has done so on the grand scale even in modern times. Our faith has to be rooted in the transforming power of love on individual and society. The decline of the virtuous life amongst humanity would entail its own destruction and also that of many creatures and plants. Our species development requires autonomous choices that are individually initiated by true adults. Individualism is not the same as individual maturing: overemphasis on `my rights`, `my happiness` and `my plans`, can signify loss of communal membership. Not just self and community, but the entire species may become spiritually stunted and bring about its own demise. Globalism's abuse may hasten this – the global community may not develop, except as an arena for rivalry and ever-spreading superficiality of living. When our inner life loses its way, the human outlook is that little bit less promising.

There are at least eleven directions for action arising from the themes in this book.

1. The expertise developed by parent and carer in early years, and refined by experts, must not be usurped by formal learning targets and rigid programme schedules. Politicians must respect professional experts who plead that the youngest are inspired to enjoy their world.

2. Parents need more time interacting with their children, developing routines and standards of behaving, thus settling them into stable expectations and a peaceable social sphere. Public information programmes can help, and a shorter working week is essential.

3. Parents need to learn to resist their child's demands arising from peer pressure, and teachers have a major part to play in educating their pupils in the dangers of valuing popularity, group acceptance, and those distracting high-tech games. School-home liaison must focus on such issues. This implies that education in good parenting requires appropriate funding, and

national publicity. Poor educational achievement often has roots in the home.

4. Teacher education requires a relevant philosophical foundation. The view that education is contemplative must replace assumptions that it is to train for work and wealth. A vision of education as the development of mind to maturity is central.

5. A coherent and secular understanding of spiritual development is essential in state education. This will not exclude an understanding of the religious traditions and why they are so important to the peoples of the world.

6. Teachers must be versed in the central place of narrative in human development. All should be enabled to envisage the stories of their own lives, the future life of their communities and of the wider world, and to play their part.

7. Pupils must be encouraged to learn in depth, which means that teachers no longer feel obliged to cover the whole programme of study, but to focus at times on learning with the motivated learner in topics that inspire. This enhances the love of learning.

8. Preoccupation with formal success, employment prospects, popularity, winning and wealth, should be understood as important but as less vital than a life of integrity and love of the world. These perceptions must be taught through the manner of life of teacher and parent as well as the content of the curriculum and life of the school.

9. Teachers require time and funding for professional improvement, which includes self-evaluation, not only in terms of measurable performance, but of their

> overall vision, assumptions and attitudes to their work.
>
> 10. The status of teaching as a profession requires radical reappraisal. New recruits must be given longer training with initial incentives and salary scales should become appropriate
>
> 11. Academic qualities of a high order are required and professional quality rewarded by means of practical school-based professorships.

A new horrific analogy might be made between the living planet and that strangling fig of my preface, its development perceived by few, yet not effectively destroyed. The slow strangling process attacks humanity. Its destruction begins within the self, spreads into the loss of local conviviality, infects our politics, perverts national culture, stunts the growth in spirit of our young, and guarantees poorer parenting for the future.

Biological evolution carries the guarantee that the fittest shall survive, if, that is, any manage to survive at all. The progression towards maturity of the human spirit has no such guarantee. It moves upwards, not by the processes of animal evolution, but by the power of learning, love and wisdom. *When these fail, the whole world is threatened.* The human race dominates the world of creatures, whose life and death are in its hands. How dare we imagine any sports star, brain surgeon, or banker to perform roles more vital than teachers?

"Voici mon secret. Il est très simple: on ne voit bien qu'avec le cœur. L'essentiel est invisible pour les yeux."

(Here is my secret. It is very simple: It is only with the heart that one can see rightly; what is essential is invisible to the eye.)

Antoine de Saint Exupery   The Little Prince 1943

BIBLIOGRAPHY

ALLPORT G.W. (1950, 1969)
`The Individual and His Religion`   Canada, Macmillan

APPIGNANESI, R. & TARRRANT, C. (1995)
`Introducing Postmodernism`   Cambridge, Icon

ARISTOTLE (ca.330 B.C.E)
` Aristotle: Ethics` 1953, rev.1976 transl.   Thompson J.A.K., Penguin

BARBOUR, I. (1974)
Myths, Models and Paradigms: Nature of Scientific and Religious Language
                                                      London, SCM Press

BERLIN, I. (1990)
The Crooked Timber of Humanity: Chapters in the History of Ideas,
                                                      London John Murray

BERGER, J. (2001)
The Shape of a Pocket   London, Bloomsbury Press

BETTELHEIM, B (1991)
The Uses of Enchantment: The Meaning and Importance of Fairy Tales   Penguin

BLACKBURN, S. (2001)
`Being Good: a short introduction to ethics`   Oxford Univ. Press

BONHOEFFER, D. (1953 1st Eng.edition)
`Letters and Papers from Prison`   London, SCM Press

BRUNER, J. (1960, rev.1977)
'The Process of Education`   Harvard Univ Press

BRUNER, J. (1968)
`Toward a Theory of Instruction`   N.Y. Norton 1968

BUBER, M. (1923, 1958)
`I and Thou `   New York, Scribner`s

CANNADINE, D. (2012)
`The Undivided Past: History beyond our Differences`   London, Allen Lane

CLAYTON, E. of Central Michigan University has contributed a very readable article
on Alasdair MacIntyre`s work in the Internet `Encyclopedia of Philosophy`

COOPER, D. (1996)
`World Philosophies: an historical introduction`   Oxford, Blackwell

CUPITT, D. (1991)
'What is a Story?'   London, S.C.M. Press

CUPITT, D. (2005)
`The Way To Happiness`   Santa Rosa, Polebridge Press

CURTIS, A, cited in Bunting M.
`Where is the Vision to Unite Us?`   Guardian Weekly, 23/6/09

De BOTTON, A. (2005)
'The Art of Travel`   London, Macmillan

De BOTTON, A. (2012)
`Religion for Atheists`   London, Hamish Hamilton

De VRIES, M.K. (2000)
`The Happiness Equation: meditations on happiness and success`   Vermilion, London

DEACON, J.   (1979)
`Tongue-tied`   New York, Scribner`s

DALLE PEZZE, B.
`Heidegger`s`Gelassenheit`
              Minerva Vol. 10 2006 at http://www.ul.ie/~philos/vol10/Heidegger.html

EDWARDS, R. (1972,)
`Reason and religion: an introduction to the Philosophy of Religion`   Harcourt

EGAN, K. (1986)
`Individual Development and the Curriculum`   London, Hutchinson

EGAN, K. (1986)
`Teaching as Storytelling`   University of Chicago Press

EGAN, K. (1988)
`Primary Understanding: Education in Early Childhood`   NY, Routledge

EGAN, K. (1991)
`Romantic Understanding: The Development of Rationality and Imagination, ages 8-15`   NY, Routledge

FAWCETT, T. (1970)
`The Symbolic Language of Religion`   London, S.C.M

FINLAYSON, J.G. (2005)
`Habermas:a very short introduction`   Oxford Univ. Press

FOLEY, M. (2010)
`The Age of Absurdity: Why Modern Life Makes it Hard to be Happy`
                                                        N.Y Simon & Schuster

FREUD, S. (1928, 1974)
`The Future of an Illusion`   London, Hogarth

GIDDENS, A. (1991)
'Modernity and Self-Identity'   Cambridge, Polity Press

GLADWELL, M. (2009)
`Outliers: The Story of Success`   Penguin

GOLEMAN, D. (1996)
`Emotional Intelligence`   London, Bloomsbury

GRAYLING, A.C. (2004)
`What is Good? The search for the best way to live`   Phoenix, London

HABERMAS, J. (1983)
`Discourse Ethics: Notes on Philosophical Justification.` in Moral Consciousness and Communicative Action   (Eng.trans. Polity 1990)

HABERMAS, J. (et.al) (2007, 2010)
`An Awareness of What is Missing: Faith and Reason in a Post-Secular Age`. Translated by Cieran Cronin.   Cambridge, Polity

HAIDT, J. (2006)
`The Happiness Hypothesis`   London, Heinemann/Arrow

HAMILTON, C (2013)
`Earthmasters: The Dawn of the Age of Climate Engineering`   Yale

HAMILTON, W., (1973)
`Phaedrus and letters VII & VIII by Plato`
                    extracts from which publ.1995 in Penguin `60`s Classics` series

HANFLING, O. (1987)
The Quest for Meaning   Open University

HEIDEGGER, M. (1932, 1962)
`Being and Time` (transl. Macquarrie J. & Robinson E.)   Oxford, Blackwell

HEIDEGGER, M. (1966)
`Discourse on Thinking`   Harper and Row Torchbooks

HICK, J, (1977)
`The Myth of God Incarnate`   S.C.M., London

HOBSBAWM, E. (1994, 2002)
`The Age of Extremes: the Short Twentieth Century 1914-1991`   London, Abacus

HOBAN, R. (1990, 2000)
`The Mouse and His Child`   Harper & Row NY

HOGAN, P. (1995)
`The Custody and Courtship of Experience`   Dublin, Columba Press

HORTON, J. and MENDUS, S. (1994)
`After MacIntyre; critical perspectives on the work of Alasdair MacIntyre`
                                                        Cambridge Polity Press

HOUSE, R. (ed.) (2011)
`Too Much, Too Soon: Early Learning and the Erosion of Childhood`
                                                        Stroud, Hawthorn Press

HUGHES, B. (2010)
`The Hemlock Cup: Socrates, Athens and the Search for the Good Life`
                                                        Jonathan Cape

HUGHES, T. (1989)
`Myth and Education` in Abbs.P.(ed.) The Symbolic Order   London, Falmer

JACQUES, M. (2009, 2012)
`When China Rules the World`   London, Allen Lane/ Penguin

JOSEPHSON, M. (1946)
`Stendahl, or The Pursuit of Happiness`   N.Y., Doubleday

KEIGHLEY, A. (1976)
`Wittgenstein, Grammar and God`   London, Epworth 1976

KELLER, H (1903, 2009)
`The World I Live in & Optimism`   NY Dover Publications

KIERKEGAARD, S. (1846, 1974)
`Concluding Unscientific Postscript` tr.
Swenson, David F. & Lowrie, Walter   Princeton University Press

KOHLBERG, L (1981).
Essays on Moral Development, Vol. I: The Philosophy of Moral Development
                                                        Harper & Row

MACINTYRE, A. (1990)
'After Virtue' (2nd. ed.)   London, Duckworth

MACINTYRE, A. (1999).
Dependent Rational Animals: Why Human Beings Need the Virtues.
                                                    Chicago: Open Court

MCCRUM, R. (2010)
`Globish: How the English Language became the World`s Language`   Viking

MCGREAL, I.ed. (1995)
`Great Thinkers of the Eastern World`   Harper Collins N.Y.

MALCOLM, N. (1966)
`Ludwig Wittgenstein: a Memoir`   Oxford Univ. Press

MARCUSE. H. (1964, 1991)
One Dimensional Man: Studies in the Ideology of Advanced Industrial Society
                                                    Routledge, London

MASLOW, A.H. (1970)
Motivation and Personality.   New York: Harper & Row.

MAZOWER, M. (2012)
`Governing the World: the History of an Idea`   Allen Lane/Penguin

MILL, J.S.   (1873)
The Harvard Classics, Vol. 25,
Charles Eliot Norton, ed.   N.Y. Collier & Son Company 1909)

MILL, J.S. (1848)
'Of the Stationary State'. In `Principles of political economy Book IV:
 Influence of the progress of society`   London: Longmans, Green & Co.

NEF UK (2010)
`Growth Isn`t Possible: Why We Need a New Economic Direction`
                                        New Economics Foundation, London

NEF UK (2010)
`21 Hours: Why a shorter working week can help us all to flourish in the 21st century`
                                        New Economics Foundation London

NEWBY, M.J. (2011)
`Eudaimonia: Happiness is not Enough`   Leicester,Troubadour/Matador

NICHOLS, A. (2009)
`G.K.Chesterton: Theologian`   Darton Longman & Todd

NORMAN, A. (2008)
`The Story of George Loveless and the Tolpuddle Martyrs`   Devon Halsgrove Press

OPIE, I. & P. (1974)
`The Classic Fairy Tales`   Oxford University Press

PALMER, R.E. (1969)
`Hermeneutics: Interpretation Theory in Schleiermacher, Dilthey, Heidegger and
Gadamer`   NorthWestern University

PAPERT, S. (1969)
`Mindstorms: Children, Computers, and Powerful Ideas`   NY Basic Books

PETERS, R.S. (1966)
Ethics and Education   London, Allen & Unwin

PETERS, R.S. (1973)
`The Philosophy of Education`   Oxford Univ. Press

PHILLIPS, D.Z. (1976)
Religion Without Explanation   Oxford, Blackwell

PLATO (c.370 BCE)
`Phaedrus` (1995 edition)   Penguin

PULLMAN, P. (2010)
`Jesus the Good Man: Christ the Scoundrel`   Canongate Books

RAEPER, W. (1987)
`George Macdonald`   Tring,Lion Books

RIPLEY, A (2013)
`The Smartest Kids in the World: And How They Got That Way`
                                                    Simon & Schuster

ROBERTSON, J. (1998)
`Transforming Economic Life: a Millennial Challenge` UKGreenbooks

RORTY, R (1989)
`Contingency, Irony and Solidarity`   Cambridge University Press

SACKS, J. (2002)
`The Dignity of Difference: How to Avoid the Clash of Civilisations`
                                                    London, Continuum Press

SANDEL, M.J. (2009)
`A New Citizenship`   BBC Reith Lectures

SANDEL, M.J.(2012)
`What Money Can`t Buy: the Moral Limits of Markets`   Allen Lane/Penguin

SCHLICK, M. (1927)
`On The Meaning Of Life` reprinted in Hanfling O.(ed.)
`Life and  Meaning`   Oxford, Blackwell
1987; also in Hanfling`s `The Quest For Meaning` 1987 pp.35-40

SCRUTON, R (1994)
`Modern Philosophy - an introduction and survey`   Arrow Books (1997)

SEACOLE, M. (1857, 2005)
`The Wonderful Adventures of Mary Seacole in Many Lands`   Penguin

SKIDELSKY, R. & E. (2012)
`How Much is Enough? The Love of Money,and the Case for the Good Life`
                                                    Allen Lane

SPONG, J. (1994)
`Resurrection, Myth Or Reality?`   London, Harper/Collins

SULLIVAN, L. (2003)
Hey, Whipple, Squeeze This: A Guide to Creating Great Ads   N.Y Wiley

TAYLOR, C. (1989)
`Sources of the Self: the Making of the Modern Identity`   Cambridge Univ. Press

THISELTON, A. (1980)
`The Two Horizons`   Exeter, Paternoster Press

WALSH, P.(1993)
`Education and Meaning: philosophy in practice`   London, Cassell

WHITE, J. (2011)
`Exploring Well-Being in Schools: a guide to making children's lives more fulfilling`
                                                                    Routledge

WILKINSON, R and PICKETT, K (2010)
`The Spirit Level: Why Equality is Better for Everyone`   Penguin

WINNICOTT, D.W. (1971)
`Playing and Reality`   Penguin

WITTGENSTEIN, L. (1922, 1961)
`Tractatus Logico-Philosophicus`   Routledge

WITTGENSTEIN, L. (1953)
`Philosophical Investigations`   Macmillan

Lightning Source UK Ltd.
Milton Keynes UK
UKOW03f0356230414

230416UK00002B/14/P